Gandhi's Wisdom

V. K. Kool · Rita Agrawal
Editors

Gandhi's Wisdom

Insights from the Founding Father of
Modern Psychology in the East

Editors
V. K. Kool
SUNY Polytechnic Institute
Utica, NY, USA

Rita Agrawal
Harish Chandra Post Graduate College
Varanasi, Uttar Pradesh, India

ISBN 978-3-030-87493-3   ISBN 978-3-030-87491-9   (eBook)
https://doi.org/10.1007/978-3-030-87491-9

Cover illustration: wpap

This Palgrave Macmillan imprint is published by the registered company Springer Nature Switzerland AG
The registered company address is: Gewerbestrasse 11, 6330 Cham, Switzerland

Preface

Plagued as the twenty first century globe is with insurmountable problems, utmost wisdom seems to be our only hope. Humankind, though at the apex of phylogeny, has played havoc with Nature, bringing in its wake, innumerable crises, both at the environmental level and at the interpersonal level. Our search for wisdom, or, if we may dare to say so, authentic wisdom, continues, with scholars from a variety of disciplines urging us forward and providing momentum. It is but natural that psychology, as the science of human behavior, bears equal if not greater responsibility in this endeavor. Mohandas Karamchand Gandhi, the half clad Indian, regarded by many as the wisest man to step on earth, provides many a clue. The need is to delve deeply into his life and work.

Gandhi is well known for his contribution to peace, justice, and nonviolence, leading to the independence of India (currently the largest democracy in the world), for sowing the seeds of freedom in South Africa, and overall, for giving shape to what we now know as "organized nonviolence" around the globe. There have been no dearth of scholars who had studied him during his life time, and many continue to do so, drawing from his wisdom in the hope of weaving the tapestry of harmonious and peaceful coexistence. In fact, more than 5000 scholarly books have been written on Gandhi's life and work. However, with a few exceptions, for example, Erikson's Pulitzer Award winning book, *Gandhi's Truth* (1969), there have been almost negligible attempts to scientifically study the ways through which Gandhi helped us internalize, and put in tandem, not only the core human psychological framework of cognition, motivation and emotion, but also to explore how they can be made congruous with people and things around us.

In our two-volume book, *Gandhi and the psychology of nonviolence* (Kool & Agrawal, 2020), we invited readers to view Gandhi's life and works from the lens of scientific, modern psychology and how it has the potential to be used across various sub-fields, both traditional, such as social and community psychology, and those that are relatively new, such as psychology of technology. While we did mention Gandhi's wisdom in that book, it was only as a passing reference at the end of the second volume.

There have been significant developments since then, including but not limited to, discussions regarding having a commonly agreed conceptualization of wisdom among psychologists (for example, a recent international conference in Canada). Further, there have been invitations to genuinely explore the scientific roots of nonviolence in the context of Gandhi (for example, Nagler's Third Harmony and Cortland's core belief in the success of nonviolent methods). Added to the above are developments in the study of human cognition (for example, Kahneman's Prospect Theory—slow and fast thinking and its applications; Nobel Laureate Thaler's nudging and boosting); neuropsychological researches in the study of self control; advances in the understanding of empathy and its neurological basis (for example, 'Gandhi' neurons); neurological findings regarding relevant brain areas and its neuro-circuitry; evidence regarding the evolutionary basis of nonviolence and its concomitants and a much greater awareness regarding the importance of nonviolent methods for resolving conflict (through the empirical findings of Chenoweth and Stephan, for example). Moreover, there are psychology's new empirical endeavors in such nuanced forms of behavior as vows, silence, sacrifice and fasting, all of them being integral parts of Gandhi's behavior contributing to the experiencing of wisdom in the context of nonviolence. And, can we disregard the growing consensus among eminent thinkers (such as Paul Krutzen, Martin Rees and Chris Rapley) on the "enormity of humanity's responsibility as stewards of the earth" during the current epoch of the anthropocene or the emphasis being laid by world bodies such as the United Nations regarding the role of humans in global warming, climate change and the creation of a sustainable ecology?

This book is about the missing link between Gandhi's wisdom, the inspiration we can draw from him to solve the problems of this century, and the practice of authentic wisdom. Psychologists have been mentioning 'authentic happiness', but where is it? Not surprisingly, when the authenticity of things and people around us has been changing exponentially, from "having a body versus being a body", to cloning, and more, it is becoming imperative to seek the mainstay of human cognition. This is where the wisdom of Gandhi could be of immense use, offering us the impeccable means of nonviolence for forming the core of coexistence. With human greed, coupled with the ever-increasing plethora of wants and the multitude of emotions disturbing the very foundation of our cognition (acquired through our cultural heritage, rightly, or even, partly so), the equipoise of human existence has never been as flimsy as it is today and the end result of our irresponsible behavior is being highlighted, like never before, during the pandemic caused by the Covid 19 virus.

While psychology, as a science, grew in the West under the leadership of William James in the USA and Wundt in Germany in the late 19th and early part of the twentieth century, Gandhi, around the same time or soon afterwards, was exploring the roots of the science of behavior in the gigantic canvas encompassing three continents (Asia, Africa and Europe), where he lived, interacted and experimented to explore the nature of human cognition through, what is commonly known as, his experiments with truth. Gandhi, in his own way, was exploring the nature of cognition, whereas the science of psychology was struggling to keep cognition as its focus of study, thanks to the anti-cognition movement led by distinguished psychologist Skinner during the mid- twentieth century.

Further, while almost all leading scholars, ranging from Skinner and Bandura to Maslow and Howard Gardner, have cited Gandhi in their works, very few, to the best of our knowledge, have afforded an in-depth coverage or tacit applications based on his life and work. In fact, when Erikson wrote in 1969, in the above mentioned book, *Gandhi's Truth* that, "...I sensed an affinity between Gandhi's truth and the insights of modern psychology" (p. 440), the science of psychology was far from ready to accept human cognition as the mainstay of its subject matter. Unquestionably, Gandhi was far ahead of his time, similar to Ebbinghaus, whose self-experiments on memory could gain attention and appreciation only several decades later.

It is contended here that for its growth, modern psychology needs Gandhi, and as regards the psychology of wisdom, there is plenty of wisdom to look for in Gandhi. Gandhi is, undoubtedly, the founding father of modern psychology in the East in as much as, if not more than, William James or Wundt in the West, unless someone ignorantly claims that exploring into the science of behavior can be confined only to the walls of a laboratory. The spotlight on Gandhi would also go a long way in overcoming the objection raised by Arnett (2008) that the dominant American psychology tends to focus only on 5% of the world's population, obscuring the behavior of the remaining 95% of the population of the world.

The need to concentrate on wisdom has grown exponentially with the unprecedented growth of technology during the previous century, enabling us to dwell on the role of human intelligence in establishing a technological evolution vis-a-vis the ongoing, biological evolution. Despite the above, the study of wisdom has not found its place in the menu of the science of psychology. We have been amazed at the potential impact of cloning, genetic engineering, artificial intelligence, and more ranging from that on our personal lives to the survival of human beings and to all things sentient in the universe. So, while earlier it was simply the biological evolution which human beings were forced to grapple with in the context of the survival of the fittest, today, we have, in addition, the extraordinary growth of the technological evolution that needs to be managed so as to safeguard our existence.

In overseeing the problems caused by both biological and techno-logical evolutions, human cognition needs to be rebooted as well and made free from the viruses of violence, greed, and the abuse of natural resources. This will enable us to scrutinize all the issues taken together, and understand how morality and moral responsibility, the anchors of the yester-years, are being pushed into isolated islands around the globe, making us wonder whether humans have been misnomered as homo sapiens (Latin for 'wise man') and should instead be called 'homo prospectus' (Seligman et al., 2016), seeing that the hallmark of human beings lies in their ability to prospect about the future. But, problems and issues do not end with this new nomenclature.

While philosophers appear reluctant to accept the recent psycholog-ical analysis of people acting rationally without deliberation or even irrationally with deliberation, their explanations fail to solve the debate between internalists who argue that the ideas central to us provide justi-fication to our beliefs in contrast to externalists who seek justification outwardly, say in factors such as the environment. Further, we find no definite answers to unprincipled virtue in the moral agency of our time. Seligman and his colleagues (ibid.) are trying to trace roots of wisdom in the deep self of human beings, but where is Gandhi, comprehensively investigated and presented, our moral man of the previous century who presented the dynamics of the deep self through his experiments with truth.

This book is about the iteration of nonviolence as the default mode, a precursor of our existence as presented by Gandhi. In so doing, we explore the operating system of human cognition loaded with wisdom, something that we say is available everywhere but are being able to find, only, in bits and pieces. Wisdom emanating from the adherence to nonviolence is needed holistically and consistently. It must be ever ready, to scroll up and down and manage problems caused by any evolution—biological, technological or the two, in interaction with each other.

While configuring this volume, we realized the need to look for Gandhi's wisdom beyond our own limited knowledge and from what we had learned from interviewing members of Gandhi family, his coworkers and scholars of Gandhian studies from multiple disciplines. With the cooperation of and excellent support from several eminent scholars from various parts of the world, we were able to carve this book on Gandhi's wisdom with the following three prime considerations.

Firstly, we have focused on the nature and measurement of psychology of wisdom, limitations in conceptualizing it narrowly and particularly in the absence of support from interdisciplinary studies such as sociology, history, political science, and economics, and more importantly, lessons from Gandhi. The case, in point, is our chapter on "Milgram's lost Gandhi: Whither Gandhi's wisdom of nonviolence in the psychology of wisdom."

The second part of the book deals with our understanding of wisdom in the context of such nuanced forms of behavior as fasting, silence, vows and more that have only recently gained attention in modern psychology, but for Gandhi, were integral parts of his behavioral repertoire, helping him to expand and reboot his psychological capital known as wisdom. Not only did he internalize the interrelationship between his cognition, motivation and emotion, but he also aligned them in the context of social good, illustrating them in such forms as non-possession (aparigraha), mitigation of us-them boundaries, anasakti (use of pure means) and the embracing technology wisely. The chapters in this section represent the contributions from a core of scholars who range from psychologists to administrators and interdisciplinary faculty, deeply interested in the life and works of Gandhi.

Finally, in the third part of this book, we have sought contributions from those scholars in the West who have found in Gandhi, an exemplar for their lives and have written extensively on him and are known for their books and for managing Gandhi related publications. For Gandhi, belief has no meaning without any action. It is heartening to note that one of the contributors, Michael Nagler has established a center of nonviolence based on Gandhian principles and is managing a harmony project. While we could have invited many others, the limitations of space constrained us from doing so.

The final chapter of this book on the relevance of Gandhi's wisdom in the twenty first century begins with the fallacy that we consider ourselves wise but create us-them dichotomies, and, in the process, are failing to benefit from the wisdom of other living beings. Further, we have argued that the psychology of wisdom needs input from other social and related sciences to expand its applications. And finally, we have raised the issue of what is good about a science if it does not illustrate its authenticity, asking the reader, subsequently, whether the volume enabled them to experience the traces of authentic wisdom in the life and works of Mahatma (the great soul) Gandhi.

We would like to thank members of the Gandhi family and his coworkers who helped us in securing relevant information on his life and work. Also, it has been a great pleasure to work with each contributor in this book, bringing in and highlighting unique aspects of Gandhi's wisdom which remained, hitherto, neglected or poorly explored. In fact, we cannot thank them enough. Further, we take this opportunity to thank everyone who read and offered comments on the chapters of our book.

As always, it has been a great experience to work with our publisher, Palgrave Macmillan, and, as we move along with the production of our fourth book with this company, we thank the current editorial team consisting of Beth, Brian, Isobel, Liam, Lynnie, Shukkanthy and others.

Los Angeles, USA   V. K. Kool
Varanasi, India   Rita Agrawal

References

Arnett, J. J. (2008). The neglected 95%: Why American psychology needs to become less American. *American Psychologist, 63*, 602-611.

Erikson, E. (1969). *Gandhi's truth*. Norton.

Kool, V. K., & Agrawal, R. (2020). *Gandhi and the psychology of nonviolence* (Vols. 1 & 2). Palgrave-Macmillan.

Seligman, M. E. P., Railton, P., Baumeister, R. F., & Sripada, C. (2016). *Homo prospectus*. Oxford University Press.

Acknowledgements

In preparing this book, we acknowledge the encouragement received from the members of the Gandhi family, his coworkers, our colleagues and the members of our family. We would like to make a special mention of the encouragement and blessings we received from His Holiness, the 14th Dalai Lama, (whose name translates to "A teacher who is an Ocean of Wisdom") in 2008 to work in the field of nonviolence and well-being. At an event in Mumbai, India, he signed the book, *Psychology of nonviolence and aggression*, authored by Professor V. K. Kool and published by Macmillan-Palgrave, 2008 (photograph below).

Contents

Notes on Contributors

Rita Agrawal is Ex-Director and Professor, FMT, Harish Chandra PG College, Varanasi, India. She has over 40 years of teaching experience at various universities and premier institutes in India and abroad. She is author of several books, including *Stress in life and at work* (Sage-Response, 2001); and *Psychology of Technology,* coauthored with V. K. Kool (Springer, Switzerland, 2016); has a large number of invited chapters in books published by internationally renowned publishers such as Wiley, Springer and Palgrave-Macmillan; and, over 90 research papers published/presented in international/national peer reviewed journals and international conferences.

Alka Bajpai is an Assistant Professor of Psychology, University of Delhi, India. She received her doctorate from the University of Allahabad and specializes in Organizational and Applied Social Psychology. Her publications have focused on emotional climate, work place spirituality and emotional labour. Her interest also lies in understanding self and cultural processes.

David Cortright is Emeritus professor at University of Notre Dame and is the author of over 20 books. He has received several awards: Publisher's Choice Outstanding Academic Title Award for Governance for Peace: How Inclusive, Participatory and Accountable Institutions Promote Peace and Prosperity 2019; Gandhi Peace Award, with Karen Jacob, by Promoting Enduring Peace 2004; Publisher's Choice Outstanding Academic Title Award for 2001; The Sanctions Decade: Assessing UN Strategies in the 1990s; Award from the Program in Research and Writing for Peace and 1990 International Cooperation of the John D. and Catherine T. MacArthur Foundation, Chicago.

Todd Davies is associate director and a lecturer in the Symbolic Systems Program, and researcher at the Center for the Study of Language and Information, at Stanford University. He has a Ph.D. in cognitive psychology, an M.S. in data analysis and statistical computing and a B.S. in statistics with honours in the humanities, all from Stanford. He has also served as a computer scientist at the Artificial Intelligence Center, SRI International, assistant professor of psychology at Koç University in Istanbul, and, most recently, faculty in residence at the Stanford Bing Overseas Studies Program in Oxford and a visiting fellow at Brasenose College. Davies has also served as Co-Director, Peace+Justice Studies Initiative. Stanford University (2013–2017). His research focuses on deliberation, technology and methods for social decision making, and information policy. Website is https://web.stanford.edu/~davies.

Matthew M. Hollander is Sociology faculty at Marion Technical College (Marion, OH). After completing his Ph.D. in sociology at the University of Wisconsin-Madison in 2017, he was a postdoctoral researcher at the UW-Madison Department of Emergency Medicine, contributing to NIH-funded projects on dementia caregiving and care transitions from emergency department to home. His current research focuses on sociology of morality, diversity and racial justice and Latin sociology (especially Mexico-U.S. historical-comparative sociology). He is currently completing a book manuscript on power, resistance and moral action in the Stanley Milgram "obedience" experiments (w/ Jason

Turowetz, under contract with Oxford University Press), and a textbook on U.S. racial diversity using a comparative perspective with the Caribbean and Latin America.

V. K. Kool Emeritus Professor of Psychology, SUNY Polytechnic Institute, USA, has taught for over five decades at eight universities. He has received three Fulbright awards and his institution's Goodell Award for research and creativity; published eight books, including *The Psychology of Nonviolence and Aggression* (Macmillan-Palgrave) and *Gandhi and the psychology of nonviolence*, volumes 1 and 2, Macmillan Palgrave, USA/UK, 2020 (coauthor: Rita Agrawal); has served on the editorial board of American Psychological Association's Peace Division journal for seven years.

John S. Moolakkattu Professor, Department of International Relations & Politics, Central University of Kerala, Kasargod, India. He was earlier Professor & Director, School of Gandhian Thought and Development Studies, Mahatma Gandhi University, Kottayam, Professor, IIT Madras, and Gandhi-Luthuli Chair in Peace Studies, University of KwaZulu-Natal, South Africa. He was a Commonwealth Fellow and Fulbright Lecturer. His publications have appeared in leading journals such as *Public Administration and Development, Asian Journal of Women's Studies, Indian Journal of Gender Studies, Cooperation and Conflict, International Studies, Economic and Political Weekly, Peace Review, Sage Open, India Quarterly*, among others. He is a founding editor of the *South African Journal Ubuntu: Journal of Social and Conflict Transformation*. He has been editing Gandhi Marg, the quarterly *Journal of Gandhi Peace Foundation*, New Delhi, for the last 15 years. His areas of interest include peace and conflict resolution studies, international relations theory, African political economy, gender, local governance and planning, and Gandhi.

Michael Nagler, Ph.D., is professor emeritus at UC Berkeley, where he founded the Peace and Conflict Studies Program and taught upper-division courses on nonviolence, meditation and other subjects. He has spoken and written on peace and nonviolence for many years, and is president of the Metta Center for Nonviolence. Among other recognitions, Michael received the prestigious Bajaj Award for Promoting Gandhian Values Outside India in 2007. He is the author of *America Without Violence* (Island Press, 1982), *The Upanishads* (with Sri Eknath Easwaran, Nilgiri Press, 1987), *The Search for a Nonviolent Future* (Inner Ocean Publishing) which won the 2002 American Book Award, *The Nonviolence Handbook* and The Third Harmony: Nonviolence and the New Story of Human Nature (Berrett-Koehler, 2020). He also wrote and directed Metta's documentary film with the same title. Michael has lived at the Blue Mountain Center of Meditation community in Northern California since 1970.

Graeme Nuttall OBE, partner Fieldfisher, London; Executive Fellow at the Institute for the Study of Employee Ownership and Profit Sharing at The Rutgers School of Management and Labor Relations, and a trustee of the Institute for the Future of Work. Author of *Sharing Success: The Nuttall Review of Employee Ownership* (Department for Business, Innovation & Skills, 2012), *EO v3.0 – Employee ownership with added Gandhian purpose* (The Gandhi Foundation, 2020) and co-author and contributor to various publications including *Employee Ownership: Legal and Tax Aspects* (with John Nelson-Jones) (Fourmat, 1987).

Doug Oman, Ph.D., is Associate Adjunct Professor in the School of Public Health, University of California, Berkeley, where he has taught since 2001. His 100+ professional publications focus primarily on the role in physical and mental health of psychosocial factors, especially spirituality and religion. A major current interest is investigating applications of self-efficacy theory to spiritual and religious growth, and he is lead author of the chapter "Spiritual modeling self-efficacy: A standalone measure," forthcoming in *Assessing Spirituality in a Diverse* World (Springer International). Oman edited *Why Religion and Spirituality Matter for Public Health: Evidence, Implications and Resources* (Springer International, 2018), and directs a traineeship at U.C. Berkeley in spirituality and public health. Oman is a former president of the Society for the Psychology of Religion and Spirituality (Division 36 of the American Psychological Association) and recipient of the William C. Bier award for integrating the psychology of religion/spirituality with other disciplines.

He coedited a 2018 special issue on spirituality for the journal, Psychological Studies (India), and has served as associate editor at Psychology of Religion and Spirituality and Mindfulness (personal website: http://dougoman.org).

George Paxton editor of The Gandhi Way (Journal of The Gandhi Foundation, UK) author of 2 books, 3 papers in Gandhi Marg (Delhi), co-editor of 1 book, many book reviews and short articles and author of *Nonviolent Resistance to the Nazis*, (YouCaxton 2016).

Chayan Poddar is currently pursuing Ph.D. at Indian Institute of Management Shillong. He obtained his B.Sc. (Hon) in Economics from the University of Calcutta and completed Master's in Development Studies at the Indian Institute of Technology, Guwahati.

Tej Prakash has seen success in both academic and administrative areas. As a Senior Fellow member, he teaches at Duke University, USA and Delhi University, India. Working as an administrator, he has served in several departments of the Government of India in the capacity of Joint Secretary. For the past two decades, he worked in the International Monetary Fund, Washington, DC. During his visit to several countries, and in consultation with their top leaders to discuss disbursing funds from the IMF, he had prepared numerous policy documents for the use of IMF. Additionally, he has also published research papers in the area of management and finance.

R. C. Tripathi is a retired Professor of Psychology of the University of Allahabad, India. He was formerly Director of the G.B. Pant Social Science Institute and currently is the Kulguru (Vice Chancellor) of Swaraj Vidyapeeth, an institute dedicated to realization of Gandhi's "Poorna Swaraj". He has co-authored and published 7 books and has published nationally and internationally. He is the Fellow of International Association of Applied Psychology and National Academy of Psychology (India) and has been a National Fellow of the Indian Council for Social Science Research.

Nachiketa Tripathi received his doctorate in Social Psychology from Indian Institute of Technology, Kanpur, India and presently working with Indian Institute of Technology Guwahati as Professor of Psychology and Management. He has over 22 years of teaching and research experience. He has published his research work in reputed journals. His areas of research are influence strategies, gender, organizational culture and organizational learning.

Jason Turowetz is a postdoctoral research fellow at the University of Siegen (Germany), with an appointment at the Garfinkel Archive (Newburyport, MA). His research focuses on social and cultural theory, inequality and identity, and health, and his recent publications include *Discovering 'culture' in interaction: Solving problems in cultural sociology by recovering the interactional side of Parsons' conception of culture* (w/ Anne Rawls) and *Documenting diagnosis: Testing, labelling, and the production of medical records in an autism clinic* (w/ Douglas Maynard). He is currently completing book manuscripts on how clinicians diagnose autism (w/ Douglas Maynard, under contract with University of Chicago Press) and power, resistance, and moral action in the Stanley Milgram "obedience" experiments (w/ Matthew Hollander, under contract with Oxford University Press).

List of Figures

List of Tables

List of Boxes

Part I

Gandhi and the Psychology of Wisdom

1

Gandhi's Truth as a Precursor of Authentic Wisdom

V. K. Kool and Rita Agrawal

If uplifting our capabilities to come to terms with people and things around us reflects wisdom, any number of experiments human beings conduct upon themselves or outside of them to search for the truth, constitutes our inveterate attempt to configure our ongoing wisdom. In his writings as well as in his works, Gandhi experimented to seek the truth with his core belief in coexistence and nonviolence.

It is no wonder that in his recent memoir, former President of USA, Barack Obama (2020), wrote that if he was asked as to whom he would like to take out for dinner, he would say "Gandhi". This seems quite surprising, knowing the frugal vegetarian meals that Gandhi had and that, too, by sitting on the floor rather than at a dining table. Well, if we think of Einstein's remark regarding Gandhi, that he was the

V. K. Kool (✉)
SUNY Polytechnic Institute, Utica, NY, USA

R. Agrawal
Harish Chandra Post Graduate College, Varanasi, Uttar Pradesh, India

© The Author(s), under exclusive license to Springer Nature
Switzerland AG 2022
V. K. Kool and R. Agrawal (eds.), *Gandhi's Wisdom*,
https://doi.org/10.1007/978-3-030-87491-9_1

3

wisest person to have stepped on earth, Obama's choice is not surprising, despite his having spent years at the White House and having enjoyed the luxuries of life. Yet, in all probability, the majority of us would have loved to have a meeting with Gandhi but maybe, not to have dinner with!

Further, we wonder what Obama would learn from Gandhi's wisdom. In his memoir, Obama has stated that Gandhi's greatness aside, he had failed to remove the curse of the caste system and solve some of the other problems in India. In other words, there is a misconception that if someone is wise, s/he should be able to offer a magic pill to solve all the problems in a community. However, in the same memoir, Obama wrote that Gandhi, who had faced two World Wars, had set the moral tone of the previous century—a great compliment, indeed! Moral engagements offer the highest form of wisdom and help us look beyond political parties, religious or community affiliations.

We may bask in the glory of having had the company of great people such as Gandhi, but to embrace the genuineness of his wisdom is totally different. In contrast to the above views of Obama, consider those of Howard Gardner, an eminent scholar of human intelligence and faculty at Harvard University, from where Obama had studied and graduated. In an interview published in the *Harvard Gazette* (2018), Gardner has stated that he enjoys reading Gandhi's autobiography frequently and wishes to be like Gandhi in any proportion.

The above provide ample evidence for the different nuances through which Gandhi, a small, half-clad person, has been viewed: Einstein's wise human being who enlightened his mind, Obama's dinner companion, and a favorite of a leading scholar of human intelligence, Gardner, who broadens his own cognition by reading Gandhi's autobiography. When intellectuals such as Einstein, leaders such as Obama, and scholars such as Gardner regard Gandhi as an exemplar, it becomes imperative that psychologists become curious in learning about his messages to humanity, for both individuals and the society at large.

Despite the above, it is unfortunate that while experts who specialize in the psychology of wisdom have mentioned Gandhi in their research, none, to the best of our knowledge, has attempted to provide an in depth analysis of Gandhi's wisdom obtained through his experiments with truth. Apparently, people might want to take Gandhi for dinner, but they appear to be reluctant to look at his menu of wisdom, forgetting why Monday was the day of his silence, why would he not order a meal, or why was he fasting. Well, there is plenty of wisdom in fasting and observing silence, but several such forms of behaviors have received scant attention in modern psychology, let alone in the more specialized field of psychology of wisdom.

Through this book, we focus on how Gandhi drew from religious scriptures of both the East and the West and coupled it with his engagements in communities across three continents—Asia, Europe, and Africa. On the basis of these, he navigated like an avatar with behaviors such as fasting, silence, exercising self control in the face of brutality by the oppressor, and resiliency, in developing in himself and others, the zenith of human psychological capital–wisdom.

Recently, we (Kool & Agrawal, 2020) have discussed our learnings regarding Gandhi through interviews with members of his family and people associated with him. One such person was Justice Chandrasekhar Dharmadhikari, a prominent Gandhian scholar who had lived with Gandhi. He narrated how fortunate he had been to be with Gandhi. His father, a close friend of Gandhi, had written a book on Sarvodaya to illustrate Gandhi's philosophy inspired by Ruskin's (1860) book, *Unto This Last*.

In the conversation with Kool (2017), Justice Dharmadhikari narrated an incident about a villager who had a physical ailment but no money for his treatment. Though he lived far away, he somehow, managed to reach Gandhi's residence. After listening to him, Gandhi advised him to come back after a few days. During this period, Gandhi consulted several physicians, but to no avail. He then decided to carry out an experiment upon himself, and to see whether it was salt that was at the root of the villager's ailment.

The interesting part of the story, besides revealing Gandhi's tacit principle of self experiments, is that when Gandhi told the villager, upon his return after a few days, that he should not take salt or at least reduce its intake, the villager burst into anger. He told Gandhi that this was something he could have been told at his last meeting itself, rather than making him travel the long distance again, and, that he was a cruel man, and a Mahatma only for the namesake. The behavior of the villager clarifies how it is, often, difficult to understand Gandhi, and even more so, the trajectory of his wisdom, and how according to Gandhi, wisdom comes in small portions if we remain earnestly committed in our search for truth.

The most significant aspect of Gandhi's wisdom is that it is experienced when we live and experiment like Gandhi. When Kool hired a human peddled vehicle in India, called rickshaw, driven by a very frail man, the driver could not drive it up the slope. Having pity for the driver, Kool got down but gave him his contracted money. Kool was shocked when the driver refused to take it, stating that since he had failed to provide the service, he had no right to take this wage. Kool was deeply moved and tried to stuff more money into the puller's pocket but he remained adamant. When Kool questioned him regarding his deep rooted convictions of morality, his answer was simple: "I am a devout Hindu and my hero is Gandhi who respected all religions. Some of my fellow rickshaw pullers are Muslims and they are also like me. Each day, we pick up children from their homes and drop them to their schools and treat them like our own children".

The behavior described above is amply corroborated by the empirical findings of one of the most recognized authorities on, and the founder of the science of human happiness, Deiner (2008), who contended that the rickshaw pullers (those who substitute machine and horse) of the city of Kolkata were among the happiest people on earth. Sadly, we mourn the loss of Diener, as we learn that he passed away on April 27, 2021, while we are finalizing this chapter.

The message from such studies is humbling, and, enables us to realize that when virtues go hand in hand with wisdom, genuine happiness is experienced. And, while within such a mode, when we go a step further, sensing that wisdom leads to happiness, authentic wisdom becomes a corollary to authentic happiness. Gandhi's life and work was bundled with experiments in seeking authenticity of human virtues, wisdom, and happiness in relation to all people and things around us.

And then, there was a British army officer's daughter, Catherine Mary Heilman, who later took on the name, Sarala Behn and traveled from UK to India simply to join Gandhi's movement. When she arrived in

India and approached Gandhi for joining his independence movement, Gandhi asked her to do the menial job of removing the night soil, a job that was traditionally assigned to the lowest caste of untouchables in India. Many Britishers thought that Gandhi was simply using a naive British girl to humiliate British pride. Gandhi knew that any such service rendered by the young British girl, or for that matter, by any Indian, would be considered an act of extraordinary service to humanity. Yet, without genuine engagement and the relentless pursuit of testing one's own means for reaching the goal, it would not make her wise. As Gandhi wrote, seeking independence for India was not enough, it had to be attained through the highest form of inclusiveness as manifested in Vasudhaiva Kutumbakam (the world is our family). What we learn from Gandhi is that gratitude, compassion and other forms of positive behavior have restricted impact if they are not accompanied by wisdom.

Gandhi's Wisdom: Lessons from the Founding Father of Modern Psychology in the East

For Gandhi, wisdom is a product of one's inner search and not of any external inducement. In fact, Gandhi was wary about external controls and particularly about Nietzche's syndrome of *umvertung aller werte*, or the vulnerability of cardinal private values to external evaluations as is often manifested among so-called "wise" politicians.

Further, Gandhi propagated that the mere understanding of wisdom is not enough. It is imperative that it is reflected in and tested through our actions. Another Harvard scholar, known for his contribution to the understanding of moral development, Kohlberg (1976), has been criticized for limiting his analysis to moral judgment and failing to show its relationship with human conduct. While he referred to Gandhi's behavior in his writings, he failed to realize that the inveterate roots of Gandhi's wisdom lay in human conduct, not simply in its rationalization.

Wisdom is an exercise for expanding our cognition and not simply for scrolling down its accumulated layers. For Gandhi, in order to understand wisdom, one has to locate its roots in truth and nonviolence, without which our very survival would be at stake. Thus, Gandhi argued that wisdom must never be loaded onto the back seat. Rather, it must be recognized as the default mode of every human being on earth. Further, for Gandhi, nonviolence is, therefore, the cornerstone of wisdom.

Gandhi, as a scientist of human cognition, not only understood the nature and purpose of the thought of nonviolence as a precursor of wisdom, but also invited us to test it in our lives. But mere thought is not enough because, for Gandhi, thought tends to divide us, for example, I am a female, or, I am a communist, socialist, a Christian, and so on. In contrast, an exercise in the search for truth helps us to understand that it is thoughts such as these which lead to dichotomization, causing "us-them" divides and inviting destruction and violence in the absence of the default mode of nonviolence. For Gandhi, thoughts have no meaning or relevance if they are not tested for the purpose of enlarging our cognition, understanding the dynamics and implications of our greed/ motivation, and consequently, triggering our impulses/emotions and getting associated with people and things around us.

Are not such scenarios relevant to modern psychology and form the core subject matter of the science of behavior?

When Gandhi wrote that his life is his message, he was referring to the wisdom of nonviolence, so arduous to cognize in daily life, particularly when away from the prescribed religious or similar places. Yet, through emotions and intrinsic motivation emanating from acts of kindness, compassion, and forgiveness, Gandhi showed us how to embrace nonviolence. Our ability to connect with others through love, compassion, and other positive forms of behavior are not mere products of our thoughts. Such behaviors are neurologically rooted in the lower levels of brain functioning and are the first responders of survival. Therefore, for Gandhi, any understanding of wisdom would require seeking a balance between freeing ourselves from ignorance through our search for knowledge and, at the same time, carving out our default mode of cognition so as to bolster our survival, based on truth and nonviolence.

Even a cursory view of the eight-volume biography of Gandhi prepared by Tendulkar (1953) and considered to be one of the most authentic documents ever prepared on Gandhi (or, even other recently prepared websites on Gandhi) shows that while embracing truth and nonviolence, he was always ready to unlearn something, only for the purpose of relearning it to reflect the genuineness and authenticity of wisdom rooted in nonviolence. Readers will be surprised to note that for almost every component of wisdom research in which psychologists are engaged in today, such as, context, uncertainty, self control or monitoring, moral grounding, emodiversity, and virtues (the list is, actually, much longer), Gandhi stands out as an exemplar.

There is so much to learn from him that we cannot help but conclude that Gandhi is, indeed, the father of modern psychology from the East as much as William James is known to be the father of modern psychology in the West. We are not alone in making this statement. Consider what Erikson (1969) of Harvard University who, after interviewing contemporaries of Gandhi era, wrote in his Pulitzer Award winning book, *Gandhi's Truth*:

> I sensed an affinity between Gandhi's truth and the insights of modern psychology. (p. 440)

The argument for presenting wisdom in the context of nonviolence is uncontested in as much as we believe in the supremacy of life, limited to not just every human being on earth but to all things sentient in nature. If nonviolence is universal, where is the problem? The problem is in developing a universal consensus, among individuals, communities, or even nations, regarding what constitutes nonviolence. While Gandhi argued that we may never be able to develop a collective universal brain, but at a minimum, we can hold such a trajectory, even in the most difficult conditions, with the hope that it would apply to others. In such a scenario, while our position may appear to be weak, it will, still, remain moral, human, and truthful. Wisdom, in this context, appears as a chimera, as Columbia University philosopher Bilgrami (2003) argues, but it remains rooted in our morals and practical relations. Box 1.1 illustrates Gandhi's wisdom at its best.

Box 1.1 Realizing the "universalizability" of wisdom (Source Bilgrami, 2003, 2020)

Illustrating Gandhi as a philosopher, Bilgrami (2003, 2020), professor at Columbia University, narrated an incident from the days of his youth. While walking with his father in India, he noticed a wallet with currency notes sticking out of it lying on the road side. His father asked him if we should pick up the wallet or not. Bilgrami replied that if we did not pick it up, someone else would. At this point, his father replied, "if we do not take it, nobody else will". Bilgrami wrote, candidly, that while at that point of time, he was too young to understand his father's message, he wonders, now, the extent to which such a level of moral character and integrity could be demonstrated while living and working in the West.

In the context of Gandhi, even if we are unable to realize the *universality* of wisdom, we can, surely, hold it onto oneself and demonstrate it in the form of *"universalizability"*, making an earnest request for its potential for universal application. While the logic underlying the above may sound weak, it provides, unquestionably, a manifestation of a universal ethic which regards the removal of someone else's property as violence, since the owner might come back to reclaim his wallet. At the same time, if the intent is to return the wallet to the legitimate owner after picking it up, there is no violence. Intentionality is the key factor in wisdom and it must be rooted in the thought and conduct based on the cognition of nonviolence.

While twenty-first century lifestyles may often repudiate the concept of any form of universal wisdom, such universality has existed from the days of Aldous Huxley, Huston Smith, and Gottfried Leibnitz and were referred to as perennial philosophy or perennialism, with the core of the belief being reflected in the statement,

If we take the world's enduring religions at their best, we discover the distilled wisdom of the human race. (Huston Smith, 1996)

Further, as pointed out by Fr. Richard Rohr (2019),

However different, all advocate the rediscovery of the wisdom traditions of the past, believing that the various visions of the great world religious traditions share the same deep truths from which all belief systems have developed.

These deep truths were, in fact, what Gandhi had advocated and practiced over a century ago, in the form of the creed of nonviolence, needed today, more than ever before, in the face of rising communalism and religious pluralism, bringing in its wake, hatred, discrimination, prejudice and even mass violence.

While psychologists have been debating about the nature and measurement of wisdom as recently as during the International Conference on Wisdom held in Toronto (2020), it is unfortunate to note that nonviolence, as a subfield of psychology, has received scant attention as described by Murray and colleagues (2014):

> Although there have been some efforts to develop a psychology of nonviolence (e.g., Kool, 2008), and the APA has had a division of peace psychology since 1988, the potential for contributions of psychology to the study and practice of nonviolence has been largely untapped. The possibilities, however, are exciting. We have only enough space to make a few suggestions. Kool (2008) gives a far more extensive discussion. (p. 179)

Let us now explore, though briefly, the construct of wisdom in the domain of modern psychology. While it would not be possible to deal with all the work that has been undertaken, we will attempt to focus on the major threads of empirical work on the definition and measurement of wisdom.

The Psychology of Human Wisdom

Despite the fact that wisdom has been at the core of almost all religions and philosophy, psychology seems to have fallen behind. The earliest mention of wisdom was as early as in 1922 by G. Stanley Hall. Thereafter, we see a fairly long gap, with research, in earnest, in this all important topic appearing only in the mid-1970s. There is, however, one exception, that of Erikson (1969), who had concluded that the successful resolution of the final stage of identity seeking, namely, integrity versus despair, is the hallmark of wisdom.

By and large, formal research on wisdom was not initiated until the beginning of this century. For the most part of the previous century, psychologists remained preoccupied with the study of human intelligence. Examples include Terman, Wechsler, Sternberg, and Gardner, who believed that their ultimate goal was to unravel this human potential. It was much later that they realized that intelligent people are not necessarily wise and that wisdom, not intelligence, is the key to understanding and solving human problems.

Over the years, one comes across two broad categories of theories of wisdom. Firstly, there are subjective or implicit theories, which are based on folk psychology and common sense and focus on what people consider wise behavior. Secondly, there are the explicit theories, which have attempted to understand wisdom through empirical studies and are concerned with unraveling the antecedents, correlates, and consequences of wisdom. While the former dominated the scene for several years, recent empirical work and measurement has led to the elaboration of various explicit theories of wisdom. We provide a brief overview of some of them.

The 1970s saw two, almost, parallel developments, one at the Max Plank Institute, Berlin, Germany led by Paul Baltes, and Ursula Staudinger and the other in California, USA by Vivian Clayton and her student, Monika Ardelt.

At the Max Plank Institute at Berlin, Germany, Baltes' interest in wisdom was whetted by wanting to identify the antecedents of expert behavior and the factors that facilitate the bringing out of the best in individuals in all walks of life (Baltes & Smith, 2008). On the basis of empirical findings, he formulated what has come to be known as the Berlin Wisdom Paradigm, according to which wisdom can be considered to be "an expert system dealing with the meaning and conduct of a good life". While the latter refers to the understanding, planning, and managing of a good life, the former, that is, expertise can be understood in terms of five criteria, two of which are general criteria while the remaining three are meta-criteria. The first category consists of rich factual knowledge (what does one know about human conditions) and rich procedural knowledge (how to handle issues in life). The meta-criteria deal with contextualism (fitting in roles and finding interconnections), relativism of values (understanding differences), and the recognition and management of uncertainty. Participants who scored above a certain point on all five criteria were considered to being wise. Later, using these five criteria, Ursula Staudinger, at the Jacobs Center for Wisdom, Bremen, developed a measure known as the Bremen measure of wisdom.

Around the same time that Baltes and his team were attempting to understand the basis of wise behavior, a developmental psychologist and neuropsychologist, Vivian Clayton, proceeded along a totally different trajectory, and focused on personal wisdom and how knowledge remains at the threshold of wisdom until it is internalized. She adopted the life span approach and developed a definition of wisdom which continues to be of relevance even today, concluding that wisdom consists of three aspects: cognition, reflection, and compassion. As individuals age, they develop higher levels of cognition, which can be used to reflect upon or gain insights which can, then, be used to understand and help others. Based on these three components, Monika Ardelt (2003), a life span psychologist in the USA, later developed a scale which could be used for the measurement of wisdom. The life span approach to wisdom continues to have its proponents although it has now been clarified that wisdom can be seen even in younger people.

A third line of thought regarding what constitutes wisdom was derived by the cognitivists. Psychologists such as Labouvie-Vief (Labouvie-Vief, 1980) contended that even the final stage of Piagetian cognitive development, namely that of the formal operations stage, fails to provide the type of thinking required by the complicated and ill-defined challenges of life. Also, individuals continued to develop cognitively, even after reaching the formal operations stage. This development was termed post-formal development and was marked by the ability to engage in dialectical thinking and reasoning, requiring intellectual humility, contextualization, and the ability to take a variety of perspectives. This approach to cognition, referred to as the Neo-Piagetian approach, has spurred wisdom research leading to the identification of the characteristics of the post-formal operations stage, on the basis of which individuals can be categorized as wise.

Another landmark in wisdom research was that by Robert Sternberg, known for his contributions to the study of intelligence. In recent years, Sternberg has professed that intelligence alone is not enough to handle the complexities of life. Sternberg views wisdom in terms of the successful application of tacit knowledge composed of a combination of creativity and intelligence. Based on the research of his team, he developed the Balance theory of wisdom, according to which wisdom requires a balance at all three levels of human behavior, intrapersonal, interpersonal, and extrapersonal (such as community work) in the context of adapting to, shaping, or choosing environments. More research is needed to demonstrate the application of his theory, albeit he is widely known for his books on the psychology of wisdom.

Notable work has also been undertaken by Howard Nusbaum, a cognitive neuroscientist at the Center for Practical Wisdom at the University of Chicago, with the primary aim of isolating how people can become wiser. According to Nusbaum, wisdom needs to be examined in the context of the community and the society and the ability for reflective decision making, self regulation, and self control (Sternberg et al., 2019).

While cognitive psychologists, such as those referred to above, focused on cognition as being the basis of wisdom, positive psychologists such as Seligman and others have attempted to understand the wisdom in terms of our striving for the positive virtues of life. They define wisdom as our ability for procuring knowledge and using it for our betterment and is reflected in five forms: creativity, curiosity, judgment, love of learning and perspective-taking.

The work of positive psychologists has received a massive impetus, recently, with even scholars in psychiatry taking an interest. Dilip Jeste, a geriatric neuro-psychiatrist at the University of California, San Diego, has attempted to bridge the gap between medicine and positive psychology. He contends that, like psychology of the early part of the twentieth century, psychiatry, too, has focused more on the analysis and treatment of mental illness than on mental health. He adds that while even William James, the father of modern psychology, proposed that positive virtues go a long way in reducing the risk of mental illness, it was not until positive psychology came into being with the writings of Maslow and others, that psychology started focusing on positive aspects of human nature. So, just as we now speak of positive psychology, the time has come for a positive psychiatry, which may be defined as that science of psychiatry which attempts to understand and nurture human well-being through the constructs of resilience, optimism, self efficacy, social engagement, environmental factors, spirituality, and wisdom (Ardelt & Jeste, 2016; Jeste & Lafee, 2020).

Perturbed by the observation that human beings survive even after they reach the stage of infertility, which goes against Darwin's theory of survival of the fittest, Jeste and his team concluded that one of the reasons for this is wisdom, which seems to increase with age, also called the "grandma factor", leading to greater well-being and happiness, in general. Jeste and his coworkers propose that wisdom is a multidimensional trait, including specific components such as social decision making, a pragmatic knowledge of life, empathy, reflection and self understanding, ability to cope with uncertainty, and even a sense of humor.

Their contribution to the study of wisdom is important because it attempts to delve into the neurological basis of wisdom. The research by Jeste and others has shown that wisdom involves both the phylogenetically newer prefrontal cortex and the older limbic system. This not only provides evidence for the evolutionary basis of wisdom but also clarifies that wise behavior involves both cognitive and emotional components.

Apart from the cognitive angle, wisdom has also been studied from the perspective of emotions by Grossmann and his team. While many researchers have focused on the ability to down regulate emotions as the hall mark of wisdom, Grossmann and his team are of the view that a differentiated and balanced focus on a variety of emotions leads to wiser reasoning. In other words, emotional diversity or, emodiversity is an important precursor of wisdom (Grossmann, 2017; Grossmann et al., 2020).

On the basis of empirical work they have concluded that when people manifest higher emodiversity, there is a greater likelihood of engaging in aspects such as intellectual humility, a willingness to consider alternative options and a search for compromise, all of which are seen as concomitants of wisdom. Not only is the concept of emodiversity important for overcoming personal hassles but it has been found to be equally potent for resolving interpersonal issues and geo-political problems.

From the above, it can be noted that while wisdom appears to be a multidimensional construct, the cognitive aspect along with its neurological substrates is of prime importance. That the affective processes have adaptive value is clarified by the finding that some parts of the phylogenetically older limbic system, have been found to play a role.

Issues with Research on the Psychology of Wisdom

Whether we look at wisdom subjectively or empirically, the fact remains that it is a virtue of the highest order, cherished for happiness and for attaining the super order goals of our lives. With wisdom around, we are able to nurture our families and communities; sustain and improvise our relationships with all things sentient in nature, and, derive meaning in life. In other words, despite the differences in defining or measuring wisdom, it is comprehended as a virtue. Adding it to the repertoire of psychological inquiry would not only be immensely worthwhile but would also make "explicit the goal of orchestrating mind and virtue towards human excellence and the common good" (Baltes & Smith, 2008).

At the same time, one major concern with psychological studies of wisdom is that as soon as the classification of the components of wisdom is attempted, the construct appears fuzzy. An example is a study at the VIA Institute (reported by Miller, 2020) revealing that 93 percent of participants selected, either, fairness, curiosity, love, judgment, or kindness as the best indicator of wisdom. This begs a question regarding the composition of the construct of wisdom and the weights to be assigned to its different components. For instance, is a high level of kindness commensurate with wisdom?

In other words,

> The richness of this emerging field has also led to confusion about the psychological conceptualization of the construct. (Grossmann et al., 2020, p. 104)

In view of the above, an international Wisdom Task Force consisting of researchers from across the globe gathered together in Toronto, Canada in July 2019 with the principal objective of describing the current status of research in the psychology of wisdom, so as to clarify the knowns, the unknowns and the areas of dispute.

On the basis of a mixed methods study, various clarifications emerged but probably the most significant was the consensus on a common definition. It was felt that while the researchers differed on a variety of nuances of wisdom, at the core was a general understanding regarding a common definition of what constitutes wisdom. This would enable the overcoming of the jingle-jangle phenomenon with which research in wisdom is currently beset and, thereby, help researchers arrive at a more coherent set of findings.

According to the experts, the psychometrically derived definition of wisdom can be said to consist of two aspects, namely, a moral grounding and social cognitive processing or metacognition.

The meaning of the above two aspects clearly reveals that Gandhi was ahead of modern psychology, and what was unearthed by this Wisdom Task Force, after considerable deliberation and by utilizing advanced statistical methods, was grasped by Gandhi through his simple experiments on truth with himself as the sole subject. A glance at the meaning of the above two aspects as constructed by the Task Force furthers our contention regarding the wisdom of Gandhi.

According to Grossmann and his team (2020),

> By moral grounding, we mean a set of interrelated aspirational (or normative) goals, balance of self and other oriented interests, pursuit of truth and orientation toward shared humanity. By excellence in social cognitive processing we specifically refer to the application of certain forms of metacognition to reasoning and problem solving in situational domains that have the potential to affect other people. (p 103)

To clarify what the researchers meant by moral grounding a survey was carried out, the results of which revealed the following (Grossmann et al., 2020, p. 108):

- "orientation towards shared humanity (i.e., no in-group vs. outgroup distinction)" (80%),
- "pursuit of truth" (69%),
- "common good orientation" (64%),
- "balance of self-protective and other-oriented interests" (56%).

It is amazing to see the close parallel between these characteristics and the virtues advocated by Gandhi. What is even more important is that Gandhi provided detailed descriptions of each of these in his writings and after verifying their veracity through experiments on himself, he guided his fellow satyagrahis in ways of attaining each of them. The wisdom engrained in them is clear from the success of his nonviolent movements and the ways in which people flocked to him despite the extreme hardships and grinding poverty.

The importance of perspectival metacognition (PMC) was also analyzed, revealing that without PMC, moral grounding would remain a mere abstract concept, far removed from their application in daily life decision making. PMC, an important aspect of which is dialectical reasoning involving the recognition of the fallibility and limits of one's knowledge, or what has been termed intellectual humility, is the ability to look at the situation through a variety of perspectives and the tendency to be able to integrate diverse viewpoints, and is now being recognized as an important cognitive feature of wisdom by several researchers including Sternberg, Grossmann, and Staudinger.

PMC can override the immediate impulse to protect self-interests (Grossmann, Brienza, & Bobocel, 2017), augmenting propositional tendencies by allowing comparison across multiple propositions and moral principles (e.g., family security vs. societal well-being). (Grossmann et al., 2020, p. 110)

Another key feature of the findings of the Task Force was that the researchers showed agreement regarding the plasticity of wisdom and the role of training. However, while theorization regarding the methodology of such training is abundant, we are still not sure about their efficacy because of the lack of empirical validation. Once again, Gandhi comes to the rescue: the very fact that he could train thousands of people, the majority of whom were illiterate, and help them enlarge their moral compass to become morally inclusive and overcome all types of "us-them" boundaries, stands evidence for the efficacy of the methods he used. Some of these, for example, the role of silence, fasting, and vows have been dealt with in detail elsewhere in this volume, while a detailed description of Gandhi's methods of training people in self control using cognitive mechanisms can be found in our earlier book (Kool & Agrawal, 2020).

As revealed by the common definition, wisdom requires a sound moral grounding, manifested through a strong societal orientation and a readiness to work toward the development of mutual understanding. While we understand that wisdom invites healthy social living, there is a clearly a dilemma, as human beings have a tendency to categorize and create "us-them" dichotomies. In other words, wisdom, often, requires mitigating such "us-them" boundaries and playing against the evolutionary mode of human survival. So, in several chapters of this book, we have raised the issue of the cost of moral inclusion in the context of wisdom.

At the same time, can we afford to undermine interdisciplinary research which has made major contributions for enhancing our understanding of the moral grounding of wisdom? For example, we have Johan Galtung, a mathematician, sociologist, political scientist, and founder of peace studies in Oslo, Norway. His differentiation of three types of violence, direct, structural, and cultural, for each of which there is a nonviolent antithesis, has helped understand and resolve countless conflicts from around the world and at the same time brought to the fore the inherent wisdom of concepts such as reconciliation, mediation, and openness (Galtung, 1996).

What about economist Kenneth Boulding, whose book, *The three faces of power*, helped people realize that power does not always mean domination of one party over another? He contended that threat power is of no use in the absence of exchange power and even more so, integrative power, once again contributing to the wisdom of moral inclusion (Boulding, 1990).

Another political scientist Gene Sharp (1960) has added to our understanding of the wisdom of nonviolence by showing how nonviolent techniques offer a pragmatic solution in many a conflict. It is not without reason that he is known as the Machiavelli of nonviolence. The above provide just three examples of how the psychological understanding of wisdom can gain through interdisciplinary research. Even a cursory glance reveals many more such gems and some of them have found their due place in this book.

When the wisdom inherent in the above is complemented by the practical steps advocated by Gandhi, considerable more can be garnered. So much so that noted researcher Johan Galtung has claimed that Gandhi is to conflict what Einstein and Newton are to physics. For example, Gandhi was a strong proponent of what Boulding was to term integrative power. Consider Gandhi's definition of power, based on the three principles of (1) respect for one's opponents as persons; (2) refusal to cooperate with unjust power; and (3) creation of alternative systems of power through nonviolent direct action.

In fact, Gandhi's ideas offer the perfect resolution for the warrior-pacifist dilemma, by exemplifying how these contradictory tendencies can be integrated through the practice of nonviolence. Gandhi's trysts with fighting oppression bring to the fore the ways in which the steadfastness of the warrior can be combined with the total abhorrence of violence of the pacifist.

Further, wisdom is useful for life in general, over and above personal ends. Work provides not only money for our livelihood, but it also brings pride and meaning in life. However, we would like to point out that, as far as wisdom research is considered, the domain of work has received scant attention. While Sternberg, Grossmann, and others have contributed through empirical findings, their research is still at a very nascent stage. In our recent book (Kool & Agrawal, 2020) and in some of our other papers (for example, Kool, 2013; Kool & Agrawal, 2013; 2018) the reader will note the ways through which several domains of life can be improved through the application of Gandhi's wisdom.

In several chapters of this book, the readers will find how worker productivity and sustainability of organizations can be enhanced by applying Gandhi's wisdom at work, through the construct of the calling orientation and trusteeship. Similarly, the wisdom engrained in Gandhi's pattern of education, Nayi Talim, has been well documented by the United Nations and has made Gandhi's thoughts on education the center piece of its Sustainable Development Goals for education. Nobel Laureates such as Paul Crutzen have discussed how Gandhian wisdom may help in finding solutions to the problems of climate change and environmental destruction.

Nagler (1990) suggested that there is a need to establish the science of nonviolence and in this context, as we have argued here, and in the following chapters of the book, that then, we will be able to understand the wisdom inherent in nonviolence intensely as well as comprehensively.

One more aspect that is found wanting in wisdom research is that it fails to provide a cross cultural perspective. This is of utmost importance when we remind ourselves that cultures vary in their description of what constitutes wisdom. A prime example of the above is the difference between the individualistic and collectivist philosophies of Aristotle and Confucius. While the international Task Force on wisdom was certainly a step taken to overcome this shortcoming, much more needs to be done. We would like to point out the contention of Arnett (2008) that the results of American psychology are far from being representative, considering the fact that while developing its constructs and theories, it fails to take into account over 95% of the global population. The need of the hour is to involve thinkers and researchers from all over the globe. Gandhi provides us with a starting point, with his vast multi-cultural experiences spanning across three continents.

While reviewing current work on wisdom, it was unfortunate to note that none of the scholars researching in the psychology of wisdom engaged in the personal emulation of Gandhi, one of the wisest human beings. To enrich the psychology of wisdom, three scholars, who have written extensively on Gandhi and have found in him, an exemplar for themselves, discuss, that unlike wisdom studies that tear apart the psychological components of wisdom, what it takes to view wisdom from the lens of Gandhi? Our contention is that wisdom research needs inputs from such wise scholars who represent the mainstream of various social sciences and are cheer leaders of Gandhi's wisdom at its best.

Easwaran (1983), a leading scholar on Gandhi, warned us several decades ago about the risks in understanding Gandhi's wisdom when viewed in an isolated context. Saints reach their sainthood through their engagements in several episodes of human activities and we, therefore, find them wise. Mere acts of compassion, empathy, or forgiveness, howsoever cherished and admired, do not make us wise, but its script and schema in our minds and subsequent resolution for its expression, certainly, lead to wisdom in the context around us. Wisdom is as much personal as it is social. This book is an invitation to the psychology of wisdom to enlarge its compass in an interdisciplinary context framed through the lens of Gandhi's life and work.

In other words, Gandhi helps us to bridge the gap between the domains of cognition, personality, motivation, emotion, and morality in order to obtain a more true to life perspective on how to solve complex problems at the personal, interpersonal, and societal levels. A focus on Gandhi will enable psychologists to bring greater ecological validity into their laboratory-based findings.

References

Ardelt, M. (2003). Development and empirical assessment of three-dimensional wisdom scale. *Research on Aging, 25,* 275–324.

Ardelt, M., & Jeste, D. (2016). Wisdom and hard times: The ameliorating effect of wisdom on the negative association between adverse life events. *The Journal of Gerontology, 73,* -8, 1374–1383.

Arnett, J. J. (2008). The neglected 95%: Why American psychology needs to be less American. *American Psychologist, 67,* 602–614.

Baltes, P. B., & Smith, J. (2008). The fascination of wisdom: Its nature, ontogeny, and function. *Perspectives on Psychological Science, 3,* 56–64.

Bilgrami, A. (2003). Gandhi the philosopher. *Economic and Political Weekly,* 38–39.

Bilgrami, A. (2020). Rationality and alienation: Themes from Gandhi. In T. Akram & S. Rashid (Eds.), *Faith, finance and economy: Beliefs and economic well being*. Springer.

Boulding, K. E. (1990). Three faces of power. In V. K. Kool (Ed.), *Perspectives on nonviolence*. Springer-Verlag.

Diener, E. (2008). *Happiness: Unlocking the mysteries of psychological wealth*. Wiley.

Easwaran, E. (1983). *Gandhi the man*. Random House.

Erikson, E. (1969). *Gandhi's truth*. Norton.

Galtung, J. (1996). *Peace by peaceful means: Peace and conflict, development and civilization*. Sage.

Grossmann, I. (2017). Wisdom in context. *Perspectives on Psychological Science, 12*(2), 233–257.

Grossmann, I., Weststrate, N. M., Ardelt, M., Brienza, J. P., Dong, M., Ferrari, M., ... & Vervaeke, J. (2020). The science of wisdom in a polarized world: Knowns and unknowns. *Psychological Inquiry, 31*(2), 103–133. https://doi.org/10.1080/1047840X.2020.1750917

Hall, G. S. (1922). *Senescence: The last half of life*. Appelton.

Jeste, D., & Lafee, S. (2020). *Wiser: The scientific roots of wisdom, compassion, and what makes us good*. Sounds True.

Kolhberg, L. (1976). Moral stages and moralization: The cognitive development approach. In T. Lockina (Ed.), *Moral development and behavior*. Holt, Rinehart and Winston

Kool, V. K. (2008). *The psychology of nonviolence and aggression*. Palgrave Macmillan.

Kool, V. K. (2013). Applications of Gandhian concepts in psychology and allied disciplines. *Indian Journal of Psychiatry, 55*, 235–238.

Kool, V. K. (2017). Personal communication during interview with Justice Dharmadhikari.

Kool, V. K., & Agrawal, R. (2013). Whither Skinner's science of behavior, his assessment of Gandhi, and its aftermath? *Gandhi Marg, 35*, 487–518.

Kool, V. K., & Agrawal, R. (2018). Gandhian philosophy for living in the modern world: Lessons from the psychology of satyagraha. In S. Fernando & R. Moodley (Eds.), *Global psychologies: Mental health and the global South*. Palgrave-MacMillan.

Kool, V. K., & Agrawal, R. (2020). *Gandhi and the psychology of nonviolence, Volumes 1 and 2*. Palgrave Macmillan.

Labouvie-Vief, G. (1980). Beyond formal operations: Uses and limits of pure logic in life-span development. *Human Development, 23*, 141–161.

Miller, K. (2020). The five character strengths in positive psychology. PositivePsychology.com.

Murray, H., Lyubansky, M., Miller, K., & Ortega, L. (2014). Toward a psychology of nonviolence. In E. Mustakova-Possardt & M. Lyubanski, et al. (Eds.), *Toward socially responsible psychology for a global era* (pp. 151–182). New York: Springer.

Nagler, M. N. (1990). Nonviolence as new science. In V. K. Kool (Ed.), *Perspectives on nonviolence* (pp. 131–139). Springer Verlag.

Obama, B., & H. (2020). *A promised land*. Crown.

Rohr, R. (2019, August 14). *Distilled wisdom — center for action and contemplation*. https://cac.orgdistilled-wisdom-2019-08-14

Ruskin, J. (1860). *Unto this last*. Cornhill Magazine.

Sharp, G. (1960). *Gandhi wields the weapon of moral power*. Navajivan Publishers.

Smith, H. (1996). *Bill Moyers: The wisdom of faith with Huston Smith*. WNET.

Sternberg, R. J., Nusbaum, H. C., & Gluck, J. (2019). *Applying wisdom to contemporary problems*. Palgrave-MacMillan.

Tendulkar, D. G. (1953). *Mahatma: Life of Mohandas Karamchand Gandhi*. Jhaveri & Tendulkar.

2

Milgram's Lost Gandhi: Whither Gandhi's Wisdom of Nonviolence in the Psychology of Wisdom

V. K. Kool and Rita Agrawal

Would you agree to deliver shocks to another human being for making mistakes while learning some very simple material? Generally speaking, we would say that it would be crazy to give shocks for the above, but you will be surprised that such cruel behavior was displayed consistently by participants in many experiments conducted around the globe. Through his pioneering research work, Stanley Milgram (1974), demonstrated, empirically, in his laboratory how ordinary human beings could be goaded into accepting his request to deliver electric shocks to an "erring learner" for a simple task. Further, it becomes even more difficult to believe that a substantial number of these participants continued to deliver shocks, at even lethal levels.

V. K. Kool (✉)
SUNY Polytechnic Institute, Utica, NY, USA

R. Agrawal
Harish Chandra Post Graduate College, Varanasi, Uttar Pradesh, India

While Milgram's experiments have been successfully replicated in many research laboratories around the globe, exhibiting consistent results since it was extensively reported in the early 1970s, a number of explanations have been offered for such human vulnerability (for example, Burger, 2009; Dolinski et al., 2017; Russell, 2011). The amount of curiosity generated was so pervasive that the official journal of the American Psychological Association, the *American Psychologist*, dedicated its entire volume to Milgram's experiment in 2008, almost 40 years after the original experiments.

While Milgram and fellow psychologists remained profoundly busy in searching for the causes of such obedient human behavior (irrational but also unethical to the extent that the replication of this experiment is now banned), there were hardly any attempts to study the behavior of those invited participants of Milgram's study who simply refused to give any shock to the learner, who defied the instructions of Milgram, and, walked away from his laboratory. Many other replications of Milgram's work have also corroborated the above, the common denominator in all such experiments being that the number of disobeying subjects was very insignificant, being less than 2%, as reported, initially, by Milgram.

Milgram and later researchers continued to ignore their disobedient nonviolent participants. The reason for this neglect could be the insignificant quantum of knowledge regarding nonviolence in the domain of psychology. It must also be kept in mind that for years together, divergent thinking of any type has failed to receive a level playing field in mainstream American psychology, especially, in the presence of the APA Division of Military Psychology.

In contrast to the prevailing neglect of the disobeying subjects, Kool attempted to analyze the reason for such disobedience. In his researches in the 1980s and the 1990s Kool (Kool, 1990; 1993; Kool & Sen, 1984) noticed that those subjects who scored high on his test of nonviolence (the NVT), were more likely to refuse to participate in the experiment or tended to deliver significantly lower levels of shocks than those who scored low on the NVT (see Kool & Agrawal, 2020; Sen, 1993).

In a recent analysis published by us (Kool & Agrawal, 2020), it has been demonstrated that in at least four variant conditions of Milgram's

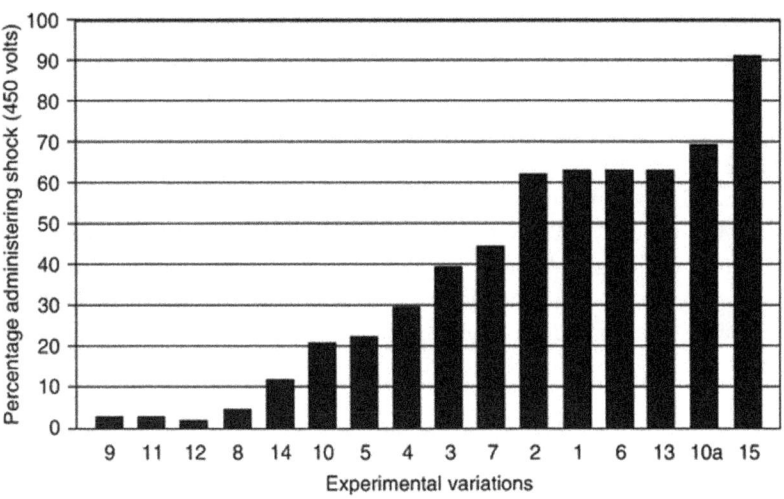

S. No	Experimental variations	S. No	Experimental variations
9.	Learner demands to be shocked	3.	Proximity
11.	Authority as victim—an ordinary man commanding	7.	Institutional context
12.	Two authorities—contradictory commands	2.	Voice feedback
8.	Subjects free to choose shock level	1.	Remote victim
14.	Two peers rebel	6.	Women as subjects
10.	An ordinary man gives orders	13.	Two authorities—one as victim
5.	Remote authority	10a.	The subject as bystander
4.	Touch proximity	15.	A peer administers shocks

Fig. 2.1 Some facts and traces of psychology of nonviolence in Milgram's study (Kool & Agrawal, 2020)

study, there were clear indications of escalation of disobedience, or, in other words, nonviolence, as illustrated in Fig. 2.1, with a fewer number of subjects delivering shocks. Probably, it is results such as these that made Jacob Appel (2019) argue that, instead of calling Milgram's study a study of obedience, it could well be called a study of disobedience (Box 2.1).

Box 2.1 Rethinking the infamous Milgram experiment in authoritarian times by Jacob M. Appel, M.D. J.D., Icahn School of Medicine at Mount Sinai, NY (*Source* Appel, 2019, scientificamerican.com)
"Some of Milgram's subjects did defy the experimenter. Like Jan Rensaleer, a Dutch immigrant who responded to the experiment's warning that he had no other choice to continue at 255 volts with the following memorable declaration:

> I do have a choice. Why don't I have a choice? I came here on my own free will. I thought I could help in a research project. But if I have to hurt somebody to do that, or if I was in his place, too, I wouldn't stay there. I can't continue. I'm very sorry. I think I've gone too far already, probably.

In some cases, the subject stood up during the experiment and walked away.

So maybe it is a mistake to view Milgram's work as an "obedience experiment"—although, he clearly did. Maybe, what he actually conducted was a disobedience experiment, showing that some people will not follow orders no matter how strong the social pressure.

They are out there, waiting the moment when history calls upon them to disobey. We should not lose sight of them in the weeds of social psychology. They are Stanley Milgram's unheralded legacy—and we may even stand among them."

For the purpose of clarity, let us now look at the first four experimental variations in which there were a fewer number of people who were ready to administer 450-V shocks, starting with the variation # 9, in which there were the least number of subjects (refer to Fig. 2.1).

1.# 9. Learner demands to be shocked (Compare it with Gandhi and his followers inviting violence from their adversaries in their satyagraha movement)
2.# 11. Authority as victim, an ordinary man commanding

3.# 12. When two authorities offer contradictory commands
4.# 8. Subjects free to choose shock level

Looking at Fig. 2.1 in this way, one finds that as conditions changed, the number of subjects, who were ready to administer high levels of shock, declined considerably, with compliance levels dropping to less than 10%. This data provides, in the process, interesting insights regarding ways of reducing aggression. Unfortunately, Milgram had not paid much heed to this aspect, preoccupied as he was, with the investigation of the dynamics of obedience to authority in terms of aggressive behavior. However, we see exciting possibilities in this part of Milgram's data and take this opportunity to extend this monumental research on the psychology of aggression to understand more about nonviolence (from Kool & Agrawal [2020]: *Gandhi and the Psychology of Nonviolence, volume 1*).

It seems that psychology at the time of Milgram, and even today, has failed to latch on to the momentum of nonviolence and embrace its wisdom.

We argue, here, with the support of additional scenarios in psychology and illustrate, why this discipline remained apathetic to the study of the human tendency to survive and flourish. Kool (2008) examined the studies of Solomon Asch, in which one dissenting observer changed the decisions of other conforming participants in judging, falsely, the size of lines, and those by Philip Zimbardo on prison guards who could not take the pressures and walked away, in the context of the psychology of nonviolence. It is, also, known that Henry David Thoreau and Gandhi were, then, considered insignificant rebels who were neither popular in the mainstream of their psycho-historical times nor rated wise as they are regarded today.

As a consequence, psychology started losing its momentum: by not attending to the behavior of people such as Henry David Thoreau and Mohandas Karamchand Gandhi—but in contrast, studying Adolph Hitler's psychological profile prepared promptly during WW II at the famous Harvard Clinic. It is, indeed, unfortunate that Gandhi, at any time or anywhere, was never evaluated. For psychology, it was considered wise to study the context of genocide, but rarely so, if any, in seeking justice and freedom for citizens across continents. As a consequence, whereas other social sciences were advancing in the company of those who sought peace and nonviolence, for example, through the monumental works of Galtung, Sharp, Boulding and several others, psychology was still battling to bring cognition, its mainstay, to the forefront and struggling for survival as a science.

Gandhi and William James' Moral Equivalent of War

William James is generally regarded as the father of modern psychology. Besides his contribution toward laying the foundation of modern psychology as an independent science, distinguishing between primary and secondary memory (which is still regarded as a classical finding), analyzing habits as our fly wheels, and exploring religion and related issues of consciousness, he is also very well known across academic disciplines for his classical essay on the moral equivalent of war (James, 1910). There is nothing more important than our own survival, argued William James, and continuously attempted to enlarge our moral compass through the repertoire of virtues. As we state in this chapter and in the previous chapter, the discipline of psychology failed to take a leaf from the wisdom offered by its own mentor. In contrast, in his lesser known book, *Talks to Teachers* (James, 1899), James describes how he was intrigued by the knowledge and behavior of students from the Eastern countries, whom he happened to meet during his visit to the UK.

The study of wisdom begins with the laying of the bricks of our experiences on the solid foundation of human existence and by treating all things sentient in our universe as our own garden, as put by Noble Laureate Paul Crutzen, or as what Gandhi called Vasudaiva Kutumbakam (the universe is our family). But, the ways through which our experiences relate to each other so as to function at a higher order was neither given any attention in Western Psychology until the last quarter of the previous century nor was James considered significant in building a psychology of cognition. In fact, veteran scholar Skinner's behaviorism had such a strong influence in the domain of psychology that cognition remained on the back seat for the major part of the previous century.

Around the same time as when James was teaching at Harvard University and was permitting Edward Thorndike to experiment with rats in his home laboratory, Gandhi, in his own way, was laying the foundations of modern psychology. Gandhi's sprawling laboratory covered at least three continents of the globe—Africa, Asia, and Europe, and there he learned, practiced, and demonstrated the efficacy of several psychological concepts, much like veteran psychologist Ebbinghaus, who searched in and researched on his own memory, establishing the nature and laws governing the associations forming in his brain. Gandhi championed several psychological concepts in nuanced forms such as moral inclusion (by integrating various communities for seeking justice), self control (by demonstrating nonviolently and without retaliation to oppression), self efficacy (by sustained efforts to believe in ourselves), empathy (to the extent of loving our own adversary), and more, leading to the expansion of human cognition.

We have presented a plethora of evidence (Kool & Agrawal, 2020) to clarify how Gandhi, inveterately, illustrated many modern psychological theories and concepts of cognitive psychology, for example, those used by Nobel Laureate Kahneman (Kahneman & Tversky, 1979) in his prospect theory; behavioral economist Nobel Laureate Thaler (Thaler & Sunstein, 2008) in conceptualizing nudging and boosting; intrinsic motivation and the neuro-social psychology of self control. There is no book of modern psychology that does not refer to the concepts we have presented here. Unfortunately, while they form the distinguishing features of Gandhi's nonviolence, they rarely find recognition and detailed analysis, leave alone appreciation, in the science of psychology, even though, they form the mainstay of our cognition and wisdom.

It is our considered opinion that by promoting Hitler's psychological profile and neglecting Gandhi, psychology lost its wisdom, in as much as its similarity to Milgram's neglect of disobedient participants, unwilling to deliver shocks to their fellow human beings.

Wisdom is not about cutting and pasting a piece of human knowledge acquired in the laboratory. Rather, it epitomizes collective and configured human experiences, in the ways in which Gandhi based them on the solid foundation of his life and experiments with truth. In fact, in our book, consisting of two volumes on *Gandhi and the psychology of nonviolence* (Kool & Agrawal, 2020), we have shown that there is hardly any subfield of psychology, from educational to community psychology, or relatively newer fields such as psychology of technology and environment, that have not been enriched by the application of Gandhi's conceptualization of human behavior. And, we wonder how psychology, a science of behavior, found him good for references only, as had been done by luminaries of psychology such as Skinner, Bandura, and others, but rarely, if any, attempted to establish him as an unquestioned father of modern psychology emerging in the Eastern part of the globe.

However, there is one notable exception, Erikson (1969), who wrote in his Pulitzer award winning book, *Gandhi's Truth*,

> …I sensed an affinity between Gandhi's truth and the insights of modern psychology (p. 440),

albeit, his widely popular book was presented in the psychoanalytic perspective. Upon reading this book multiple times, we learned how deeply Erikson engaged himself to the understanding of Gandhi. The book reveals how Gandhi's moral and ethical perspectives were blended with the caring and justice considerations such that he was able to resolve his follower's identity struggle in a violent world, yet, stayed strong as a rock to exercise nonviolence and demonstrate wisdom, in the context of what Gandhi called, his experiments with truth.

Whereas, we acknowledge that great researches emanate from sophisticated establishments and laboratories, there is considerable to be learned from outside their walls and by integrating, sensibly and prudently, the available segment of such knowledge. Here, the remarks of Arnett (2008) are useful, stated so succinctly, yet, categorically, that there is a serious problem with the leadership of American psychology as it tends to ignore roughly 95% of global human behavior in its academic pursuits and related publications.

Both Gandhi and James, in their own ways, advocated the human need for survival and preached the significance of nonviolence, James through his writings on war against war and Gandhi through his activism. Both were thinkers of the human mind and deserve to be called the founding fathers of modern psychology, one in the West and the other in the East.

There is enough reason to argue for their common cardinal goal in unraveling the dynamics of the human mind. What is good about a science that leads to destruction but offers no wisdom for its management?

We take pride in our technological achievements, housing developments, and broadly speaking, consider ourselves modern and sophisticated, but do we think about the new habits that are emerging and creating gaps between us and nature, among human beings, and in retaining our cultural heritage that has brought us to cherish our current existence after surviving thousands of years of struggle? Our fly wheels, known as habits, need rebooting with all the bugs being fixed through our wisdom, in the context of the emerging noosphere in the changing world. Call it collective wisdom, cultural wisdom, or anything, wisdom will remain wisdom, not out there but residing within us, and only, thereafter, can we nomenclature it, societal, personal, or both. Recently, in a similar tone, Nagler (2020) echoes it in the form of the third harmony mentioned elsewhere in this book.

We believe that for both Gandhi and James, nonviolence was the lever which could provide a jump start to any psychology—Western or Eastern, experimental, or non experimental, though, certainly, not one which is not tested and experienced within ourselves. They guided and illuminated us and suffused us with immense wisdom for the establishment of a new enterprise of human knowledge, known as psychology, and suggested that through its inspired and ingrained use, we can link our wisdom to war against war or to experimenting with truth. French scholar Bruno Latour's (1993, 2013) question, "are we really modern", points to the complex ways through which the layers of our wisdom are earned through membership in the culture around us.

Nonviolence as Wisdom

Let us begin with the following two scenarios (Kool, 2008). First, is it wisdom to use violence when an issue can be resolved through nonviolent methods? The answer is simple: no rational human being would use violent methods to solve a problem if it could be resolved peacefully.

In contrast, the answer to the second question is not that simple: is it wisdom to use nonviolence when it is failing (or likely to fail) to resolve a conflict?

According to Gandhi, violence can never be wiped out from this world (Iyer, 1983), but at the same time he argued, is it not wisdom to try to avoid violence, because he firmly believed that an eye for an eye would make the entire world blind? To prepare an answer to the second question, Gandhi advocated focusing on just and fair means and, at the same time, beginning to learn how to detach ourselves from the ends. This is significant because it is only then that we will be able to keep our emotional equipoise and not get swayed by temptations to reach our goals. For Gandhi, following nonviolence is the cardinal means to achieve an end and affords an opportunity for navigating through life with wisdom.

Gandhi's Understanding of Human Cognition

Gandhi was very particular about scripting and creating schemas of nonviolence. These two psychological features have great relevance for our cognitive functions and are considered, relatively, newer entries to our understanding of human cognition. Schemas are mental plans with scripts feeding its elaboration. Gandhi, as an applied psychologist, understood the importance of schemas for booting our cognition, just as we do not expect to be asked about seating in a fast food restaurant, but will do so in a formal restaurant. Gandhi trained his freedom fighters to remain resolutely nonviolent even in the face of immense adversity and to not lose focus on the nonviolent means. For developing such an ability to focus on nonviolent means and for keeping the schema of the freedom fighters firm, Gandhi and his followers were powered by their reengineered cognition enabling them to face, any or all, the unexpected forms of aggression displayed by the adversary and, yet, keeping their own heads high.

Our ability to elicit schemas of nonviolence needs patience. With the passage of time, the nonviolent schema grows stronger, affording us time to evaluate options and leading to the emergence of sublimated responses from the oppressor. In the context of nonviolence, the chances of nurturing wisdom among both the aggressor and the victim for resolving a conflict are far greater than in the case of violence which is often swift and sudden and escalates fast, without allowing other virtues to elicit any alternate schema. When Gandhi professed that the practice of nonviolence is difficult and that in more incidents than one, we tend to choose violence over nonviolence, he probably understood, implicitly, the complex ways in which human cognition operates, making him comment that,

We are helpless mortals caught in the conflagration of himsa (himsa means violence). (Gandhi, 1927, pp. 427–428)

It was only at the turn of the twentieth century that noted cognitive scientist and Nobel Laureate Daniel Kahneman put forth his theory regarding two systems of thinking, one fast and used more often, helping us to deal with exigencies, and, the other much slower, allowing us time to think rationally (Kahneman, 2011, *Thinking Fast and Slow*). The faster System I forces us to retaliate at the spur of the moment, but if we allow our rationality to take over, decisions are slower, but far-reaching, bringing in its wake the true resolution of the problem and satisfaction for all stake-holders (Kool, 2008; Kool & Agrawal, 2020).

Returning back to the two groups of Milgram's subjects, namely, those who accepted instructions to deliver shocks versus those who declined and walked away from his laboratory, Table 2.1 shows the usefulness of the prospect theory of Kahneman in the context of Gandhi and the psychology of nonviolence.

In the processing of information, if a person fails to focus on the relationship between means and ends, the behavior of the participating subjects in the experiment seems to be restricted to System 1 level

Table 2.1 Milgram's lost Gandhi and Kahneman's System 1 and 2

FOCUS GIVEN BY PARTICIPANTS	INSTRUCTIONS TO DELIVER SHOCKS	
	Punishment	No punishment
Willingness to participate	Accepted[a]	Rejected
Means used for research (deliver shocks)	Accepted[a]	Rejected
Purpose of study served	Accepted[a]	Rejected
VIEWING THE MORAL TRAJECTORY OF THE EXPERIMENT		
Affording *justice* to the learner	No	Yes
Affording *caring* to the learner	No	Yes

[a]Participants in the Milgram experiment were operating at the System 1 level

thinking. On the other hand, those subjects who refused to deliver shocks were operating at System 2 level thinking, for they were less concerned about the ostensible purpose of some research at the prestigious Yale University, but more with the means of treating the learner in the experiment with electric shocks. To them, such means do not justify the ends, a principle that Gandhi always insisted upon in his experiments with truth.

Were those Milgram's subjects who delivered shocks less than human? From Fig. 2.1 it is abundantly clear that they were not so because as Milgram changed the conditions of the experiment, for example, when there was another participant refusing to deliver shocks, they, also, reduced their aggression. In short, while all human beings are equipped with a sense of justice and caring for others, Milgram's experiment is a challenge posed to the participants to tap and regulate the psychological capital of nonviolence coexisting with their proneness to deliver shocks for reaching a goal without focusing on the means being used for the purpose. Therefore, we agree with Appel (2019) that Milgram's experiment could well be viewed as an experiment on disobedience.

Box 2.2 The "why" of obedience to immoral orders: Revelations from studies of brain function

When Milgram started his famous obedience to authority experiments, most people insisted that they would never administer electric shocks to innocent people. However, when actually placed in the experimental scenario, a large number of subjects did administer the shocks, even to, supposedly, lethal levels. The question which arose was "why did these people obey?" Various explanations had been offered by Milgram himself, but the curiosity continues to date, forcing psychologists and others to attempt to find answers for this seeming mystery.

More recently, attempts have been made to study the brain processes behind obedience/disobedience through the use of ERPs (Event Related Potentials). One such very innovative study (Fabre et al., 2021) placed subjects in a scenario in which they were told that they were UAV operators and that their defective drone was about to crash. They had the option of either allowing it to land on a military site which would cause the damage of a large amount of material but with no human deaths or to land it on a civilian site which would cause death of a large number of civilians. The subjects were placed in either of two conditions, the command condition or the no-command condition.

"While in the no-command condition, participants decided according to their own preferences, in the command condition they were ordered to protect the military material at the expense of civilians for undisclosed strategic reasons. The results revealed that in the no-command condition participants almost always crashed the drone on the military site (96%), whereas in the command condition they chose to obey orders and sacrifice civilians to protect the military material 33% of the time. In the command condition, participants were longer to make their decisions, mobilizing greater attentional and cognitive resources (i.e., greater P300 responses) to resolve the conflict between their internal moral values and the orders they were given (i.e., greater N200 responses) than in the no-command condition, where they automatically applied the 'you shall not kill' rule. Participants also showed a greater negative affective response (i.e., greater P260 amplitudes) after choosing to disobey than to obey orders. This result suggests that disobeying authority could be perceived as a greater moral violation than obeying and sacrificing civilians, suggesting that individuals may sometimes choose to obey malevolent authority to avoid the negative affective reaction triggered by disobedience" (Fabre et al., 2021, p. 2).

The authors of the study explain the above results in terms of the two systems of thinking forwarded by Kahneman (2011), to reveal that conflict created by moral dilemmas take greater attentional resources and more time, because they bring into play System II thinking which is rational but also slower. This could well explain the behavior of the German soldiers during the Holocaust, and, that of many other people who simply obey unjust or immoral orders because of the greater latency and negative affect produced through disobedience. It would also explain the large number of people who were ready to obey Milgram's orders, unjust though they were. But then, there were those who disobeyed, small though their numbers were.

Can we use the findings presented in Box 2.2 to explain the behavior of people in South Africa, who continued to obey unjust laws? It was probably easier, both cognitively and emotionally, to obey such laws than trying to disobey them. Yet, when Gandhi was told to leave the first class compartment of the train, despite having a ticket for the same, he refused. What ensued is known to all: he had to be literally thrown out of the compartment at the Pietermaritzburg station, because he refused to obey unjust orders.

This was Gandhi's first incidence of disobedience, to be followed by many more, both at the personal level and by his followers. The ways through which he could get thousands of people to disobey is ample evidence of Gandhi's wisdom, and, his ability to understand the human psyche. He realized that while human beings generally believe in the "you shall not kill" principle, they tend to act violently, retaliating to every blow with another blow. The task faced by him was to show the world that the opponent can be won over without blows and bullets by following the path of nonviolence (ahimsa) which was the ultimate truth (satya).

Through his experiments with truth on himself and others, he perfected a methodology (namely, satyagraha) making it easier for people to disobey authority and unjust laws propounded by the British, both in

South Africa and in India. Almost half a century before Kahneman and other cognitive psychologists, he preempted several forms of behavior (such as vows) which reduced the cognitive and emotional burden of disobedience. By careful priming of schemas and scripts for nonviolence, he reduced the amount of scarce attentional resources being used (in a way, shifting people from the slow System II thinking to the almost automatic System I thinking). Further, by creating an alignment between the "you shall not kill" instinct and the orders being given by Gandhi to stick to nonviolence, no matter how great the instigation to do otherwise, he was able to reduce any conflict in the minds of his satyagraha followers. In other words, Gandhi attempted to make nonviolence the automatic or default mode of thinking. That he succeeded in doing so is well evidenced by the success of his satyagrahas and the ways through which he was able to convince the British to repeal unjust laws.

We add, further, that Milgram's unsung Gandhian subjects have considerable to offer to modern psychology, opening new vistas of research in the psychology of nonviolence, and broadening the interdisciplinary impact of psychology as in explaining the behavior of over one billion people engaged in activism around the globe (*Time*, Stengel, 2011). As Bilgrami (2003, 2020) of Columbia University argues, with the prefix non in nonviolence, there are no opposites involved and thereby, makes its study robust and meaningful. We contend, here, that Gandhi sought to present cognition not as a response to a conditional context, but as an element of consciousness unhinged from the desirabilities around us, in contrast to Milgram's subjects who succumbed to his goading for delivering shocks to the innocent learners. Whether you take Milgram's subjects or Kahneman's prospect theory of cognition, there is so much to learn from Gandhi for understanding cognition and for developing the science of human behavior.

Gandhi's Understanding of Human Motivation

But, first things first: Gandhi, always, insisted that every participant listen to his or her inner voice before joining his movement. Essentially,

he was referring to their intrinsic motivation, a very useful psychological concept with wide applications across all subfields of psychology,
ranging from industrial psychology to environmental psychology, and
more. In short, Gandhi was a master technician of the mind and, thereby,
enriched the science of psychology by expanding and demonstrating in
the real world, two key areas considered to be the sine qua non of human
behavior—cognition and motivation.

Gandhi's life and work also helps to explain the diffidence shown
by some subjects in Milgram's experiment. Wisdom without action,
as popularly stated in Buddhism, is like wearing a fetter but claiming
to be free. Conceiving wisdom appears question-begging and highly
constricting in the context of the purely utilitarian criterion of its
measurement, as psychologists often tend to engage in, with rare exceptions such as the analysis offered by Erik Erikson.

In expressing his wisdom, Gandhi was not like a clergy, not even like a
saint who, unlike a clergy, can look beyond advocating and reinterpreting
scriptures in the context of changing times. Gandhi acted more like a
hermit, combining the wisdom of the serpent with that of a dove (Iyer,
1983). He invited us to examine wisdom in the light of our mental world
which is capable of transcending to all things sentient in nature and to,
thereby, create Vasudaiva Kutumbakam. For him, service to humanity is
the direct corollary of wisdom and can be experienced only through our
action.

Following the tradition of philosophers like Hume and Adam Smith,
our moral values and sentiments are understood, and supposedly derived,
from the states of mind. However, what if we consider them, instead, as
responses to the values around us and pose a challenge to the natural
scientist by asking, for instance, are values valuations? Are not desires,
asks Bilgrami (2003), themselves responses to desirabilities that we
perceive around us? In this sense, argues Bilgrami, we might be able to
better understand well being versus poverty, kindness versus cruelty, or
in the context of wisdom, maximizing survival through this apex form
of our thinking and behavior. It is imperative for the growth of modern
psychology to widen its compass and Gandhi's wisdom is one such trajectory to be comprehended from the lens of our "experiments with truth"
during the course of our lives.

Iyer, a noted Indian scholar on the life and philosophy of Gandhi and who had, also, taught in the USA, stated categorically, that while it would be difficult for Western intellectuals to comprehend Gandhi in the above context, Gandhi was, truly, a genuine thinker, challenging us to test our wisdom through experiments with truth on ourselves and on the rest of the world.

In the psychological conceptualization of nonviolence, as offered by Kool (2008), wisdom can be construed in terms of minimizing aggression, opening vistas of moral concerns both theoretically and practically, and integrating our actions with the experience of power with people. In terms of our analysis of Gandhi and nonviolence, it is clear that when these moral concerns are coupled with internal locus of control (what Gandhi termed "inner voice"), we witness nonviolence at its zenith, with justice and care orientations existing side by side with the ability for self blame and the resoluteness of the nonviolent means being used (for details, see Kool & Agrawal, 2020). In Fig. 2.2, the blue oval at the lower right hand corner of the cuboid shows the location of the wise person.

In other words,

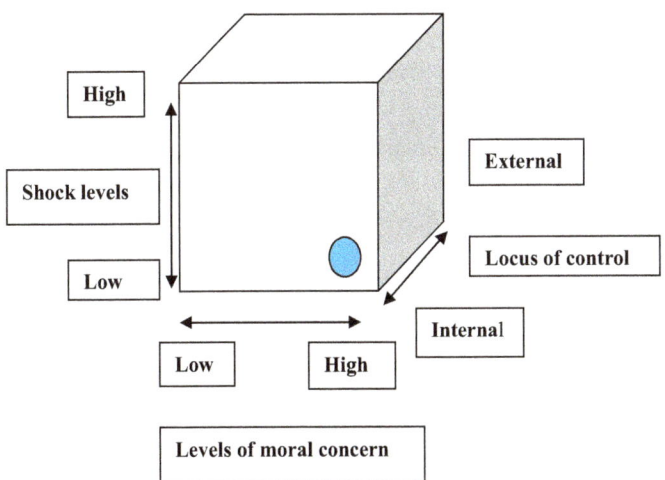

Fig. 2.2 The three dimensional model (Kool, 2008) in terms of obedience/disobedience (from Kool & Agrawal, 2020)

- High moral concerns + Internal Locus of Control (LOC) + Low obedience = conscious objector = nonviolent protester, much like the Milgram's disobedient subjects
- Low moral concerns + External LOC + High obedience = violent person, such as those who obeyed Milgram's orders

Is this not a manifestation of the ripening of wisdom, allowing the person to cognize nonviolence and to be motivated to stick to nonviolent means, no matter what the level of external provocation? In the words of the Mahatma,

> A votary of ahimsa, therefore, remains true to his faith if the spring of all his actions is compassion, if he shuns to the best of his ability, the destruction of the tiniest creature, tries to save it, and thus incessantly strives to be free from the deadly coil of himsa. (Gandhi, 1927, pp. 427–428)

This compassion is rooted in the moral concern for the other, while the steadfastness of purpose can become possible through an internal locus of control (the "inner voice"). Is this not evidence that Gandhi, through his emphasis on the "inner voice," preempted the concept of locus of control brought to the forefront of psychological research many decades later?

When legendary psychologist Skinner (1987) wrote his well known essay, *What is wrong with the Western society*, he was convinced that the management of reinforcements would induce the development of an ideal community. But in reality, his community, based on the tacit concepts of his own theory, could not last for long for several reasons, including the issues of the identity of those who opted to join his community based on reinforcements. Erikson (1969) was so correct in stating that identity without affiliation has no meaning. And, this affiliation must be deeply rooted in our culture and traditions and ready to jump start our schemas and harmonize our dedication to and faith in the nonviolent means. Gandhi did not merely visualize nonviolence as wisdom, but tested it continuously to seek its efficacy in community work, and aligned it with his personal goals to test his own psychological capital.

In order to understand how Gandhi built his psychological capital, we need to closely examine and explore how he developed some nuanced forms of his own behavior through vows, fasting, silence and more in forging the unity of core psychological components of cognition, motivation, and emotion, a major issue in the current research on wisdom in psychology. In his seminal work, Kris Kirby (2013) has analyzed how vows helped Gandhi in the maintenance of his self control. After promising his mother to remain a vegetarian, Gandhi often vacillated when tempted by a nonvegetarian meal placed in front of him while he was a student in England. Using the delay discounting theory of Ainslie, Kirby has shown how the window of vulnerability at point c in the graph could be handled with the bundling effects of vows in the long term reward (l) as compared to a temporary reward at the short term (s) level. Instead of having to choose between s and l on a daily basis, vows help us to decide once and for all the bundling effect of summative values that we create around us. We believe that such seminal research highlights the genuineness of Gandhi's wisdom and stands as an exemplar to address the dilemmas in understanding the relationship between cognition, motivation and emotion in modern psychology. We had invited Kris Kirby to write about the implications of his research and his response is reproduced in Box 2.3 and illustrated in Fig. 2.3.

Box 2.3 Gandhi's vows as an anticipated solution to modern psychology

In his personal communication (April 26, 2021) to us, Kris Kirby, PhD (Harvard) and Professor of Cognitive Psychology at Williams College, USA, wrote:

> The central problem in the psychology of self-control is that temptations offer tangible, immediate rewards, whereas the rewards of self-control are more diffuse and long term. Consequently, we are least motivated to exercise self-control

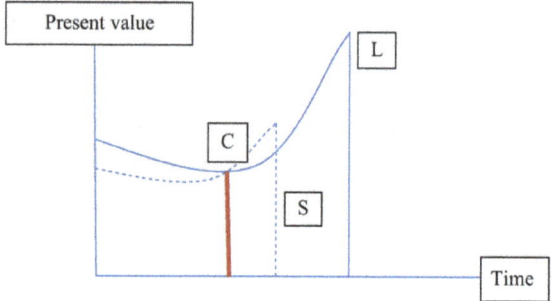

Fig. 2.3 How vows guard us against temptation (adapted from Kirby, 2013)

at precisely those moments when we most need it. In his practice and writings on the use of vows, Gandhi anticipated modern psychology's solution to this problem: private vows (vrata, or sacred promises made to oneself) can 'bundle' together many future choices—each fraught with temptation—into a single choice, the choice to make and keep the vow. Moreover, the making and keeping of vows can be motivated by higher goals than merely enhancing rewards. For Gandhi, self- control, and the vows one takes to achieve it, is dharma, and thus, an end in itself. 'God is the very image of the vow... We should, therefore, never doubt the necessity of vows for the purpose of self-purification and self-realization' (Letter to Naraindas Gandhi, 14 Oct 1930). Whether about small matters like not eating sweets, or large matters like ahimsa, Gandhi saw keeping vows as a sacred duty, not only for one's own benefit, but for the common good of humanity through one's exemplary effect on others.

Nonviolence as a Science and Precursor of Wisdom

At a conference organized by Kool in Wisconsin (1988), a young scholar from the University of California, Berkeley, Michael Nagler surprised the audience by stating that the laws of nonviolence could be postulated and that we must investigate them for enhancing the quality of our survival. He stated,

But nonviolence is a science. It has precise rules, and we have to learn them, even though some of them tell us we have to think and feel and love differently, which is very hard. (Nagler, 1990, p. 138)

Nagler, further, contended that Gandhi could be best exemplified in his ability to

conceptualizing nonviolence as a non-something to a something but from a something to the basis of everything. (ibid., p. 138)

Gandhi's initiative to alter the consciousness of millions of people symbolizes the rare cognitive revolution unseen and unheard of in recent history. As a dedicated follower of Gandhi's life and work, Nagler (2020) has discussed his ideas in a recent book, *The Third Harmony: Nonviolence and the New Story of Human Nature*, containing ideas well supported by scientific research on quantum physics and brain science.

Basically, as the product of evolution we define our organic existence along with the natural forces that sustain and nurture us. By creating a parallel evolution through technology, as in cloning, the organic human body finds a symbiosis with those unfamiliar "biotech" compatible elements, supposedly implanted to enhance our survival. We, then, marvel at our creativity in the unprecedented broadening and deepening of our knowledge in many sciences, and take pride in our degrees and credentials attesting our competencies.

But, did any of those renowned institutions offer us a degree in human wisdom to address the problems posed by our so called "material growth" leading to our imbalanced equipoise? For Gandhi, the roots of wisdom lie in the primary institution known as family, a place for the child's initial education (as he postulated in Buniyadi talim), and continue in the community. Through these important socializing agencies, the child has continued exposure to what Erikson describes as generativity. In other words, Gandhi was appreciating the true influence of our culture in its noblest form. Deficits in the above lead to the inability to solve many of the inherent problems and such deficits could well be the reason for why artificially designed communities, such as those of Skinner, failed.

A zombie needs a repertoire of experiences for its interaction unless it is—as in the case of Artificial Intelligence—controlled from somewhere or through an artifact. Outsourcing our human cognition has its own risks, with several brilliant scholars such as Kurzweil (2005), widely and openly, expressing their concerns over the kind of social order that is emerging in the face of technological growth. According to the National Science Foundation (Rocco & Bainbridge, 2002), it is not possible to predict the impact of technology beyond 20 years, and our own life time provides ample attestations for the above. Had you ever imagined that a power point presentation would provide you such ease as going to the classroom without priming the schemas of your lecture? For more information on technology related issues, please refer to our chapter, "Turing Testing and Gandhi's Wisdom in the Era of Cognitive Computing" (Chapter 10 in this book).

We argue that any restructuring of cognition will have consequences for living with the wisdom we cognize, and for deploying it in the new social order. For Gandhi, if we follow nonviolence as a means for seeking truth, our acquired wisdom will never fail. With nonviolence at the core of our cognition, we will always find ourselves in the driver's seat, managing the direction and speed of our activities in conjunction with, or independent of, the two evolutions we are wrestling with, namely, the biological and the technological. Nagler is so correct in concluding that Gandhi "thought and functioned precisely as a scientist" (ibid), and even argued that his approach to nonviolence is tougher than the laws of physics.

In fact, our contemporary cognition is at the cusp of being hijacked. We rarely need to remember telephone numbers any more, finding them instantly on our mobile phones. Are we ready to mortgage our wisdom, too, or for convenience, put a moratorium on it, like many politicians do for their self interests? Authentic wisdom, then, would remain totally illusive.

In Gandhi's authentic wisdom, there is a clear invitation for bridging the gap between our thinking, feeling, and action so as to view our existence in the company of everything sentient in nature and of finding ways of enhancing our well being. Before closing this chapter, we invite readers to test the limits of their wisdom in the following context. Think of a two-year-old baby, sitting in a cart and moving along with her mother in a grocery store, hitting you, much as a number of toddlers do, simply to spark excitement. What would you do? We guess that you will share her joy and fun. However, supposing you find someone 6, 8, 10 16, 25 or 40 years old, engaging in the same kind of behavior? Our guess is that you would respond as per the context, depending on the age of the person.

Surprisingly, such a schema can be reengineered, as demonstrated by Bonta (1993) in his study of nonviolent cultures and witnessed personally by Kool in a remote village, Malana, deep in the Himalayas (Kool & Agrawal, 2020; Piazza & Dote, 2013). Both found that nonviolent cultures emphatically teach their young ones to avoid violence and, unlike other mainstream communities of our modern world, let their kids know that they are not special in comparison to those of others around them. Their "us-them" boundary is mitigated and othering, as a natural human response, is unothered with the initiation of the child into the community. In Gandhi's carving of human cognition, such wisdom glows in all forms of behavior, including those identified as being adverse. Cultivating mutualism in the face of acute adversarialism is wisdom at its best and nonviolence affords a means for fostering it.

Like emotions, wisdom is relished in the company of others and in our own mental world, by engaging in behaviors such as silence, fasting, vows, and more, that Gandhi demonstrated so uniquely, and presented so succinctly by positing that, "my life is my message." We hope that for modern psychology, the variety of nuances of Gandhi's nonviolent behaviors will be an invitation to further explore the range and depth of wisdom, without categorizing such behaviors as being exotic or positioned beyond the scope of what we know as the science of psychology.

References

Appel, J. M. (2019, September 9). Rethinking the infamous Milgram experiment in authoritarian times. *Scientific American.* blogs.scientificamerican.com

Arnett, J. J. (2008). The neglected 95%: Why American psychology needs to become less American. *American Psychologist, 63*, 602–611.

Bilgrami, A. (2003). Gandhi the philosopher. *Economic and Political Weekly*, 38–39.

Bilgrami, A. (2020). Rationality and alienation: Themes from Gandhi. In T. Akram & S. Rashid (Eds.), *Faith, finance and economy: Beliefs and economic well being.* Springer.

Bonta, B. D. (1993). *Peaceful peoples: An annotated bibliography.* Scarecrow Press.

Burger, J. M. (2009). Replicating Milgram: Would people still obey today? *American Psychologist, 64*, 1–11.

Dolinski, D., Grzyb, T., Folwarczny, M., Grzybala, P., et al. (2017). Conducting the Milgram experiment in Poland, psychologists show that people still obey. *Society for Personality and Social Psychology, 8*, 927–933.

Erikson, E. (1969). *Gandhi's truth.* Norton.

Fabre, E. F, Causse, M., Othon, M., & Vanderhenst, J. B. (2021). The dilemma of disobedience: An ERP study. bioRxiv.

Gandhi, M. K. (1927/2003). *An autobiography or The story of my experiments with truth.* Navjivan Publishing House.

Iyer, R. (1983). *Moral and political thought of Mahatma Gandhi.* Concord Grove Press.

James, W. (1899/1983). *Talks to teachers on psychology and to students on some of life's ideals* (F. H. Burkhardt, Ed.). Harvard University Press.

James, W. (1910/1995). The moral equivalent of war. *Peace and Conflict: Journal of Peace Psychology, 1*, 17–26.

Kahneman, D. (2011). *Thinking, fast and slow.* Farrar, Straus and Giroux.

Kahneman, D., & Tversky, A. (1979). Prospect theory: An analysis of decisions under risk. *Econometrica, 47*, 263–291.

Kirby, K. (2013). Gandhi, vows, and the psychology of self control. *Gandhi Marg, 35*, 519–540.

Kool, V. K. (Ed.). (1990). *Perspectives on nonviolence.* Springer-Verlag.

Kool, V. K. (Ed.). (1993). *Nonviolence: Social and psychological issues.* University Press of America.

Kool, V. K. (2008). *The psychology of nonviolence and aggression.* Palgrave MacMillan.

Kool, V. K., & Agrawal, R. (2020). *Gandhi and the psychology of nonviolence,* Volumes 1 and 2. Palgrave-Macmillan.

Kool, V. K., & Sen, M. (1984). The nonviolence test. In D. M. Pestonjee (Ed.), *Second handbook of psychological and sociological instruments* (pp. 48–54). Indian Institute of Management.

Kurzweil, R. (2005). *The singularity is near.* Viking Books.

Latour, B. (1993). *We have never been modern* (C. Porter, Trans.). Harvard University Press.

Latour, B. (2013). *An inquiry into modes of existence: An anthropology of the moderns* (C. Porter, Trans.). Cambridge, MA: Harvard University Press.

Milgram, S. (1974). *Obedience to authority.* Harper.

Nagler, M. N. (1990). Nonviolence as New Science. In V. K. Kool (Ed.), *Perspectives on nonviolence* (pp. 131–139). Springer Verlag.

Nagler, M. N. (2020). *The third harmony: Nonviolence and the new story of human nature.* Berrett-koeler audio

Piazza, E., & Dote, D. (2013). Modern psychology, Gandhi and peace cultures with special reference to Malana. *Gandhi Marg, 35,* 619–630.

Rocco, M. C., & Bainbridge, W. S. (Eds.). (2002). Converging technologies for improving human performance: Nanotechnology, biotechnology, information technology and cognitive science. *NSF/DOC-sponsored report.* National Science Foundation.

Russell, N. J. C. (2011). Milgram's obedience to authority experiments: Origins and early evolution. *British Journal of Social Psychology, 50*(1), 140–162.

Sen, M. (1993). An empirical study of nonviolence in India. In V. K. Kool (Ed.), *Nonviolence: Social and psychological issues.* Springer-Verlag.

Skinner, B. F. (1987). Whatever happened to psychology as the science of behavior? *American Psychologist, 4,* 780–786.

Stengel, R. (2011, Wednesday, December 14). Introduction: Person of the Year. *Time.*

Thaler, R., & Sunstein, C. R. (2008). *Nudge: Improving decisions about health, wealth and happiness.* Simon & Schuster.

Part II

Gandhi's Wisdom in the Interdisciplinary Perspective

3

On Seeking Wisdom in Gandhi's Silence

V. K. Kool and Rita Agrawal

The problem with modern psychology has been that most of its growth has emanated out of observations of some negative aspect of human behavior. The psychology of silence is no exception, with the effects of noise being abundantly investigated while its counterpart, namely, silence, has generally been put in the back seat and used, if needed, as a control condition in researches on noise.

At the same time, it is no secret that in almost every religion and culture, silence has been viewed as a virtue. Yet, silence, along with topics such as self-control, happiness, flow, resiliency, and more specifically, all that constitutes the subfield of positive psychology in modern psychology, has not been paid much heed to until the onset of the current millennium. It was this which made Valle (2019) remark,

V. K. Kool (✉)
SUNY Polytechnic Institute, Utica, NY, USA

R. Agrawal
Harish Chandra Post Graduate College, Varanasi, Uttar Pradesh, India

© The Author(s), under exclusive license to Springer Nature Switzerland AG 2022
V. K. Kool and R. Agrawal (eds.), *Gandhi's Wisdom*,
https://doi.org/10.1007/978-3-030-87491-9_3

Although silence is a common and potentially powerful human experience, the number of professional publications in psychology regarding silence has remained small and essentially unintegrated. (Valle, 2019, p. 219)

This chapter focuses on silence as a self-controlled activity and reflects on the virtue of remaining quiet, both verbally and non-verbally, in order to find space for inner reflection. It is an internal exercise for seeking control on our vocal apparatus and all forms of macro- or micro-behaviors, understanding comprehensively and also implicitly, that no action, in itself, is some action and that it, often, speaks louder than words (see Box 3.1). This is also in line with observations regarding gait, posture and other micro-forms of behavior, which, often, carry meanings far deeper than our words.

In their book, *Qualitative Studies of Silence: The Unsaid as Social Action*, Murray and Durrheim (2019) have pointed out the relevance of silence in the context of social interaction involving what is said versus what is not said, with scenarios having implications for intentionality of those who spoke or remained silent. Along with other contributors in this edited book, they have reflected on the issues of silence and its impact on the identity of individuals or related cohorts.

Box 3.1 Silence Speaks Louder Than Words

While waiting for the announcement of boarding the plane at the airport lounge, a professor laid down a bag of potato chips on the table and began to read his book. Soon, he noticed that a lady, sitting in front of him, was picking up chips from his bag that he had placed on the table in front of him. The munching of chips by the lady continued until she heard the announcement of boarding of her plane. No wonder, besides her own carry-on bag, she also picked up the bag containing the remaining potato chips, to place it in her bag, but soon realized that she had forgotten to take out her own bag of chips and was continuously consuming the chips from the bag of the professor sitting in front of her. She apologized for her inadvertent behavior and also offered to exchange her own bag of chips with the professor.

> During the entire incident, the professor remained silent. This professor was none other than Roy Baumeister, author of *Evil* and several other books and publications. He is widely known for his pioneering, experimental work on self-control, a precursor of silence.

Gandhi's Silence

If there is any one person who can be said to be a true votary of silence, it is the half-clad Indian, Mohandas Karamchand Gandhi. For Gandhi, silence meant much more than the mere absence of words or external interference. He used silence for his own contemplation, reflection and beyond. Tendulkar (1953), in his eight-volume biography of Gandhi has clarified that over a period of time, Gandhi found an increasing usefulness of silence. Six volumes of Tendulkar's work prominently refer to Gandhi's stance on and his practice of silence, indicating the abundance of wisdom in his use and expression of silence. Realizing the strength in observing silence, Gandhi stated,

> My greatest weapon is my mute power. (Gandhi, in Tendulkar 1953, Volume 5, p. 21)

Those who are acquainted with the life and work of Gandhi know that not only was he a great advocate of silence but that he also observed it every Monday. Yet, he was not rigid regarding this adherence, and would communicate if there was urgency, or if he felt it necessary to break his silence for expediting a task.

Even during meetings and conferences, he was known for his silence, but he never hesitated to speak out when it became necessary to intervene. For example, during the first day of the Round Table Conference meeting at St. James' Palace, London, on Monday, September 14, 1931, Gandhi remained silent and did not speak even a single word, despite it being such an important meeting, slated to determine the fate of his country, and he was there as the leader representing his country.

However, on the next day, that is, Tuesday, he delivered his first speech regarding the change of British control of India. Observers believed that Gandhi intended to listen to the other side before offering his plan and, in the process, he positioned himself as a seeker of peaceful negotiation.

Yet, his attitude toward his vow of silence was extremely practical and we quote his words on this occasion,

> If the meeting is held on Monday, I will be in the most embarrassing position. Monday is my day of silence. When I took the vow, I made three exceptions: first, if I am in distress and can only be assisted by my speaking; second, if some one else is distressed; and third, exceptional circumstances such as an unexpected call from the Viceroy or other high official who must be seen in the interest of the cause. Further, he added that his presence in the meeting on Monday was due to the third exception. (Tendulkar, 1953, Volume 3, p. 116)

In 1938, Gandhi observed silence in order to purge his organization. He stated,

> I took silence over a fortnight ago for an indefinite period. It has given me peace I cannot describe. And it enables me to commune with nature. (ibid., 1953, Volume 4, p. 273)

Soon after the departure of Cripps, who represented the British rulers and offered merely limited freedom to India in 1942, Gandhi, along with other leaders, was deeply frustrated. How did he cope with this difficult situation? In the words of Gandhi,

> It was during my Monday day of my silence that the idea was born in me. From that silence arose so many thoughts that the silence possessed me and also the thoughts possessed me .... (ibid., 1953, Volume 6, p. 100)

Gandhi observed silence from May 24 to 29, 1944 and later, he stated at a community meeting that,

> What a good thing is silence! I have personal experience of it. The joy one derives from silence is unique. How good it will be, if everyone observed

silence for some time every day! Silence is not for some great men; I know that whatever one person is able to do can be done by everyone, given the effort. There is a saying amongst us that through silence everything can be achieved. (Gandhi, 1956/1983)

But, Gandhi's stance on silence has also been criticized, especially at the critical juncture of the atomic bombing of Hiroshima and Nagasaki in 1945. When asked why he refrained from commenting on or condemning the cruelty perpetrated on humanity, he, simply, remained mute. When foreign newspapers began to perceive Gandhi's silence as an endorsement to the horrific event, he merely clarified that he had not made any statement. Such a response in the face of his deafening silence was not considered enough by many (see Box 3.2 for more on Gandhi and silence).

Should Gandhi's silence be taken as a form of protest? While journalists found his silence as an endorsement of the worst form of violence perpetrated by the aggressor, those who believed in Gandhi thought otherwise (see Box 3.2). Given the fact that he made nonviolence the cardinal goal of his life, any conclusion, regarding his silence as attesting to violence, is preposterous. Conversely, for a common human being, his unique stance based on silence on the atomic bombing is intriguing and more so, in sharp contrast to his position on killing the terminally ill calf, because its mother could not stop crying.

In a recent article, Rajeev Kadambi (2020), a political scientist, attempts to explain Gandhi's silence on the bombings, through the words of Gandhi himself, narrating how, when asked by a US correspondent in October, he replied,

> The more I think of it, the more I feel that I must not speak on the atomic bombing. I must act if I can.

And later, in the same article, Kadambi suggests how Gandhi could transform the tragedy into a spiritual action in line with ahimsa, through Gandhi's reply to a correspondent, Bourke-White, a few hours before his assassination.

He said, "The pilot could not see our faces from his great height, I know. But the longing in our hearts … would reach up to him and his eyes would be opened."

Box 3.2 Gandhi's Silence: John S. Moolakkattu

According to John S. Moolakkattu, noted Gandhian scholar and Professor and Editor, *Gandhi Marg*, silence for Gandhi was vastly different. In a personal communication to the editors of this volume (Moolakkattu, 2020), he writes,

> Even though Gandhi was practicing mauna, it was not detachment from the world as he went about his routine works such as writing letters, taking notes and passing notes to the queries of people. So, it was not total silence, but one that could be practiced without being shut out from the world, by any one.

Nor was it a purposeless renunciation or an act of cowardice.

> Coming to the atom bomb, I feel that Gandhi was trying to find some kind of solace at a personal level by remaining silent, rather than involve in a debate of sorts. There are occasions when people try to reconcile themselves with things at a personal level, may be based on a vicarious feeling of individual responsibility for what had happened or as a kind of penance.

But probably, the most important purpose served by silence was that it allowed Gandhi to listen to that "still voice within."

Given the above scenarios of Gandhi's paradoxical behavior and what we have learned from our ancient wisdom on silence, his silence on the atomic bombing needs further scrutiny. Simply put, Gandhi's silence on this matter was, undoubtedly, a symbolic protest. The position that Gandhi took in such cases appears to indicate that when an action is not within our reach or if, for some reason, one is unable to take some action, there is wisdom in silence, however, or by who so ever, it is misunderstood, misjudged or misperceived. In 1938, when a visitor, Professor Tao, attempted to get a message from Gandhi regarding Japan, Gandhi, simply stated,

A nation in arms cannot all at once give up arms and accept non-violence as its weapon … our enemies are not Japanese people but the Japanese militarists. (Tendulkar, 1953, Volume 4, p. 268)

Gandhi was always of the view that if the words used to condemn violence are perceived as inflammatory, there is no need to respond immediately, for patience has its own rewards. Until reason prevails and the numbing caused by violence subsides and leads to renewed appraisal, silence allows for temperance and provides for a state of human ripening. Therefore, understanding Gandhi's silence appears simple at times, but it is extremely complex and, seemingly, paradoxical in many scenarios.

Gandhi was amply aware of the significance of silence in various religions of the world, including Hinduism, Jainism, Buddhism and even Christianity.

The familiar words of Mother Teresa stretched it further,

The fruit of silence is prayer.

Gandhi, thus, realized and stated that one should speak only if it improves upon silence. Very succinctly, he wrote in his newspaper, *Harijan*,

When one comes to think of it one cannot help feeling that nearly half the misery of the world would disappear if we, fretting mortals, knew the virtue of silence. Before modern civilization came upon us, at least six to eight hours of silence out of twenty-four were vouchsafed to us. Modern civilization has taught us to convert night into day and golden silence into brazen din and noise. What a great thing it would be if we in our busy lives could retire into ourselves each day for at least a couple of hours and prepare our minds to listen in to the Voice of the Great Silence. The Divine Radio is always singing if we could only make ourselves ready to listen to it, but it is impossible to listen without silence. St. Theresa has used a charming image to sum up the sweet result of silence: "You will at once feel your senses gather themselves together; they seem like bees which return to the hive and shut themselves up to work without effort or care on your part." (Gandhi, *Harijan*, 1938, pp. 24–29)

The Neuropsychology of Silence

Let us begin with research on the effects of silence among primates. Cognitive and neurobiology scholar, Joe Tsien (2007), found that, during silence, our brain tends to manage and organize information. By monitoring the brain activities of mice under varying conditions, he noticed that "the brain appears to use these durations of silence to encrypt information." Tsien identified a group of cell assemblies in the cortex and hippocampus areas of the brain that are triggered when we need to attend intensely and get ready for some action. Speaking requires attention and during the pause, our neural circuits function like the deeper layers of an, apparently, calm sea.

Some of the well-known neuropsychological research on silence has emerged almost in serendipity. Luciano Bernardi et al. (2006) was interested in the impact of different types of music on brain processes by playing six musical tracks to his participating volunteers and studying its arousal effects reflected in the elevation rates of blood pressure and circulatory processes in the brain. The surprising finding was that the random periods of silence between presentations (that were considered irrelevant) had dramatic effects in the opposite direction, that is, they led to a release from high concentration leading to deeper relaxation, a state much more beneficial than relaxing music or pre-experimentally induced silence. Based on neuropsychological studies, it is now firmly concluded that the diastolic blood pressure, heart rate and breathing rates are lowered during silence and so are cortisol levels (Bernardi et al., 2006; Trappe & Voit, 2016).

From the evolutionary psychology perspective, periods of sleep provide relief to brain mechanisms and during this default mode, silence helps to rebuild and conserve energy. Yet, our brain is alert during silence allowing us to detect sounds and signals of dangers. Conversely, when continuous sound is stopped, the neurons in our auditory cortex fire at the onset of silence. In other words, silence, in its default mode, has evolutionary significance.

The person may seem to be doing nothing but considerable meaningful activity is going on in the brain which Raichle terms intrinsic activity enabling reflection and creativity (Raichle, 2010, 2015). Delving into the neuroscience of mindful meditation, researchers, such as Tang et al. (2015), clarify that it leads to heightened attention, improved emotion regulation, greater present moment awareness, self-awareness and stress management. While not using these terms per se, Gandhi wrote of similar effects of his days of silence.

Another way to look at the neuropsychology of silence begs the question—does the absence of sound really mean silence? Let us assume that we are playing our favorite song and when it is stopped, do we really stop cognizing and mimicking the song? We don't stop at Frank Sinatra's "Let it snow", but continue by repeating it to experience the flow. Otherwise, simply bringing this song back to our verbal repertoire may seem insipid and casual.

The above examples prompt us to argue that even though the external sound has been stopped, the inner representation caused by it in our brain, may continue. And, it could even lead to the illusion of listening to the actual sounds. In other words, our brain is highly creative and with sensory input absent, it tends to create a symphony of its own. Technically, there is no sound signaling our silence!

Imaging studies of the human brain, clarify that tasks requiring intense concentration cause an increase in the cortical activities of the connected areas of our brain, but at the same time, reduce the firing rate of neurons in the other areas. Such findings caution us that the background activity of the brain must not be underestimated, as it consumes considerable energy, which gets depleted over time.

While Gandhi converted the practice of silence into a normal ritual observed every Monday, the implications of this ritual go much beyond our limited current neuropsychological discoveries that have only started to confirm the positive impact of silence in the neurogenesis of the hippocampus (Kirste et al., 2015), the functioning of the frontal cortex and, in fact, the entire brain, along with replenishing our mental resources and tapping the brain's default network (Gregoire, 2017).

The Psychology of Silence

Silence Is Sleep That Nourishes Wisdom: Francis Bacon

From the point of view of psychology, silence places us in an actor-observer dyadic relationship. While it is not possible to separate the two approaches, our focus will be primarily on the former in the context of Gandhi's wisdom. The issues of collective silence, such as those of marginalized groups, have been clarified by sociologists, political scientists and others in the context of what is known as the spiral of silence, that is, why we refrain from saying what we think. While the two approaches are not unrelated, we will delve into the psychological effects of silence on the individual, in whom psychology, as a science of human behavior, is primarily interested.

Now, returning to Gandhi's silence on the atomic bombing of Japan. By not condemning a genocide, we might construe such silence in many ways: as an excuse to detach ourselves from the event; our fear of retaliation; no obligation to speak in the absence of global citizenry; our own personality trait or pathological state of anomie, or simply, because of the familiar pattern of un-connectedness, popularly known as the bystander effect.

For Gandhi, it was none of the above, for he was morally engaged with, and included in his fold, all forms of life and things sentient in the universe. Also, abstinence based on religious ground was not the hallmark of Gandhi's behavior, for he believed in a sound moral discourse that approximated his ideal of truth and sound pragmatism. While journalists and other writers in the West concluded that Gandhi's vows, such as fasting and silence, were tactical with a purpose of creating moral shaming in his opponent, Gandhi refrained from anything short of deliberate commitment to some worthy moral principle in all endeavors, including those personal in nature or tested in public domains.

Gandhi's silence was an exercise in mindfulness. For him, there must be some action well thought out to serve humanity and powerful enough to convince the perpetrator of wrongdoing; otherwise, silence was golden to allow time to seek a nonviolent solution. According to Gandhi, when one desists from speech, silence speaks (see Box 3.3).

Gandhi was an applied psychologist, par excellence. He knew that his silence on moral grounds, and based on self-sacrifice or penitence, might be misunderstood for tactical purposes, as stated above. So, he adhered to a variety of vows, in the efficacy of which he had a firm belief and, in fact, believed that vows act as an anchor for the ship of life, despite the fact that many of his close friends, including Kumarappa and Andrews tended to differ from him (Iyer, 1983). They preferred the term self-determination, chiefly because, in the course of time, a vow connotes observance or activity elevated to "the position of sacrosanctity and unquestionable authority, and thus refers to some social obligation" (Iyer, ibid., p. 80).

Box 3.3 The Motive Underlying Silence

It has often occurred to me that a seeker after truth has to be silent. I know the wonderful efficacy of silence. I visited a Trappist monastery in South Africa. A beautiful place it was. Most of the inmates of that place were under a vow of silence. I inquired of the Father the motive of it and he said the motive is apparent: 'We are frail human beings. We do not know very often what we say. If we want to listen to the still small Voice that is always speaking within us, it will not be heard if we continually speak.' I understood that precious lesson. I know the secret of silence (Gandhi in *Young India*, August 8, 1925).

So, why did Gandhi emphasize silence as a vow rather than as a mere determination? For Gandhi, his search for truth led to the realization that the moral platform on which one stands and operates for engaging in and for seeking common social good, allows no place for mere determination (Box 3.3). A personal pledge converts determination into an unquestionable faith and in the context of community service resonates with some higher purpose in life. Gandhi was always skeptical of external influences leading to compromising our evaluations based on sound moral grounds and therefore, he preferred vows to mere determination. As clarified by Kool and Agrawal (2020),

Gandhi was skeptical about how privately appealing values can become subservient to external social evaluations, often constructed by the corrupt media, self-serving politicians and religious leaders. For Gandhi, the exaltation of conscience, as Iyer wrote, was "the supremacy of the individual and of his role in society cannot be grasped without turning to his fundamental concept of conscience." (p. 119)

When Gandhi was unable to communicate his condemnation of the bombing of Hiroshima, could he be said to be in a state of zombie, totally taken aback, by an experience which took only seconds to annihilate scores of other fellow human beings? No, he certainly was not.

A vow of silence, unlike states of zombie, is taken with total consciousness signaling "the fullness, intensity and authenticity of personal commitment to chosen ideals and social ends" (Iyer, p. 75). Gandhi was against using vows as psychological crutches for the purpose of self-discipline. Rather, he felt that they must be used as a tool for seeking satyanishta, that is, constancy in absolute loyalty to truth and a deliberate commitment to a higher purpose in life, reflecting both social good and the strength of human conduct.

As noted by Erikson (1969), Gandhi had an uncanny ability to not only provide the opponents with opportunities for change but to also equip them with avenues for being in the mode of change. Gandhi knew that the Allies would soon realize the impact of their grueling operation and as Erikson pointed out, "... indeed, only faith gives back to man the dignity of nature" (p. 435).

Coming to empirical research, Barnwal and Kulshresta (2011) found evidence of positive effects of silence on the self-actualization scores of subjects practicing silence, indicating that the period of silence affords an opportunity to realize one's own potential, to find ways of maximizing it and to seek the higher stages in the hierarchy of human needs.

Research has also focused on the mnemonic effects of silence, and has clarified that silence can either enhance memory or may cause forgetting depending on the cross-play between various factors, one of which is intentionality. The effects of intentional silence, such as that used by Gandhi are far different from when the silence is unintentional (Stone et al., 2012) and conclude that,

Our discussion here indicates that experimental psychology can offer new insights into the mnemonic consequences of silence. (p. 49)

Our Appraisal of Silence in Everyday Life

In his seminal work, Valle (2019) has clarified several "distinguishable forms of silence that are layered from the most external worldly manifestations to the subtlest and most inwardly attuned discernments", that is, from the control of sound to the acquisition of the transcendent.

As we are writing, we are also feeling the entrapment of modern psychology—thinking about the opposite of silence and its negative connotation. Verbal discourses are mostly indicative of self-satisfying expressions and could be experienced as rewarding, but what if we are unable to control them? As stated earlier, our speech entails high levels of attentional resources leading to a decrease in brain functioning over a period of time (Kool & Agrawal, 2016). So much so, that a period of two minutes of silence has been found to infuse remarkable positive effect in tasks involving high mental concentration.

On the other hand, simply because one is not communicating, does not mean that one is not listening. Silence involves reducing the levels of sensory input. To initiate its practice, we commonly learn to reduce our own verbal output and, at the same time, try to listen with one ear only to throw it out of the other. In everyday life, if a person is able to cultivate this habit, he or she is perceived by others as being wise. At the personal level, this person is likely to experience the sense of self-control, ripening and maturity (Kool, 2008).

While Gandhi's vows appear insurmountable to average human beings, what if, without following any ritual or religion, one attempts to test the impact of silence on himself or herself, say for ten days. Here are some of the observations in this type of scenario.

The first reaction that, often, emerges is that silence is difficult and scary and that people may construe it as a sign of rudeness. The second thought could be that if we don't have to speak, there is nothing to prepare, because all we have to do is listen. Silence could, also, lead to denial and isolation, perhaps causing even anger or depression. Finally, when a person begins to override his or her negative feelings and learns to focus on the brighter side, she/he discovers the illuminating mode, the fruition of silence—not being vulnerable, feeling strong and be in control. Silence, then, has its own rewards. Believe it or not, Gandhi had gone through many of the above-stated stages, as cited and highlighted elsewhere in our books, *Gandhi and the Psychology of Nonviolence* (2020).

For Gandhi, the search for truth was sacred and the vow of silence was a tool to reach a state of natural peace, a stage in which mental and sensory inputs are integrated to experience quietness. This stage helps us in two ways, first absence of reactivity and control over mental turmoil, and second, affording an opportunity to identify "with the observer or witness of the mind and its content" (Valle, 2019), known as absolute silence.

Gandhi was pragmatic in the use of silence in as much as it helped him to maintain wisdom, including, but not limited to, non-cowardice and seeking the truth; experiencing an everlasting flow rather some flux in life; finding a positive phenomenon to augment and co-constitute verbal discourse and leading to healing without disruption. While Gandhi understood the power of silence and its underrated value in social inter-action, he opposed negative silence, that is, refusing to speak due to an inflated ego or to negative feelings, as these have no place in fostering human relationships.

In the form of a vow, the human brain, as a supercomputer, also needs some time to encode the data accurately. Gandhi wrote,

> A vow is to all other indifferent resolves what a right angle is to all other angles. And just as a right angle gives an invariable and correct measure, so too a man of vows, rightly followed, gives of himself an invariable and correct measure. (Gandhi, *Young India*, June, 1919)

It takes considerable courage to remain silent in a social setting and particularly more so, when we are provoked in some familiar or unfa-miliar situation. The virtue of silence is a form of nonviolence, unlike violence that erupts in the form of a tongue as a weapon and words as arrows. Silence is bliss that a person experiences phenomenologically and affords a chance for appraising oneself. When Gandhi did not condemn the atomic bombing of Japan immediately, he knew that the bomb could never kill our spirits of wisdom. In the context of getting trapped in an instant response, loss of self-control and provocation, he preferred a calling to overcome our numbing and to maintain our poise with measured equanimity.

As stated in the introductory chapter of this book, and, as clarified by Baltes, a leading authority on the psychology of wisdom, there is no single criteria for judging human wisdom because it represents the potential pragmatism to plan, manage and understand good life (Baltes & Smith, 2008). Among the several criteria offered by Baltes, procedural knowledge, that is, the using of a strategy to navigate through a situation is significant for explaining silence. Is there wisdom in speaking out in an unfamiliar scenario? With no earlier exposure to such a horrific loss of lives in the context of the atomic bombing of Hiroshima, and the trauma it afflicted globally, Gandhi was right again: if you have no solution, find a solution and show it in your conduct, not merely in your judgment. His silence was the answer, a nonviolent gesture of moral awareness to show that where faith in religions and other forms of virtuous living, both in spoken and preserved forms, fail to mend human behavior, silence might offer a strong symbolic message to raise the levels of human consciousness. His faith in the power and wisdom of silence is revealed in his consistency: on all occasions of his nonviolent movement, in moments of adversity, he tended to revert to silence, as if, waiting to find an answer.

While using the example of a knife may sound odd here, please note that a knife need not be used for slicing only, but it is good enough to even spread butter. Similarly, Gandhi never asked his follower satyagrahis, to remain silent in their protest against their adversary, but to speak the practiced slogans, as per their free will, and to focus on their mission of nonviolence for the elimination of injustice. Was it symbolic to let everyone know that though words were available, and so was the physical force for retaliation, but the expanded self of a satyagrahi was, both morally and spiritually, far superior to that of their violent perpetrators. If you had watched carefully, the scene of the Dandi March in Lord Attenborough's movie, *Gandhi*, you cannot miss the comment of the

American journalists covering the episode, stating that the moral position of Gandhi that had descended on the West, had won freedom for India on that very day of his movement. There was far more action, coupled with the silence of the nonviolent satyagrahi (other than for a few slogans), as compared to the loud and vulgar expressions that we often notice in the protests of today.

Gandhi firmly believed that when we start appreciating the value of silence, it would be difficult to break away from it. "When I began observing silence", wrote Gandhi, "it meant an effort on my part. Now it has become a part of my nature, and to break my silence means an effort." In other words, for Gandhi, silence need not be practiced in any exotic form, but it could be used as a routine coping mechanism for the purpose of navigating in, and managing, situations confronting our lives.

But it will require patience and rigorous training. There are religious groups, nondenominational organizations and commercial or noncommercial entities offering a wide variety of programs for learning the virtues of silence and making it an integral part of our life. One of the most notable of such programs, based on the Buddhist tradition, is known as Vipassana (for details, see Agrawal, 2001).

As explained by Gandhi,

> Before one is able to listen to that voice, one has to go through a long and fairly severe course of training, and when it is the inner voice that speaks, it is unmistakable. The world cannot be successfully fooled for all time. There is, therefore, no danger of anarchy setting in because a humble man like me will not be suppressed and will dare to claim the authority of the inner voice, when he believes that he has heard it. (Gandhi, *Harijan*, March 18, 1933, p. 8)

References

Agrawal, R. (2001). *Stress in life and at work*. Response/Sage.

Baltes, P. B., & Smith, J. (2008). The fascination of wisdom: Its nature, ontogeny, and function. *Perspectives on Psychological Science, 3*, 56–64.

Barnwal, S. L., & Kulshreshta, S. (2011). The impact of Maun of vag indriyas (organ of speech) on self-actualization. *Indian Journal of Ancient Medicine and Yoga, 4,* 151–155.

Bernardi, L., Porta, C., & Sleight, P. (2006). Cardiovascular, cerebrovascular, and respiratory changes induced by different types of music in musicians and non-musicians: The importance of silence. *Heart (british Cardiac Society), 92*(4), 445–452. https://doi.org/10.1136/hrt.2005.064600

Erikson, E. (1969). *Gandhi's truth.* Norton.

Gandhi, M. K. (1919, June). *Young India.*

Gandhi, M. K. (1925, August 8). *Young India.*

Gandhi, M. K. (1933, March 18). *Harijan,* p. 8.

Gandhi, M. K. (1938, September 24). *Harijan.*

Gandhi, M. K. (1956–1983). *Collected works of Mahatma Gandhi* (Vol. 83, p. 44). Navajivan.

Gregoire, C. (2017). Why silence is so good for your brain. *Science.* 03/05/2016 07:00 am ET Updated Jan 9, 2017.

Iyer, R. (1983). *Moral and political thought of Mahatma Gandhi.* Concord Grove Press.

Kadambi, R. (2020, August 5). The meaning of Gandhi's silence. *The Hindu.*

Kirste, I., Nicola, Z., Kronenberg, G., et al. (2015). Is silence golden? Effects of auditory stimuli and their absence on adult hippocampal neurogenesis. *Brain Structure & Function, 220,* 1221–1228. https://doi.org/10.1007/s00 429-013-0679-3

Kool, V. K. (2008). *The psychology of nonviolence and aggression.* Palgrave Macmillan.

Kool, V. K., & Agrawal, R. (2016). *Psychology of technology.* Springer.

Kool, V. K., & Agrawal, R. (2020). *Gandhi and the psychology of nonviolence* (Vols. 1 & 2). Palgrave Macmillan.

Moolakkattu, J. (2020). Personal communication to V. K. Kool.

Murray, A. J., & Durrheim, K. (Eds.). (2019). *Qualitative studies of silence: The unsaid as social action* (pp. 1–20). Cambridge University Press.

Raichle, M. E. (2010, April). Two views of brain function. *Trends in Cognitive Sciences, 14*(4), 180–190. https://doi.org/10.1016/j.tics.2010.01.008

Raichle, M. E. (2015). The brain's default mode network. *Annual Review of Neuroscience, 38,* 433–447. https://doi.org/10.1146/annurev-neuro-071 013-014030

Stone, C. B., Coman, A., Brown, A. D., Koppel, J., & Hirst, W. (2012). Toward a science of silence: The consequences of leaving a memory unsaid. *Perspectives on Psychological Science: A Journal of the Association for Psychological Science, 7*(1), 39–53.

Tang, Y. Y., Hölzel, B. K., & Posner, M. I. (2015). The neuroscience of mindfulness meditation. *Nature Reviews Neuroscience, 16*(4), 213–225. https://doi.org/10.1038/nrn3916

Tendulkar, D. G. (1953). *Mahatma: Life of Mohandas Karamchand Gandhi,* Volume 5. Jhaveri & Tendulkar.

Trappe, H. J., & Voit, G. (2016). The cardiovascular effect of musical genres. *Deutsches Arzteblatt International, 113*(20), 347–352. https://doi.org/10.3238/arztebl.2016.0347

Tsien, J. Z. (2007). The memory code. *Scientific American, 297*(1), 52–59.

Valle, R. (2019). Toward a psychology of silence. *The Humanistic Psychologist, 47*(3), 219–261.

4

Nonviolent Self-Efficacy for Social Transformation and Health: Theoretical and Empirical Bases

Doug Oman

I have not the shadow of a doubt that any man or woman can achieve what I have, if he or she would make the same effort and cultivate the same hope and faith.—Mahatma Gandhi (1967, pp. 13–14, originally 1936)

The history of science is rich in the example of the fruitfulness of bringing two sets of techniques, two sets of ideas, developed in separate contexts for the pursuit of new truth, into touch with one another.—J. Robert Oppenheimer (1953, quoted in Oman, 2014, p. 584)

Gandhi considered himself to be a "practical idealist," and conducted many experiments to adapt modern technical innovations to benefit the masses of ordinary people (Gandhi, 1967, p. 23, original statement in 1920). Could tools from modern psychology prove similarly useful to

D. Oman (✉)
School of Public Health, University of California, Berkeley, USA
e-mail: DougOman@post.harvard.edu

© The Author(s), under exclusive license to Springer Nature
Switzerland AG 2022
V. K. Kool and R. Agrawal (eds.), *Gandhi's Wisdom*,
https://doi.org/10.1007/978-3-030-87491-9_4

modern social movements informed by Gandhi's achievements? Oman (2014) argued that some outputs from modern psychology have been so powerful and flexible that they merit serious scrutiny and exploration of their practical value for preparing nonviolent campaigns and fostering cultures of nonviolence. In particular, he argued that the modern psychological construct of *perceived efficacy*, more commonly called *self-efficacy*, merits attention as an aid for cultivating and organizing nonviolence, enabling advances in "wisdom [and] ahimsa in action" (Gandhi, 1967, p. 127 [1947]; here and later, dates of original publication indicated by [square brackets]). This chapter provides a brief and condensed version of Oman's (2014) argument, plus highlights from subsequent supportive empirical research.

Understanding and fostering perceived efficacy was a major life work of Albert Bandura (1925–2021), the most influential and highly cited psychologist to have lived in the 21st century (Bandura, 1997; Oman, 2014). In Bandura's (1986) language, self-efficacy refers to an individual's judgment of his or her "capabilities to organize and execute courses of action required to attain designated types of performances" (p. 391). A person's perceived self-efficacy varies between skill areas, such as doing algebra, driving a car, managing an illness, empathically sensing another's feelings, or responding nonviolently when provoked. People low in one skill area may be high in others.

As developed by the global community of human service professionals over the past 40 years, dozens if not hundreds of self-efficacy scales now exist to measure individual efficacy perceptions in domains of human functioning ranging from education, health promotion, and athletics to organizational management (Bandura, 1997, 2006). Some scales measure facets of a subtype of self-efficacy called *self-regulatory efficacy*, the ability to control one's own behavior—such as by regularly adhering to a program of physical exercise. Importantly, efficacy perceptions are also held by groups, ranging from families and neighborhoods to organizations and nations. Group-level efficacy perceptions, termed *collective efficacy*, have been found to predict outcomes such as lower crime rates in city neighborhoods (Oman, 2014).

The present chapter applies perceived efficacy approaches to skills in Gandhian nonviolence. We first review the major features of the self-efficacy approach, emphasizing its robust empirical basis as well as the constructive dynamics of its practical application. Next, we show application to nonviolence by sketching three clusters of skills that comprise Gandhian nonviolence and generating corresponding perceived efficacy scale items. We also report new findings from a pilot study that corroborates the viability of nonviolent perceived efficacy assessment. Finally, we discuss implications and future directions, both scholarly and applied. An expanded version of this chapter's argument, with fuller discussion and citation information on Gandhi and other sources, is available in Oman (2014).

Self-Efficacy Approaches: Major Contours

Major contours and dynamics of the self-efficacy approach were described by Oman (2014). Decades of research have identified major sources of efficacy perceptions as well as primary pathways through which efficacy perceptions influence skill levels and other outcomes of interest. According to Bandura (1986), efficacy beliefs, "whether accurate or faulty" (p. 399), are based on four principal sources of information: performance attainments, vicarious experiences of observing the performances of others, social persuasion, and physiological and affective states. The dynamics and implications of each of these sources are described in Bandura's writings and also in Oman (2014). Importantly, decades of research document that by skill-building through methods such as exposure to social models and mastery experiences, many facets of self-efficacy can be raised by effective programs in education, health care, athletics, and many other fields of human functioning.

Efficacy perceptions, in turn, affect major outcomes of interest through diverse pathways related to how people think, feel, and are motivated. For example, self-efficacy perceptions may strongly influence a person's motivation to undertake activities and persevere in the face of difficulties, tendency to think optimistically versus pessimistically, and ability to manage aversive emotions and interpret relevant events as benign versus emotionally perturbing (Bandura, 1997). Through such pathways, efficacy perceptions may influence a person's acquisition of specific skills as well as his/her overall life-choices and life-trajectory.

Bandura's approach to perceived efficacy was summarized in tabular form by Oman (2014; see his Table 1.1, p. 586). Importantly, when self-efficacy approaches are applied to a particular skill domain, they can catalyze several beneficial spirals and feedback loops that enable people in diverse roles to apply their existing competencies more effectively. Developing a self-report scale to measure the level of perceived self-efficacy is typically an initial step (Bandura, 2006). Different items are developed to assess different aspects of the skill.

According to Bandura (1997, 2006), the list of items on a perceived efficacy scale should offer reasonable coverage of the skill domain—thus, Bandura (1997) suggests that "researchers must draw on conceptual analysis and expert knowledge of what it takes to succeed in a given pursuit" (p. 43). In such distillation, the practical wisdom and views of different experts must sometimes be reconciled or balanced, a process that may lead to better mutual understanding among experts and greater insight among researchers.

Actually administering scales and computing scores may also produce insight that fosters knowledge and encourages wisdom. For example, pre-to-post change data from brief or prolonged training regimens can shed light on whether participants have experienced gains in self-perceived skills, facilitating refinement of training methods (Oman, 2014). Innovations in training may in turn clarify the nature of the needed skills or suggest improved measures of self-efficacy.

Thus, over time, the perceived efficacy approach builds on pre-existing expert practical wisdom and knowledge, yet facilitates additional mutually synergistic progress in theory, measurement, and training. Such progress is greatly needed in the field of nonviolence.

Skills for Gandhian Nonviolence: Three Clusters

What skills are needed for nonviolence? The term "nonviolence" has been defined in diverse ways, each implying a somewhat different skill set. Here, we focus on Gandhi's own approach, discussing three major clusters of required skills: (1) adhering to personal nonviolence, often called *ahimsa*, as a way of life, (2) actively participating in an offering of *satyagraha* to combat injustice, and (3) engaging in activities of constructive program (These correspond to what Sharp, 1979, p. 81, called the "three main parts" of a comprehensive program of nonviolent social change.). Most existing measures of nonviolence have focused on personal ahimsa, so the present approach substantially broadens the toolkit for measuring components of nonviolence most directly relevant to group action (Oman, 2014).

For each cluster, we offer efficacy assessment items for skills needed by both individual and group actors, often called "agents" in self-efficacy theory. We take texts by Gandhi as points of departure for characterizing major requisite skills. In some cases we also discuss common instrumental practices or *means* that an agent might use to cultivate each core cluster of skills in nonviolence. Yet, because Gandhi never claimed to be a systematic thinker, our analyses should be viewed as preliminary and suggestive rather than definitive and comprehensive. Translating Gandhi's wisdom into specific novel contexts requires bearing in mind that a key component of wisdom is doing what is "contextually appropriate for the specific situation and people—sensitive to such things as the nature of the relationship, the social and cultural context, and also people's psychological needs and capacities" (Walsh, 2015, p. 286). Our tabulated example self-efficacy items are, therefore, not intended to be usable "off the shelf," but are intended to prod each reader to reflect on how such an item, or a similar item, might potentially be adapted to the contexts and struggles of greatest concern to the reader.

(1) **Skills for Ahimsa as a Way of Life**

The very first step in non-violence is that we cultivate in our daily life, as between ourselves, truthfulness, humility, tolerance, loving kindness … . [I]t is not mere policy. Policies may and do change. Non-violence is an unchangeable creed.—Gandhi (1967, p. 114 [1938])

According to Gandhi, a cornerstone of his nonviolent approach is the practice of ahimsa, a Sanskrit word often translated as "non-hurting," also possessing rich, positive, connotations related to compassion and benevolent action. Ahimsa in thought, word, and deed was a creed that Gandhi wanted his close disciples, such as those living at his ashram, to embrace not as a mere slogan, but as "an ideal which we have to reach…. if we are capable of doing so" (Gandhi, 1999, v. 15, pp. 168–169 [1916]). Yet, Gandhi also held out ahimsa as an ideal to be pursued by the masses, stating that it is a "profound error" or indeed a "blasphemy to say that non-violence can only be practiced by individuals and never by nations which are composed of individuals." (Gandhi, 1967, pp. 114 [1936], 128 [1938])

As an individual characteristic, ahimsa holds a number of similarities to character strengths, such as love and kindness, which have recently been cataloged and studied in the emerging field of *positive psychology* (Peterson & Seligman, 2004). However, Gandhian ahimsa is clearly distinctive, and a perceived efficacy scale for nonviolence must target capability, not values (Oman, 2014). An example item might be "I can refrain from verbally insulting a coworker, even when they have made a costly mistake" (see Table 4.1, item 1).

Self-efficacy items pertaining to *physical and verbal* ahimsa are relevant to both movement leadership and the general population (e.g., Table 4.1, item 1). However, both Gandhi's nonviolent approach and the logic of nonviolence as a technique of struggle require that leaders should assimilate nonviolence to a greater depth than ordinary movement participants. Items related to ahimsa *in thought* (e.g., Table 4.1, item 8) are more demanding and possess special relevance to movement leaders or leaders-in-the making.

In addition to nonviolence in interpersonal interactions, Gandhian ahimsa requires ethical lifestyle choices, such as choosing an occupation that is not founded on violence (e.g., Table 4.1, item 2). Gandhi

Table 4.1 Example Items to Assess Perceived Individual or Collective Efficacy for Skills Related to Gandhian Nonviolence

#	Agent[a]	Example Item ("How confident are you that...")
		Ahimsa skills
1	I	... I can refrain from verbally insulting a coworker, even when they have made a costly mistake
2	I	... I can consistently rely for my livelihood on an occupation that does not involve manufacturing or using weapons
3	I	... I can live in an ecologically sustainable manner
4	I	... I can minimize my consumption of products produced by exploiting labor
5	I	... I can regularly choose to endure suffering myself rather than inflict harm on others
6	I	... I can regularly recognize in my actions that maintaining my honor does not require retaliation
7	I	... I can regularly recognize in my actions that maintaining my honor requires upholding the common welfare and my sacred responsibilities
8	I/A	... I can refrain from mentally insulting a coworker, even when they have made a costly mistake
9	I/A	... I can regularly engage in activities to develop fearlessness with regard to losing my wealth
10	G	... our group can continue to collectively refrain from violence, even if its main leaders were all arrested
11	G	... our group can effectively support and motivate almost all its members to divest from businesses based on selling harmful products
12	G	... our group can refrain from violence, even if provoked by agents of the opponent
		Satyagraha skills
13	I	... I can act with trust toward an opponent who has previously deceived our group, if our group leaders declare that trust is appropriate
14	I/A	... I can follow all jail rules, even when very physically demanding, except when they are intended to undermine my self-respect
15	I/A	... I can endure blows without retaliating
16	I/L	... as a group leader, I can refrain from prematurely launching a satyagraha campaign involving civil disobedience
17	I/L	... as a group leader, even when members of my own family criticize me, I can maintain the level of purity of life that will give power to my words as a leader

(continued)

Table 4.1 (continued)

#	Agent[a]	Example Item ("How confident are you that…")
18	G	… our group can make adequate decisions for guiding the satyagraha campaign, even if all the main group leaders are arrested
19[b]	G	… our group can effectively identify and implement methods to reduce grounds for its members to capitulate to the threats of the opponent group
		Constructive Program skills
20	I	… I can regularly remember, when engaged in constructive program activities, that I should be open to learning from people who differ from me in age, ethnicity, economic status, or gender
21	I/L	… as a group leader, I can develop a constructive program that will help create the social changes we seek, as well as provide on-going opportunities for training our group members in nonviolent character strengths
22	I/L	… as a group leader, I can develop a constructive program that enacts the principle of trusteeship in ways that are appropriate to our cultural and political context
23	G	… our group can enact a constructive program that will contribute to the social changes we seek, and also provide on-going opportunities for training our group members in nonviolent character strengths
24	G	… our group, through its collective wisdom and leaders, can enact a constructive program that will contribute to our group's solidarity during times of struggle
25	G	… our group can enact a constructive program that is well-managed in its details
26	G	… our group can effectively discern when a new constructive program is necessary to augment pre-existing constructive efforts
		Spiritual skills
27	G	… our group can support our members' engagement with courage-enhancing spiritual practices in ways that respect cultural diversity

Notes In Bandura's approach, responses are typically given on a scale from 0 (*cannot do at all*) to 50 (*moderately certain can do*) to 100 (*certain can do*). Table adapted from Oman (2014)

[a]Items especially appropriate for self-efficacy among all individuals in the movement (I), individuals actively engaging in challenging movement work (I/A), individual leaders of the movement (I/L), or for holistically assessing collective efficacy of the group (G)

[b]Suggested by analyses by Gene Sharp

wrote that "whoever believes in ahimsa will engage himself in occupations that involve the least possible violence.... he will not engage in war or war preparations... [or] exploitation or envy of others" (Gandhi, 1967, p. 265 [1940]).

Means

How are individuals expected to *cultivate* ahimsa? Two common themes are the cultivation of endurance and the cultivation of fearlessness. According to Gandhi,

> The votary of non-violence has to cultivate the capacity for sacrifice of the highest type in order to be free from fear.... we should learn to dare danger and death, mortify the flesh, and acquire the capacity to endure all manner of hardships. (Gandhi, 1967, p. 126 [1940])

Table 4.1 (item 5) shows an example item on sacrifice, framed in contemporary language. Furthermore, following the *Bhagavad Gita* and other Hindu scriptures, Gandhi saw fearlessness as arising from non-attachment (e.g., Table 4.1, item 9), a construct of emerging interest to psychologists (see Oman, 2014). For Gandhi, one source of non-attachment is the development of *wisdom*—he stated, for example, that if Indian self-rule "is to be won through the non-violent strength of the millions, they must in some measure develop in them the qualities of a *sthitaprajña* ... the man of steady wisdom ... [who] will remain equally unaffected by adulation or abuse ... [and will] never wish ill to anyone" (Gandhi, 1999, v. 90, pp. 187–188 [1946]). Indeed, across religious traditions, consistent with Gandhi's view, a key component of wisdom is a skillful response to the "central existential issues of life [such as] ... confronting suffering ... and death" (Walsh, p. 285).

In Gandhi's view, another important means of cultivating fearlessness is a correct understanding of honor. Gandhi advised giving up false honor, but, repeatedly, affirmed the importance of preserving self-respect and authentic honor (Gandhi, 1951/1961, p. 55 [1910]; 1967, p. 142 [1920]; 1999, v. 33, p. 93 [1925]). Gandhi regularly asserted and exemplified the belief that self-respect does not require retaliation.

At a deep level, satyagrahis must abandon retaliation-based honor codes, and, instead, regard a sound foundation for honor as courageously but nonviolently defending one's sacred responsibilities (Table 4.1, items 6, 7). As will be discussed later, Gandhi also viewed spiritual practice as a means to cultivate fearlessness, stating that "perfect fearlessness can be attained only by him who has realized the Supreme" (Gandhi, 1967, p. 59 [1930]).

Collective Efficacy

Gandhi regarded collective nonviolence as a crucial condition of satyagraha. For example, it is well-known that Gandhi called off the national non-cooperation movement in 1922 after a mob killed almost two dozen police officers at Chauri Chaura. Thus, organizers of nonviolent social capacity must attend not only to individuals but also to a group's *collective* efficacy for ahimsa. They might seek to assess a group's perception of its own ability to remain nonviolent if its leaders were arrested (Table 4.1, item 10), or a group's ability to divest all of its financial resources from businesses deemed violent (e.g., manufacture of weapons or of cigarettes) (Table 4.1, item 11). Evidence indicates that collective efficacy perceptions share many of the same determinants and effects as individual self-efficacy perceptions—in Bandura's (1997) words, the "sociocognitive determinants operate in much the same way at the collective level as they do at the individual level" (p. 482). Collective efficacy is often assessed by aggregating individual appraisals of the group's capability as a whole, an approach called *holistic assessment* (Oman, 2014).

(2) **Skills for Acting in Satyagraha**

> The term Satyagraha was coined by me in South Africa to express the force that the Indians there used … . Its root meaning is holding on to truth, hence truth-force … . But on the political field the struggle … mostly consists in opposing error in the shape of unjust laws … . Hence Satyagraha largely appears to the public as Civil Disobedience or Civil Resistance.—Gandhi (1951/1961, pp. 6–7 [1920])

Satyagraha was the method developed by Gandhi for redressing injustices nonviolently by, in the words of Gene Sharp (1979), "taking the initiative in active struggle" (p. 14). A useful starting point for cataloging individual satyagraha skills is Gandhi's 1939 list of seven "illustrative" qualifications of a satyagrahi. These qualifications included several types of faith (in nonviolence, human nature, truth, and God) as well as other characteristics related to self-regulation (does not consume intoxicants) and capacity for self-sacrifice (ready and willing to give up one's life and possessions). The list also mentioned group-struggle-specific qualities, such as the willingness to obey "rules of discipline" that may be promulgated for satyagrahis by their leaders (analogous to military orders) as well as willingness to obey jail rules "unless they are specially devised to hurt his self-respect" (Gandhi, 1967, pp. 171–172 [1939]). Each listed satyagrahi qualification can be converted into one or more self-efficacy items. Many are similar to ahimsa items (e.g., Table 4.1, items 1, 6, 9). However, additional satyagrahi skills that pertain especially to group conflict situations—such as jail behaviors or the capacity to endure blows—generate clearly distinct self-efficacy items (e.g., Table 4.1, items 14, 15).

Beyond this illustrative list from 1939, Gandhi also enunciated the qualities of a satyagrahi on numerous other occasions. For example, Gandhi stated that because he or she is fearless and has an "implicit trust in human nature," a satyagrahi is "never afraid of trusting the opponent ... if the opponent plays him false twenty times, the Satyagrahi is ready to trust him the twenty-first time" (Gandhi, 1967, p. 170 [1928]) (Table 4.1, item 13). At other times, group conflict situations demand expressions of ahimsa that are distinctive and merit systematic attention (e.g., Table 4.1, item 12):

> The first indispensable condition precedent to any civil resistance is that there should be surety against any outbreak of violence, whether on the part of those who are identified with civil resistance or on the part of the general public. It would be no answer in the case of an outbreak of violence that it was instigated by the State or other agencies hostile to civil resisters. (Gandhi, 1967, p. 166 [1939])

Satyagraha, therefore, requires wise leadership, so that campaigns are not launched prematurely or using inappropriate strategies or tactics. Discerning *boundary conditions* for civil disobedience is, therefore, a key satyagraha leadership skill (Table 4.1, item 16). Using a military analogy, Gandhi also asserted that "There must be power in the word of a Satyagraha general—not the power that the possession of limitless arms gives, but the power that purity of life, strict vigilance, and ceaseless application produce" (Gandhi, 1951/1961, p. 97 [1938]) (suggesting Table 4.1, item 17). Yet, if the leaders in planning a satyagraha campaign have been arrested (or killed), the followers must rely on other sources of guidance, suggesting additional collective efficacy items (Table 4.1, item 18). Sharp (1973) also articulated a variety of other group-level skills to promote effectiveness, such as generating incentives and reducing grounds for capitulation, suggesting additional items (Table 4.1, item 19).

(3) Skills for Constructive Program

> Training for military revolt means learning the use of arms ending perhaps in the atomic bomb. For civil disobedience it means the Constructive Programme.—Gandhi (1945, p. 5 [1945])

A third commonly occurring component of Gandhi's approach is his constructive program, which in the Indian independence struggle was "designed to build up the nation from the very bottom upward" (Gandhi, 1945, p. 5 [1945]). It included components such as the revival of village spinning industry, the removal of untouchability, uplift of the status of women, and the establishment of understanding ("communal unity") between the various religious and ethnic groups in India. A 1945 pamphlet by Gandhi listed 17 constructive program points designed to meet India's needs. Although the precise composition of the program changed over time, its central component of spinning, sometimes called its "central sun," had been envisioned by Gandhi as early as 1908 (Gandhi, 1967, pp. 406, 408 [1946]). In Gandhi's view, spinning and the constructive program in general served both economic and social functions.

> Spinning has the greatest organizing power in it because it has itself to be organized and because it affects all India. If khaddar [village-spun cloth] rained from heaven it would be a calamity. But as it can only be manufactured by the willing co-operation of starving millions and thousands of middle class men and women, its success means the best organization conceivable along peaceful lines. If cooking had to be revived and required the same organization, I should claim for it the same merit that I claim for Khaddar. (Gandhi, 1999, v. 38, p. 210 [1927])

One overarching function of the constructive program is, therefore, to stimulate or directly implement desired social and economic changes in the larger society.

In addition, Gandhi saw a well-designed constructive program as performing a second vital function, preparation for satyagraha (see epigraph that begins this section). Cultivating individual and collective perceived efficacy for constructive program should thus be of interest to Gandhi-inspired leaders adhering to principled nonviolence as well as those emphasizing nonviolence as a policy (Table 4.1, items 20, 21, 23, 24).

One of the most challenging aspects of constructive program is discerning what should be its proper *content*. Identifying the high and low priority content of constructive program may be viewed as a group-level skill that in India's case was often delegated to Gandhi, sometimes at his insistence. Assessments of collective self-efficacy for enacting an appropriate constructive program could include items that address one or more program functions, with other items focusing on process (e.g., Table 4.1, items 24, 25).

Formulating a constructive program also requires separating the constructive program itself from allied principles that are offered as a *means* for enacting the program. For example, one point in Gandhi's Constructive Program, entitled "Economic Equality," was aimed at "abolishing the eternal conflict between capital and labour," "levelling down of the few rich," and "levelling up of the semi-starved naked millions" (Gandhi, 1945, p. 20 [1945]). In enunciating this point, Gandhi offered his "doctrine of trusteeship" as a means to promote economic equality. According to this doctrine, "those who own money now, are asked to behave like trustees holding their riches on behalf of the poor" (Gandhi, 1945, p. 21; 1967, p. 260 [1935]). Gandhi regarded such an attitude of trusteeship, sometimes called stewardship, as emerging from "true religion" (Gandhi, 1967, p. 111 [1945]), and also enunciated other principles to guide movement work, such as equitable distribution, non-possession, universal sharing of physical labor ("bread labour"), and relying on what is local ("swadeshi"). The degree and manner for best including each principle in a future constructive program is a key discernment skill (e.g., Table 4.1, item 22). A related issue is whether or not a particular nonviolent campaign requires the complement of a constructive program (e.g., Table 4.1, item 26).

Role of Spirituality

[W]hen my courage had all but gone.... I bowed over the kitchen table and prayed aloud ... . I experienced the presence of the Divine as I had never experienced Him before. ... an inner voice saying: "Stand up for righteousness, stand up for truth; and God will be at your side forever." ... My uncertainty disappeared. I was ready to face anything.—Martin Luther King (1964/1958, pp. 114–115 [1958])

Gandhi, often, referred to spiritual and religious qualities as a necessary element of his approach to nonviolent resistance. For example, as noted earlier, Gandhi declared that perfect nonviolence (perfect ahimsa) requires fearlessness, which, in turn, requires God-realization. Gandhi, at times, listed faith in God as a qualification for a satyagrahi. Other nonviolent leaders such as Martin Luther King have also attested to drawing courage from faith (see epigraph that begins this section). Should, therefore, the capacity to believe in God be assessed in scales for perceived efficacy for Gandhian nonviolence? We argue that the answer depends on how the scales will be used, and especially the cultural beliefs held by the respondents (i.e., the target population). In modernized cultural contexts, we suggest that there may be advantages to assessing spiritual efficacy items in ways that make very clear the rationale for their inclusion, in order to prevent potentially divisive misunderstandings. Jonathan Schell (2003) pointed out that "Gandhi's asceticism ... which he regarded as essential to the practice of satyagraha, seems unlikely to serve as a model for very many," suggesting that crucial questions are "what it is about religious faith that enables it to serve as a foundation for nonviolence and whether, outside religion, there may be other foundations" (pp. 117–118).

Gandhi's assertions about the necessity of faith and realization flowed from his view of the *psychology of fearlessness*. Gandhi's psychology of fearlessness resonates with the perennial spiritual view that "the moment one has a glimpse of the Imperishable [living presence of God within], one sheds the love of the perishable body" (Gandhi, 1967, p. 126 [1940]). Yet, while Gandhi often used orthodox religious language, he respected the diversity of individual pathways, repeatedly affirming the validity of all major religious traditions, and expressing openness to atheism when he saw it producing equivalent fruit in daily character and conduct (see Gandhi, 1967, pp. 66 [1927], 67 [1928]; 1999, v. 75, pp. 215–216 [1939]; Oman, 2014).

The underlying logic of the traditional view of dedication to the divine as the root source of fearlessness, which also seems to be Gandhi's view, may benefit from fuller articulation, as it is not widely grasped in modern society. This traditional perspective has seldom been articulated as fully as by Huxley (1945/1970, p. 145):

Fear cannot be got rid of by personal effort, but only by the ego's absorption in a cause greater than its own interests. Absorption in any cause will rid the mind of some of its fears; but only absorption in the loving and knowing of the divine Ground can rid it of all fear. For when the cause is less than the highest, the sense of fear and anxiety is transferred from the self to the cause as when heroic self-sacrifice for a loved individual or institution is accompanied by anxiety in regard to that for which the sacrifice is made. Whereas if the sacrifice is made for God, and for others for God's sake, there can be no fear or abiding anxiety, since nothing can be a menace to the divine Ground and even failure and disaster are to be accepted as being in accord with the divine will.

Gandhi (1967) asserted that "one can always progress toward this goal [of fearlessness] by determined and constant endeavor and by increasing confidence in oneself" (p. 59 [1930]). Thus, if the perennial spiritual perspective is correct, then fearlessness may be progressively cultivated through spiritual disciplines such as selfless service, meditation, and repetition of a mantram or holy name, practices existing in analogous forms in all major religious traditions (Oman, 2014; Oman et al., 2020; Walsh, 2015). Empirical studies corroborate that such spiritual practices may reduce fear (Sedlmeier et al., 2012). Gandhi's view that self-efficacy ("self-confidence") is related to fearlessness is also consistent with the *psychology of courage*, an emerging subfield of modern positive psychology (Pury & Lopez, 2010), and there is no need to view Gandhi's affirmations of his experience of divine support as inherently contradicting science (Bandura, 2003; Oman, 2014). Yet, in most or all modern nonviolent movements, we submit it may also be helpful or necessary to recognize respect for spiritual diversity as a component of collective nonviolent efficacy (e.g., Table 4.1, item 27).

Pilot Survey

To explore the viability of the nonviolent efficacy approach outlined above, Oman (2014) launched an anonymous online pilot survey focused on nonviolent efficacy perceptions, publicized via his original paper and messages to education and research groups for peace and/or nonviolence. From July 2014 to January 2015, completed surveys ($n = 204$) were received from respondents residing in the US or Canada ($n = 133$), Western Europe ($n = 17$), post-communist Europe, Australia/New Zealand, Latin America, East Asia, and India. Respondents were more often younger (18–39 years, $n = 55$) or middle-aged (40–64 years, $n = 82$) than older (65+ years, $n = 39$). Surveys assessed individual nonviolent self-efficacy (items 1–6 in Table 4.1 with minor rewording) plus collective efficacy for performing either nonviolent action (adaptations of items 10–12, 18, 23–24, and 17 in Table 4.1) or education in nonviolence (six novel items). Almost all participants who began a scale completed almost all its items, suggesting that items were understandable (one or zero items were skipped by 204/204 for individual efficacy, 85/90 for action group efficacy, and 19/22 for education group efficacy, with full completion by 190/204, 85/90, and 18/22). Half or more respondents, and usually more than 80%, also affirmed that each individual and group action item was "quite a bit" or "very" "relevant to exercising nonviolent power." Finally, although no relation was observed between individual and education group efficacy perceptions ($r = 0.07$, $p > 0.20$, $n = 19$), a modest and statistically significant positive correlation was found between individual and action group nonviolent efficacy perceptions ($r = 0.34$, $p < 0.002$, $n = 85$), underscoring that these are coherently related yet distinct dimensions of efficacy perception (fuller analyses of these data will be published elsewhere).

The solid completion rates, affirmations of relevance, and cogent patterning of responses to a survey designed for a very general global audience support the viability of the nonviolent approach as explicated in this chapter. Furthermore, such viability suggests that surveys tailored to particular movements and/or localities could plausibly generate the assessment-to-practice synergies described above and by Oman (2014).

Discussion

In the previous sections, we reviewed major skills for nonviolence as described by Gandhi himself, mapping these skills onto preliminary items for perceived efficacy assessment of both individuals and groups. The resulting set of questions (Table 4.1) is suggestive rather than definitive: It shows the logic of applying self-efficacy theory to nonviolence and could be expanded and refined for application to particular cultural, social, and political contexts. To our knowledge, the paper by Oman (2014), from which the present chapter is adapted, was the first systematic application to nonviolence of Bandura's self-efficacy framework, one of the most influential and practical psychological approaches of the past century (for more circumscribed applications see Oman, 2014; Thomas & Louis, 2014; Young, 2020). The approach outlined here contributes to several psychology subfields, including the psychologies of nonviolence, perceived efficacy, and courage.

Oman (2014) described a range of directions for future research and practice that due to space limitations can only be summarized here. First, the track record of self-efficacy approaches across many domains of human functioning suggests that their systematic application might prove useful for activists for peace, justice, health, and global human and environmental well-being. Specific applications might include evaluating training programs, preparing groups for functioning in various conditions, and integration into social media. Application to diverse public-health-related efforts to foster environmental justice, health equity, and consumer protection may be of special interest (Oman, 2014).

More broadly, Oman (2014) suggested that a self-efficacy approach to nonviolence might support improved integration of the teaching of nonviolent skills into mass education, which could be viewed as a constructive program. Further research is also needed on the relation between nonviolent efficacy and the psychology of courage. Ironically, despite Gandhi's emphasis on courage/fearlessness as a foundation of nonviolence, courage has been almost entirely neglected in the development of self-report questionnaire scales for nonviolent personality, none of which contain subscales for fearlessness (Kool & Agrawal, 2020, "Measurement of Nonviolence," pp. 167–193). The present analysis suggests that more psychometric attention should be given to fearlessness as a pivotal constituent of Gandhian nonviolence. Further work on fearlessness might also help clarify related issues of emotional dynamics, such as Gandhi's (1967) claim that he had "learnt through bitter experience the one supreme lesson to conserve my anger, and as heat conserved is transmuted into energy, even so our anger controlled can be transmuted into a power which can move the world" (p. 16 [1920]). Finally, perceived efficacy approaches may also be helpful for identifying common ground and fostering cooperation between adherents to diverse policy-based as well as principled forms of nonviolence (see Sharp, 1979, "Types of principled nonviolence," pp. 201–234). For example, perceived efficacy assessments could play a key role in institutionally managing the progressive integration of nonviolent sanctions into national defense, a process sometimes called "transarmament" (see Oman, 2014).

Conclusion

Using Gandhi's approach as a prototype, this chapter has sketched how to apply self-efficacy theory to nonviolence, describing requisite first steps and plausible outcomes, including enhanced effectiveness in nonviolent conduct (ahimsa), constructive program, and satyagraha. Gandhi was identified by Martin Luther King (1964/1958) as "probably the first person in history to lift the love ethic of Jesus above mere interaction between individuals to a powerful and effective social force on a large scale" (p. 79). We hope that the ideas presented here may assist anyone seeking to systematically follow the innovative trail blazed by Gandhi and his movement.

Acknowledgements The author is grateful to *Gandhi Marg* for permission to adapt portions of his 2014 paper for use in this book.

References

Bandura, A. (1986). *Social foundations of thought and action*. Prentice Hall.

Bandura, A. (1997). *Self-efficacy: The exercise of control*. W. H. Freeman.

Bandura, A. (2003). On the psychosocial impact and mechanisms of spiritual modeling. *International Journal for the Psychology of Religion, 13,* 167–173. https://doi.org/10.1207/S15327582IJPR1303_02

Bandura, A. (2006). Guide for constructing self-efficacy scales. In F. Pajares & T. C. Urdan (Eds.), *Self-efficacy beliefs of adolescents* (pp. 307–337). Information Age Publishing.

Gandhi, M. K. (1945). *Constructive programme: Its meaning and place*. Navajivan.

Gandhi, M. K. (1951/1961). *Nonviolentresistance*. Schocken.

Gandhi, M. K. (1967). *The mind of Mahatma Gandhi* (R. K. Prabhu, U. R. Rao, Eds.; Rev. ed.). Navajivan.

Gandhi, M. K. (1999). *The collected works of Mahatma Gandhi* (Electronic Book; 6th rev. ed.). Publications Division Government of India.

Huxley, A. (1945/1970). *The perennial philosophy.* Harper & Row.

King, M. L. (1964/1958). *Stride toward freedom: The Montgomery story.* Harper & Row.

Kool, V. K., & Agrawal, R. (2020). *Gandhi and the psychology of nonviolence, volume 1: Scientific roots and development.* Palgrave Macmillan.

Oman, D. (2014). Building nonviolent self-efficacy to foster social transformation and health. *Gandhi Marg, 35,* 583–617.

Oman, D., Bormann, J. E., & Kane, J. J. (2020). Mantram repetition as a portable mindfulness practice: Applications during the COVID-19 pandemic. *Mindfulness* (online before print, 16 November 2020). https://doi.org/10.1007/s12671-020-01545-w

Peterson, C., & Seligman, M. E. P. (2004).*Character strengths and virtues: A handbook and classification.* American Psychological Association.

Pury, C. L. S., & Lopez, S. J. (2010). *The psychology of courage: Modern research on an ancient virtue.* American Psychological Association.

Schell, J. (2003). *The unconquerable world: Power, nonviolence, and the will of the people.* Metropolitan Books/Henry Holt.

Sedlmeier, P., Eberth, J., Schwarz, M., Zimmermann, D., Haarig, F., Jaeger, S., et al. (2012). The psychological effects of meditation: A meta-analysis. *Psychological Bulletin, 138,* 1139–1171. https://doi.org/10.1037/a0028168

Sharp, G. (1973). *The politics of nonviolent action.* Porter Sargent.

Sharp, G. (1979). *Gandhi as a political strategist.* Porter Sargent.

Thomas, E. F., & Louis, W. R. (2014). When will collective action be effective? Violent and non-violent protests differentially influence perceptions of legitimacy and efficacy among sympathizers. *Personality & Social Psychology Bulletin, 40,* 263–276. https://doi.org/10.1177/0146167213510525

Walsh, R. (2015). What is wisdom? Cross-cultural and cross-disciplinary syntheses. *Review of General Psychology, 19*(3), 278–293. https://doi.org/10.1037/gpr0000045

Young, L. E. (2020). Who dissents? Self-efficacy and opposition action after state-sponsored election violence. *Journal of Peace Research, 57,* 62–76. https://doi.org/10.1177/0022343319886000

5

Significance of Gandhi's Fasts: An Interdisciplinary Perspective

John S. Moolakkattu

Introduction

From early times, fasting has been associated with health and spiritual development. In ancient Greece, fasting preceded many rituals aimed at invoking the divine. In the Old Testament, fasting was seen as a preparatory prayer that prophets undertook for divine revelation. The 40 days' fast by Christ in the desert did not leave any clues to its nature and effects except the advice that he gave to his followers that it should be observed privately and with all humility. In the early Christian monastic tradition, fasting was, largely, seen as a penitential act of prayer for reaching communion with God. At the same time, the health benefits of fasting were, also, recognized by many, with obese people, often, fasting for reducing their weight (Kerndt et al., 1982).

J. S. Moolakkattu (✉)
Department of International Relations and Politics, Central
University of Kerala, Kasargod, Kerala, India

© The Author(s), under exclusive license to Springer Nature
Switzerland AG 2022
V. K. Kool and R. Agrawal (eds.), *Gandhi's Wisdom*,
https://doi.org/10.1007/978-3-030-87491-9_5

Although, fasting has been associated with different religions either for the purification of oneself or for the glorification of God, it came to be employed as a means of political struggle in places like Tsarist Russia and Ireland and, among others, by suffragettes in the UK and Indian immigrants in Canada. In all these cases, the intention was to obtain certain goals of a tangible nature. But the name of Gandhi rings louder than all of the above, since he had experimented with fasting and commented on its use and abuse more than anyone else, considering it as one of the methods of Satyagraha.

Pratt and Vernon write:

> "So embedded was fasting in Gandhi's everyday life that it is difficult to neatly separate its practice as a regime of the self from its performance as an act of national significance". This practice was intended "to inscribe the self upon the nation, and the nation upon the self, in ways that elevated Gandhi's claims to moral leadership." (2005, p. 95)

Further, Pratt and Vernon call fasting as a "dietary equivalent of *brahmacharya*, the supreme exercise of self-denial" (ibid., p. 96).

Fasting is routinely employed by people belonging to different religions, who practice it by abstaining from various types of food, and over the years, this practice has become embedded in various cultures. Though, it sits uneasily with the assumptions of economic theory rooted in utilitarianism and its pleasure principle, which is associated with consumption rather than abstinence, Etzioni (1986) is of the view that utility could assume different dimensions. Although fasting may produce disutility in terms of being deprived of the natural craving for food, a new form of utility may emerge when one is convinced that it is being done in supplication of God's will. There are others who claim that the pain of fasting can be overcome by the prospective likelihood of eating with pleasure once the fast ends (Loewenstein, 2000). Those who engage in fasts for their health effects such as for improving beauty and reducing overweight are also looking for results. But this is applicable when the fasting is of a relatively short duration. Fasting can be undertaken by, even, non-religious people for the reasons mentioned above as well as for achieving some kind of self-control. There is, also, evidence to suggest that fasting practices emerged not in the context of scarcity, but in the context of affluence accompanied by religious fervor. The fasting practices of both Christians and Muslims are cited in support of this idea with the former resorting to fasting after a period of abundant eating and drinking and the latter feasting after the fast (Baumard et al., 2015).

The Cultural Context of Gandhi's Fasts

Certain aspects of Gandhi's biography, which have a bearing on his fasting experiments, could be considered here. Born into a Vaishnava family and deeply attached to a mother who kept some hard vows and observed fasts routinely, the practice was very much a part of Gandhi's ethos. The Modh Baniya, the merchant caste to which he belonged, was known for its nonviolent ethic, the Indian equivalent of the Protestant ethic. Kathiawad, the region where Gandhi grew up was, also, influenced by Jainism, the most nonviolent of Indian sects. Both his parents were religious, with his mother leaning towards an ascetic life of fasting and prayers. Thus, this kind of self-suffering, which became the anchor of Gandhi's Satyagraha and fasting, emanated, directly, from his own home. When one is angry towards someone or something, it is expressed through self-imposed penalties such as the giving up of food. Turning the other cheek is a compelling version of self-suffering and this line of the Gospel impressed Gandhi. Self-suffering was also a weapon of the Brahmin, who often resorted to fasting, self-injury, or even suicide leaving the burden or consequences of such actions on the oppressor, for having caused the death of a Brahmin (Gandhi, 1927; Rudolph, 1963).

Gandhi, often, recommended the use of fasting for health reasons, derived from his faith in naturopathic practice. Gandhi was, already, used to the Hindu fast, which allowed milk and fruit, but later he started complete fasting in which water, alone, is permitted (M.K. Gandhi, Collected Works of Mahatma Gandhi [hereafter CWMG], 39, p. 264). According to Gandhi, fasting could, at times, arouse a sexual urge and add to one's appetite for food. Hence, it has to be accompanied by self-restraint. Moreover, physical fasting has to be accompanied by mental fasting (CWMG, 39, p. 266).

At the same time, Gandhi's fasting was closely allied to Jain practice. Gandhi himself had acknowledged his debt to Srimad Rajachandra, an honest Jain businessman turned sage, who died at the age of 33. It is claimed that "fast unto death" is in the Jain tradition since it is aimed at moral persuasion rather than moral pressure. Gandhi always insisted that the famous political fasts that he undertook were not aimed at coercing people to behave the way he wanted them to. Instead, fasting was intended for his personal self-purification and, simultaneously, for atoning for his own faults and of those around him, forcing them to mend their ways (Alter, 2000). In other words, "Gandhi's political fasts, then, were fundamentally like those of a virtuous Jain parent seeking to protect his or her family" (Laidlaw, 2005). It was a form of "vicarious atonement" (Merriam, 1975, p. 292).

In the Indian renunciatory tradition, a fasting person who has moral authority and is respected by both rulers and subjects has a right to protest for legitimate causes. In the event of the fasting person losing his life, the survival of the ruler becomes precarious, posing a moral threat to the ruler. This has parallels with Gandhi's fasts, which created anxiety in the political class belonging to the British Raj due to the similar consequences that could emerge in the event of his death (Thapar, 2020).

The monotheistic religions like Judaism, Christianity and Islam see fasting not only as a religious act but also as a means of affirming community solidarity and brotherhood. Not only Gandhi but also practitioners of the political fast have drawn on this religious dimension when using fasts as a protest act (Bala, 2007, p. 81). Gandhi acknowledged that Hinduism, Vaishnavism and Jainism are all steeped in nonviolence although he admitted that this virtue is not exclusive to them. He also warned that one need not take nonviolence to its extreme point of fast unto death as some Jain practices suggest, but rather confine oneself to "fighting peacefully through voluntary suffering" (CWMG, 20, p. 33).

Fasting for the Sins of Others

In Gandhi's ashrams, be it Phoenix in South Africa or Sabarmati in India, Gandhi fasted for seven days each, because of misconduct on the part of the Ashramites. These fasts did not have any political connotations. They were aimed at purification of the Ashram community. In both these fasts, Gandhi had set a definite period and the fasts were unconditional in nature. No specific action was expected, it was only for self-examination and the purification of all concerned. But this was not the case when Gandhi undertook fasts on behalf of the striking mill-workers. He had set no deadline, although, the fast ended after three days. It was indefinite and had the potential for becoming a fast unto death, although, Gandhi never made use of such an expression. In the mill-workers' case, his fast was aimed at both the mill-owners and the workers. Gandhi, often, referred to the fast as one that brought forth some degree of coercion on the owners and to that extent, was not a perfect fast.

Gandhi moved between these two types of fasts, throughout, besides prescribing fasting for health reasons. Fasting as a form of nonviolent action on public issues intensified after the 1930s, especially the number of conditional fasts of an indefinite nature with a potential for leading to death (Jordens, 1998). As far as Gandhi was concerned, there were three arenas of public fasts, namely, fasts against the government, untouchability and violence.

Fasting as a Weapon of Nonviolence

Although fasting was a key weapon employed by Gandhi during the freedom struggle, it did not catch the imagination of many nonviolent activists who were more enamored by its strategic advantages than by its spiritual and moral connotations. So, in many nonviolent movements, fasting was not popular. But as part of movements not committed to nonviolence, many have employed hunger strikes for deriving concessions from the authorities.

One exception to the above was the fast undertaken by Cesar Chavez. His first penitential fast for nonviolence was on March 10, 1968, in order to persuade the members of the United Farm Workers not to abandon nonviolence. This fast has close similarities to Gandhian fasts, in that, it had a spiritual streak. Although the fast was indefinite, there was good progress and was concluded in 25 days. In 1981, the Irish Catholic political prisoners engaged in a hunger strike with ten of them starving themselves to death, forcing the British government to give in. This was a case of using human suffering for political ends, suffused with a religious overtone, or, a case of self-imposed martyrdom (Baumann, 2009).

The Power of Fasting

A fast is able to communicate more than what human speech or reasoned negotiation is capable of doing. It works as a "method of influencing political policy and social attitudes by creating an emotional impact difficult to achieve through ordinary speech and negotiation" (Merriam, 1975, p. 293). Further, even as Gandhi weakened his body through fasting, it "strengthened his grip on the mass mind" (ibid., p. 297). According to Jordens, "fasts used to be exercises in atonement and purification with a certain influence of moral persuasion on a close public; they had become methods of unleashing spiritual power that could move masses, because they were dictated by God and they activated divine power" (Jordens, 1998, p. 219). According to Gandhi:

> The weapon which has hitherto proved infallible for me, is fasting. To put an appearance before a yelling crowd does not always work. It certainly did not last night. What my word in person cannot do my fast may. It may touch the hearts of all the warring elements even in the Punjab if it does in Calcutta. (CWMG, 89, p. 132)

The psychology of fasting is intimately linked with the psychology of the person undertaking it, the perceptions of the spectators and the target groups. It is "a fundamentally dialogical process, which is guided by the interaction of the opponents just as much as it is by the personal intentions of the fasting persons" (Bala, 2007, p. 86).

Gandhi was, also, sensitive to the fact that his stature would provide his fasts a global reach beyond the importance that it had in India. Further, fasting undertaken by him alone would be much better than a multitude doing so. As Gandhi explained:

> The purpose of this fast is not of merely local importance. It has significance not only for the whole of India, but for the whole world. The sacrifice here of fifty humble persons cannot carry as much weight as the sacrifice of one world-famous figure. And if the problem gets solved through such a sacrifice, the sole sacrifice, namely, of myself will be enough. (CWMG, 73, p. 175)

Using the fast as a method of bargaining was anathematic to Gandhi. He stated that if "his willingness to break the fast is tied up with a conceding of all the demands, it would be a form of cowardice" (CWMG, 14, p. 267). Although many of his fasts were aimed at his own fellow-workers, he was aware of its impact on the adversary. Gandhi was, also, very particular that people who break a pledge after taking it should be dealt with strongly as such an act amounts to forsaking one's God. Gandhi felt that he should fast on such occasions. He said: "I don't suffer when I fast; fasting hurts me less than that people should deceive me by breaking their pledge" (CWMG, 14, p. 278).

Fasting can, also, be viewed as an "example of the politics and performativity of restraint and refusal, which is a core part of nonviolent protest" (Bala, 2007, p. 76). It is the "fundamentally theatrical relationship between the actor and the spectators that made fasting into a nonviolent method" (ibid., p. 78). Explaining the performativity dimension of the fast, Bala says that Gandhi did not recognize the authenticity of any other person engaged in fasting and would dub it as intended for "stage effect." She, however, admits that Gandhi's own fasts were not altogether free of "stage effect." Instead, "it was negotiated with the spectators and required their participation in order to establish Gandhi's authority" (Bala, 2007, p. 135). The reins of control always rested with Gandhi. In other words, it was akin to engaging in a conflict in a controlled way.

Much as in the case of conflicts, Gandhi's political fasts were enacted in such a way so as to pass through different stages of negotiation, interaction and communication. When he engaged in fasts, it became the responsibility of others to keep him alive. While the fast seeks to achieve certain goals, it does not stop with them. When Gandhi used his body as a weapon of nonviolence, he was claiming monopoly as the signifier. However, he saw the efforts of others to do likewise as intended for stage effect with suicidal overtones (Bala, 2008, p. 303).

Distinction Between a Fast and a Hunger Strike

Apparently, Gandhi wanted to make a distinction between political hunger strikes of a routine nature and Satyagraha. Although he acknowledged the legitimacy of the former, he was of the view that the accompanying attitude of those engaged in hunger strike had streaks of violence about it, with self-suffering accompanied by rancor and hostility towards the authorities. This aspect is absent in Satyagraha. While renouncing food can become one of the virtuous ways of engaging in resistance, it can also be treated as not so virtuous when it assumes an adversarial form. Gandhi wrote:

> The fast is not to be regarded, in any shape or form, in the nature of a hunger-strike, or as designed to put any pressure upon the Government. It is to be regarded, for the satyagrahis, as the necessary discipline to fit them for civil disobedience, contemplated in their Pledge, and for all others, as some slight token of the intensity of their wounded feelings. (CWMG, 15, p. 145)

As far as public demonstrations are concerned, Gandhi found fasting to be more potent than a *hartal* (closure of shops and offices) and felt that it could move even the hardest of hearts. Those who fast voluntarily become gentle, pure and noble. But, Gandhi, also, warned against its misuse. He cited the case of the beggars threatening to fast or pretending to do so until they get what they were asking for. Such a fast degrades the person undertaking it and it is only proper not to be kind to those who try to obtain what they want through pressure. As Gandhi clarified:

> A person who fasts before another's house in order to get money will only starve to death. Anyone who gives him money out of misplaced pity because of his fasting will have done no virtuous deed either. (CWMG, 19, p. 375)

On suffragette Emmeline Pankhurst's hunger strike in prison, Gandhi commented:

> Even in gaol, these ladies are bent on harassing the authorities and so getting themselves released. … This kind of fighting is not Satyagraha. A Satyagrahi's object is to get into a prison and stay there. He will not even dream of harming others. If, however, we leave aside her mode of fighting and only think of the suffering she has borne, we shall find much to learn from her. Despite numerous difficulties in their way, she and her companions do not yet feel dispirited, nor are they likely to do so. They will struggle on till death. Though a woman, Mrs. Pankhurst is as manly as any man. Indians should emulate all this courage, for the British women being without the franchise is nothing compared to the disabilities we suffer. (CWMG, 13, p. 81)

Drawing inspiration from Gandhi, four functionaries of the anti-nuclear fast for life movement engaged in fasting in an attempt to end the nuclear arms race on Hiroshima Day, that is, August 6, 1983. It continued for 41 days with the functionaries subsisting only on water. However, it failed to receive the kind of widespread support as had been envisaged (Harvey, 2015). Prisoners in Northern Ireland belonging to the Irish Republican Army staged hunger strikes in 1980 and 1981 seeking status as political prisoners resulting in death of ten inmates. But such deaths are not common outside the prisons.

One of the most prolonged fasts unto death was the one by Irom Sharmila of Manipur in India. Her fast lasted for, a record, 16 years. She had claimed that her method was Gandhian and the intention was to repeal the Armed Forces Special Powers Act. Her decision to fast unto death was deemed suicidal. But the consent that she gave to being fed using a Ryles tube suggested that death was out of question. Since she, also, practiced yoga to keep her bodily functions intact, it was clear that she had no desire to die. Although the AFSPA is an Act that affects everyone in Manipur including the Nagas, she became a symbol of Meitei nationalism alone. Her courageous act and persistence made her a cult figure, which was her undoing. When she ended the fast, she expressed her desire to contest elections and become the Chief Minister of Manipur (Haksar, 2016). What is lacking in a fast like the one described above is that it was aimed at putting pressure on the national government without the necessary elements that one finds in a Gandhian fast. It was a hunger strike, pure and simple. Gandhi stated:

> If my fast was fixed as an unconditional one, it is obvious there can be no coercion about it, for nothing that the public may do or not do could suspend my fast. Therefore, if a conditional fast is held to be coercive, it would be so considered because of the condition. (CWMG, 52, p. 306)

As a protest, fasts can be seen as a secular form of nonviolent resistance reducible to the category of hunger strike. But as "a personal ritual of spiritual purification, sacrifice, and penitence, fasting worked on a level much deeper than the hunger strike" (Harvey, 2015, p. 98).

Fasting as a Science

Gandhi's approach to the issue of fasting was accompanied by a certain degree of claimed expertise on the subject. He wanted many, who desired to undertake fasting, to consult him before venturing into it. He explained:

> I wish to give you my experience in this direction as a specialist par excellence. I do not know any contemporary of mine who has reduced fasting and prayer to an exact science and who has reaped a harvest so abundant as I have. I wish that I could infect the nation with my experience and make it resort to fasting and prayer with intelligence, honesty and intensity. (CWMG, 17, p. 101)

That he was the ultimate authority on fasting was made clear even more forcefully:

> A friend writes that he has gone on an indefinite fast. All that I can say is that it is not right for him to fast. To resort to a fast thus is a sin. While I am alive I should be consulted because I have much experience of fasting. I shall not go into the matter further. (CWMG, 98, pp. 189–190)

Gandhi did not recommend fasting to everyone because he was aware that it cannot be observed by one and all. One's physical capacity to fast is a lesser consideration as compared to one's abiding faith in God. Indirectly, this would exclude those who do not believe in God. But this argument may be simplistic because Gandhi did not rule out any one as long as one recognized the existence of a spiritual force guiding the world. Yet, since the urge to fast should come from the depths of one's soul, he considered it rare. The type of patience required in fasting, the determination to undertake it, the calmness and absence of any ill will are of a very tall order beyond the capacity of ordinary mortals and Gandhi was all, too, aware of it.

As Gandhi wrote:

> Fasting is a fiery weapon. It has its own science. No one, as far as I am aware, has a perfect knowledge of it. Unscientific experimentation with it is bound to be harmful to the one who fasts, and it may even harm the cause espoused. No one who has not earned the right to do so should, therefore, use this weapon. (CWMG, 73, p. 91)

Gandhi compared his suffering in fasting to that of a mother undergoing birth pangs and asked his followers to see it in that light rather than being anxious. He states that: "It is the woman giving birth to a child who suffers the pains, others only help. I, too, wish to give birth to the ideals of nonviolence and truth, so that I alone need bear the pains of fasting" (CWMG, 22, p. 397). Further, he added: "Please do nothing out of pity for me. I shall fast for as many days as I can and if it is the will of God that I should die then I shall die" (CWMG, 98, pp. 249–250).

Fasting: Public or Private?

Gandhi made a distinction between private fasts and public fasts and preferred the former, generally, and the latter in specific situations such as after the Chauri Chaura incident. He clarified:

> All fasting and all penance must as far as possible be secret. But my fasting is both a penance and a punishment, and a punishment has to be public. It is penance for me and punishment for those whom I try to serve, for whom I love to live and would equally love to die. They have unintentionally sinned against the laws of the Congress though they were sympathizers if not actually connected with it. Probably they hacked the constables- their countrymen and fellow beings-with my name on their lips. The only way love punishes is by suffering. I cannot even wish them to be arrested. But I would let them know that I would suffer for their breach of the Congress creed. I would advise those who feel guilty and repentant to hand themselves voluntarily to the Government for punishment and make a clean confession. (CWMG, 22, p. 420)

He was, also, against publicized atonement. The post-ChauriChaura fast was, however, publicized by him because it had two purposes, one private and the other public. Privately, it was a kind of personal atonement while, publicly, it was one way of punishing the people of ChauriChaura.

Fasting and Love

Gandhi's fasts were never undertaken to embarrass and defeat those against whom they were targeted. In fact, he found fasting quite useless against an insensitive person. Fasting is expected to stir the better part of a human being. Gandhi was of the view that a tyrant would only see the fast as another form of violence against him and respond in a ruthless manner. Fasting should target a lover but not for securing rights through pressure, but to reform him/her. Thus, fasting against one's father to rid him of a bad habit is in order but not fasting to get an inheritance (CWMG, 23, p. 420). Additionally, if the fast is undertaken with a mixed motive, although the material goals may be accomplished, there would not be any spiritual gain. Gandhi considered all religions other than Protestantism to be favorably disposed to fasting. Gandhi, also, found undergoing pangs of hunger as a means of identifying oneself with the starving millions and for gaining a first-hand experience of their lives (CWMG, 31, p. 319).

Many Ashram inmates and the members of the public sought Gandhi's permission and fasted. Compared to the number of persons whose requests were conceded, there were more who were asked to desist from fasting or to stop an already begun fast because they did not meet the standards that Gandhi had set for the exercise. Gandhi stated:

> A satyagrahi's first concern is not the effect of his action. It must always be its propriety. He must have faith enough in his cause and his means, and know that success will be achieved in the end. (CWMG, 23, pp. 517–518)

Fast Unto Death as the Ultimate Weapon

Gandhi displayed a certain degree of ambivalence towards fast unto death. He said it was not to be undertaken in prison. None of his fasts had lasted more than 21 days. This is because most of his fasts were unconditional. If a person engages in a conditional fast having the potential to starve to death, it would amount to a kind of suicide, which may sit uneasily with the spirit of nonviolence. Fasting is an affirmation of life itself though authorities may use the pretext of suicide to arrest the person undertaking it. Unlike dieting, which is purely physical, fasting has an ethical and symbolic aspect (Visvanathan, 2014). However, Gandhi did not rule out the possibility of fast unto death. He elaborates:

> If and when the call comes to fast unto death, I will do so irrespective of others joining or not. Fasting unto death is the last and the most potent weapon in the armoury of satyagraha. It is a sacred thing. But it must be accepted with all its implications. It is not the fast itself but what it implies that matters….But such a fast should not be undertaken inside the prison. (CWMG, 85, p. 147)

He, further, clarified:

> I have not taken up the fast to die, but I have taken it up to live a better and purer life for the service of the country. If, therefore, I reach a crisis (of which humanly speaking I see no possibility whatsoever) when the choice lies between death and food, I shall certainly break the fast. (CWMG, 25, p. 216)

Writing to CF Andrews, Gandhi explained:

> I told you that hitherto all my fasts have been conditional; even the last one was conditional. I can well understand anybody being repelled by an unconditional fast unto death, though I have told you that in my scheme of life even an unconditional fast, under very extraordinary circumstances, has a place, but I don't need to argue out that extreme position. All I want to say is that in your discussion with Gurudev you should take care to avoid arguments around a 'fast unto death', taking the expression literally. (CWMG, 56, p. 53)

Gandhi, also, had a revulsion to the term fasting unto death. Instead, he preferred fasting unto a new life (CWMG, 54, p. 328) because every fast unto death is not suicide. Writing to George Joseph in January 1933, Gandhi clarified:

> My fast was not a fast unto death in its literal sense. The Roman Catholic priest, who is a visitor to this prison, knows me, and when I was on the eve of taking that fast, he came over to me in his kindly manner just to say one word, and he said how he drew the distinction between a suicide and a sacrifice. A suicide carried with it a certainty of destruction. A sacrifice meant risking life, the greater the risk, the greater the sacrifice. But there should be nothing beyond risk. I had no hesitation in agreeing with the distinction, and my fast being conditional was not a fast amounting to suicide, but it was a fast involving the greatest risk, but still a risk and no more. (CWMG, 53, p. 44)

Yet, Gandhi saw fast unto death as an important part of Satyagraha to be used only in the rarest of rare circumstances by people qualified to undertake it.

Other Considerations

Over and above the facets of fasts and fasting elaborated upon in the previous pages, there are some other issues which also need to be touched upon. One such was the issue of untouchability. According to Gandhi, the issue of untouchability was not a matter for engaging in a struggle on the part of the affected castes, but one where compensatory acts and change of mindset on the part of the upper castes were deemed necessary. In other words, he did not favor a dissociative approach to the question as Ambedkar had suggested (Bala, 2007, p. 129). Nonetheless, Gandhi talked about a chain of fasts starting with him for removing untouchability and vitalizing the activities of the Harijan Sevak Sangh, though, he felt that a "lot of spade work" was needed before such action could be undertaken (CWMG, 81, p. 119).

Fasts demand greater qualifications than what is needed when people engage in civil disobedience. Gandhi claimed that his fasts were undertaken on the "promptings of an unseen power," which could be called the "inner voice" or "God" (CWMG, 73, p. 156). Gandhi emphasized that fasting is not to be confused with otherworldliness. It is to be employed for problems of the here and now. He stated: "All virtue ceases to have use if it serves no purpose in every walk of life" (CWMG, 76, p. 318).

Undertaking a fast is a sort of intervention of the body without emphasizing its physicality. Even when the body is placed at the center, the soul is given greater importance (Bala, 2007, p. 115). Gandhi was always skeptical of crowd behavior and whenever he had to tame it, fasting was the means adopted to do it. Although Gandhi did not recommend political fasts for women, most of his fasts could be seen as the valorization of feminine qualities. The fasting bodies, however, were not seen as representing feminine qualities, but a new form of courage, heroism and power (Bala, 2007, p. 126). This new courage was to be harnessed through self-control, celibacy and vegetarianism. The control over the body is needed for "control over the body of the nation" (ibid., p. 112). However, many in the national movement, such as Nehru and Tagore, did not find his fasts particularly appealing, the former because of its emplacement in an unappealing religious idiom and the latter because the idea of fast unto death did not agree with his understanding of Hinduism (Chandra, 2011).

Conclusion

How, then, do we evaluate Gandhi's fasts? Apparently, in a political fast, Gandhi combined the concerns of the personal, the national and the colonizer in a single sweep. A fast provided Gandhi an opportunity to test the extent to which he had acquired self-control or swaraj. It amounted to a kind of atonement for the sins and inadequacies of his fellow compatriots forcing them to mend their ways. Further, it was an attempt to morally challenge the colonizer to engage in a process of reflection about the immorality of colonialism. In other words, Gandhi sought to transform what may appear as a political struggle determined by its own idioms into a moral struggle. When we analyze the history of nonviolent action, Gandhi was the first to make fasting both a spiritual and political pursuit. As in the case of nonviolence, fasting was a science for Gandhi and he claimed that he was an expert at it, capable of advising others. However, he was very ungenerous in recommending it to others. He made it an esoteric practice, which can be legitimately undertaken in rare circumstances, by rare people like Gandhi himself.

Unlike the other tools of Satyagraha, Gandhi, alone, claimed to possess the final authority for advising people on whether they should use fast as a weapon in Satyagraha. Gandhi used his body as a symbol of resistance to the indiscipline of the mob in the course of various nonviolent actions. He saw his fasts as the result of a divine call, and not just a willful initiative on his part. He claimed that he had "priceless peace and unending joy" during the fasts and if God's grace is not there a fast would merely be "useless starvation" (CWMG, 69, p. 11). In other words, Gandhi elevated fasting to a pedestal beyond the reach of ordinary human beings and was averse to its practice at a mass level. In doing so, he ended up prescribing fasting as a nonviolent weapon of the spiritually inspired adherents of principled nonviolence, which deprived it of its élan to be used by ordinary people as a mode of resistance. Further, while Gandhi said fasting is based on an inner call, he discerned that such a call came quickly in certain matters, but was surprisingly slow to come on matters like untouchability, a development that is difficult to fathom.

References

Alter, J. S. (2000). *Gandhi's body: Sex, diet, and the politics of nationalism*. University of Pennsylvania Press.

Bala, S. (2007). The performativity of Nonviolent Protest in South Asia (1918–1948), unpublished MPhil dissertation, Johannes Gutenberg University Mainz, 2007. Available from https://openscience.ub.uni-mainz.de/handle/20.500.12030/4342

Bala, S. (2008). The dramaturgy of fasting in Gandhian nonviolent action. In M. Wagner & W. D. Ernst (Eds.), *Performing the matrix: Mediating cultural performances* (pp. 289–306). ePODIUM.

Baumann, M. M. (2009). Transforming conflict toward and away from violence: Bloody Sunday and the hunger strikes in Northern Ireland. *Dynamics of Asymmetric Conflict, 2*(3), 172–180. https://doi.org/10.1080/1746758090344024

Baumard, N., Hyafil, A., Morris, I., & Boye, P. (2015). Increased affluence explains the emergence of ascetic wisdoms and moralizing religions. *Current Biology, 25*(1), 10–15.

Chandra, S. (2011). Gandhi's twin fasts and the possibility of non-violence. *Economic and Political Weekly, 46*(23), 37–42.

Etzioni, A. (1986). The case for a multiple-utility conception. *Economics & Philosophy, 2*, 159–183. https://doi.org/10.1017/S1478061500002619

Gandhi, M. K. (1927). *An autobiography, or, the story of my experiments with truth*. Navajivan.

Gandhi, M. K. (2017). *Collected works of Mahatma Gandhi* (100 volumes). Government of India, Publications Division.

Haksar, N. (2016). Irom Sharmila's struggle against military repression: A critique. *ANTyAjAA: Indian Journal of Women and Social Change, 1*(2), 169–181.

Harvey, K. (2015). Prayer or protest? The radical promise of voluntary poverty in the anti-nuclear fast for life, 1983. *Journal for the Study of Radicalism, 9*(1), 95–124.

Jordens, J. T. F. (1998). *Gandhi's religion: A Homespun Shawl*. Macmillan.

Kerndt, P. R., Naughton, J. L., Driscoll, C. E., & Loxterkamp, D. A. (1982). Fasting: The history, pathophysiology and complications (Medical Progress). *Western Journal of Medicine, 137*, 379–399.

Laidlaw, J. (2005). A life worth leaving: Fasting to death as telos of a Jain religious life. *Economy and Society, 34*(2), 178–199. https://doi.org/10.1080/03085140500054545

Loewenstein, G. (2000). Preferences, behavior and welfare—Emotions in economic theory and economic behavior. *American Economic Review, 90,* 426–432. https://doi.org/10.1257/aer.90.2.426

Merriam, A. H. (1975). Symbolic action in India: Gandhi's nonverbal persuasion. *Quarterly Journal of Speech, 61*(3), 290–306.

Pratt, T., & Vernon, J. (2005). "Appeal from this fiery bed ...": The colonial politics of Gandhi's fasts and their metropolitan reception. *Journal of British Studies, 44*(1), 92–114.

Rudolph, S. H. (1963). The new courage: An essay on Gandhi's psychology. *World Politics, 16*(1), 98–117.

Thapar, R. (2020). Renunciation, dissent and satyagraha. *Seminar*, No. 725. Retrieved from https://www.india-seminar.com/2020/725/725_romila_thapar.htm

Visvanathan, S. (2014, September 6). Body as a site of protest. *The Hindu.*

6

Self- and Other-Purification as Gandhi's Way of Un-othering

R. C. Tripathi and Alka Bajpai

It is widely recognized that Gandhi was, quintessentially, a peacebuilder. Many around the world know him as an apostle of peace. Obama (2020) believes that Gandhi set the moral tone of the twentieth century. His adherence to nonviolence in conflict situations epitomized the method that he used for restoring peace. While there is little to dispute about Gandhi's method, more needs to be understood about the psychological processes that informed Gandhi's method to establish intergroup peace. His method had elements of empathy. But recent studies have shown that empathy has its limits (Bloom, 2016). There is a need to look for factors that were associated with Gandhi's method of establishing a harmonious relationship between groups.

R. C. Tripathi (✉)
University of Allahabad, Uttar Pradesh, Allahabad, India

A. Bajpai
University of Delhi, New Delhi, India

© The Author(s), under exclusive license to Springer Nature
Switzerland AG 2022
V. K. Kool and R. Agrawal (eds.), *Gandhi's Wisdom*,
https://doi.org/10.1007/978-3-030-87491-9_6

In this chapter, we will attempt to understand the psychological process that underlies Gandhi's way of developing warm-hearted and amicable relationships between members of groups that are involved in intractable and immutable conflicts. We call this process un-othering. Our focus will be on two sets of groups that remained central to Gandhi's concern throughout his life, namely Hindus and Muslims, and Shudras (the untouchables) and the high-caste Hindus. Gandhi's 'satyagraha' was as much directed at resolving the enduring conflict between these groups as it was directed at changing the terms of relationship with the British. So far as the relationship between Hindus and Muslims and between the high-caste Hindus ('savarnas') and Shudras ('avarnas') is concerned, Gandhi understood that the basis of mutual othering that took place in both these cases in the Indian society lay in the categorization based on the concept of impurity. This resulted in pushing members of certain groups to the margins and eventually outside the boundaries that define self and one's own group. They, then, became the other.

One may ask on what grounds this became possible. It is well known that groups develop normative structures to maintain their integrity and these normative structures tend to support othering (Pettigrew, 1991). Those who subscribe to such norms are considered pure, and 'us', the rest are considered impure and 'them'. The less prototypical members are either pushed out to maintain the purity of the group or kept at a distance. Srinivas's concept of 'sanskritization' explains how those placed lower down in the caste hierarchy sought to move up by emulating the Brahmanical rituals (Srinivas, 1952). Gandhi's wisdom turned the concept of impurity on its head. He used its antithetical concept, purity, for the un-othering of the two groups, but in a different way. The two methods that he used for this purpose were self-purification and other-purification. Gandhi used both of these synchronously for un-othering of the other and to build a harmonious relationship between the groups involved in intractable conflicts in India. We have attempted in this chapter to understand how Gandhi made use of these two processes to enable the groups to find social and moral inclusion and to 'enfold' each other (Gearhart, 1982).

Othering and Its Nature

Othering appears to be a human predicament if one were to go by what neuropsychologists have come to believe. Branan (2010) believes that our brains are hard-wired for engaging in categorization. He points out that humans have so evolved that visual inputs relating to living and non-living objects get processed in different areas of our visual cortex.

Humans learn to engage in social categorization which makes them classify individuals based on features that are similar to members of their own group and features which differentiate them from the members of other groups. Studies by Tajfel have shown that individuals tend to classify other individuals in terms of minimal criteria for categorization of individuals into groups (Tajfel et al., 1971). Tajfel and Turner's (1979) theory of social identity has been used extensively to understand intergroup behavior. The theory alludes to the concept of othering when it suggests that individuals try to hold on to their positive self-concept by attributing more positive attributes to their own group when compared to another group that their group competes with. From this, it follows that they engage more in negative differentiation. This results in seeing the members of the competing group in negative terms. Over time these feed the prejudices and stereotypes which the group members hold toward members of the other group. Such recurrent attribution of negative qualities to the other group holds the essence of the process of othering. Once stereotypes about groups are formed, they become veridical, socially as well as psychologically. However, the divide between 'us' and 'them' is created by the social identity of individuals. Tripathi (2016) points out how these result from the interplay of the processes of 'ascription' and 'inscription'. Othering has more to do with the processes of 'ascription' which involve not granting recognition, respect and dignity to members of a group which results in their feeling humiliated (Guru, 2009).

In the process of identity formation, younger members of the groups learn to view the members of the other group through the negative cognitive frames of the older and respected members of their group. Studies show that such prejudices peak in children between the ages of five and seven years (Raabe & Beelmann, 2011). The question that gets raised is how cognitive and affective frames that develop early in life remain stable and inflexible over the later years. They should have changed in the face of any positive experiences they might have had with the other out-group members, but they continued to retain their frames. As Benbassa and Attias (2004) point out, the other is another self that acts both as a 'mirror and a foil' to the self. The cognitive frames do not change because as children grow various cognitions that form the other get firmly glued by negative emotions of hate, resentment, fear and anxiety. The two frames, cognitive and affective, feed each other. This can be readily seen in the case of the two sets of groups that were of concern to Gandhi in his life, namely Hindus and Muslims, and the high-caste Hindus and the untouchable (Shudras) Hindus.

The pertinent question to ask here is how such emotions are evoked in the first place. It is our view that the major reason for this is the differentiation that groups make based on purity. Group members come to believe and act in a manner that they are, indeed, 'holier' than the members of the other group they are competing against socially and otherwise. This is particularly true when comparisons involve religious, social or political groups. Tripathi (2016) discusses how purity is used for othering by Hindus, Christians and Jews. The same holds in the case of other religious groups in India, such as Sikhs, Buddhists and Jains. Purity in different religions, however, does not carry the same connotations nor do members of different groups use the same grounds for othering or engage in it with the same degree of intensity. This can be seen in the case of Gandhi who avoided using purity for engaging in othering which has been the grounds for many religious conflicts around the world. For him, God was one. Although he grew up in the Hindu tradition, he was greatly influenced by the Jain religion which believes in the unity of life and spiritual and 'karmic' purity rather than ritualistic purity that one witnesses in Hinduism. He also, repeatedly, pointed out that there is a great deal of difference between what is professed in the religious books and what one sees being practiced by people belonging to these groups when they relate to members of religious groups other than their own.

Muslims as the Other

Gandhi struggled to save Hindus and Muslims from becoming each other's symbolic other throughout his life. But they did become each other's other during his lifetime. The behavior of the collectives always has multiple causes but if there is one factor, out of many, which has historically stood out to explain othering involving ethno-religious groups, as we have observed above, it is purity. The term connotes not only moral inclusion but also social and physical inclusion. In the case of othering, the mindset is characterized not by indifference but by negative emotions of hate, anger, fear and anxiety which support exclusionary behavior. One only has to recall the Crusades that took place during the medieval period, the annihilation of Jews in Nazi Germany, the war between Iran and Iraq, and whatever the world has witnessed in the name of 'ethnic cleansing'. This attitude is also witnessed in the treatment that is routinely meted out to the slaves, lower classes and 'untouchables' of the world.

Both Hindus and Muslims have their specific ways of defining what they consider clean or not clean, pure or not pure. Their relationships with groups come to be defined by what they consider impure. So, for Muslims, Hindus are '*kafirs*' (infidels) and deserve to be condemned, and for Hindus, Muslims are '*mlechhas*' (barbarians). Both see each other as 'dirty' and 'unclean'. A large number of studies on intergroup attitudes that have been carried out by psychologists on Hindus and Muslims in India bear this out (Ghosh & Kumar, 1991; Sen & Wagner, 2009; Singh, 1989).

Shudras as the Other

One category of people who have been othered on the grounds of purity in Hindu society is the 'Shudras', called 'untouchables' ('*achhoot*' in Hindi). Hindus believe that their mere touch leads to pollution. They rank the lowest in the Hindu caste and social-status hierarchy which is based on the relative purity of the occupation associated with a caste group. Thus, the Brahmins, whose main occupation is to teach and to serve as priests, are ranked the highest in terms of purity. Shudras are ranked the lowest because they are or were till recently involved in occupations that are considered essentially polluting, such as carrying and cleaning human excreta and many other similar acts. The tragedy is that in traditional India someone who is born into the Shudra caste is not able to beat this occupational trap.

Othering shows up in various forms and domains. Shah et al. (2006) studied the practice of untouchability in 565 villages in 11 states of India. They found that, even after six decades of India's independence, untouchability was present in 80% of the villages in some form or the other. The most common ways in which untouchability was practiced against people belonging to the Shudra caste were denying their entry into temples as well as into homes of people of other castes, not allowing them to fetch water from a common source and preventing them from inter-dining. They were even denied access to burial and cremation grounds of villages and forced to live at some distance away on the village periphery. Guru's (2009) book details the humiliation that is meted out to the Shudras in various contexts and the structures that support such humiliations. One can only imagine how much worse the situation must have been in Gandhi's time.

Gandhi's first confrontation with untouchability took place in his own home when he was scolded by his mother for touching a person named Uka, who used to clean the latrines of his house. There are other instances of similar confrontations that took place involving his wife which left his 'Vaishnav' moral mind questioning whether we all were, indeed, children of one God. It was under Gandhi's leadership that the Indian National Congress, in its session held in the year 1920, passed a resolution to 'rid Hinduism of the reproach of untouchability' (Kapur, 2010). What especially needs to be noted is that this call, along with the call for Hindu-Muslim unity, was made a part of Gandhi's first non-cooperation movement post-Jallianwala Bagh massacre. That it was not merely a part of Gandhi's rhetoric and that he meant it was reflected in his Vykom Satyagraha in Kerala where Shudras were not allowed to use the road surrounding the Shiva temple (King, 2015). It was Gandhi's 'satyagraha' that made the Maharaja of Travancore open the use of roads surrounding the temple to the Shudras. The othering of the Shudras and their un-othering remained one of Gandhi's enduring concerns throughout his life.

Un-othering and Its Nature

Othering, generally, has a historical basis. If two groups are locked in intractable conflicts over a long period, they develop cognitive structures which justify their categorization as the other. This was supported in a recent study by Bano et al. (2018) who found that the majority of Hindus preferred 'separation' as the preferred form of relationship with Muslims in comparison to 'accommodation', 'assimilation' and 'integration'. Like othering, un-othering also needs to be understood within a context. Tripathi (2016, 2021) sees un-othering as a process that involves the transformation of both personal as well as social selves of members of a group. The other becomes more agreeable with whom a warm relationship is possible with the process of un-othering. It allows for the creation of conditions that make it possible for the members of the two groups to share spaces that they had once closed off to the members of the other group.

Un-othering is somewhat different from a situation where two groups come together merely to maximize each other's gains as has been shown by some social psychologists who have studied the resolution of intergroup conflicts. It is also not achieved through ensuring equal rights for the minority or the othered groups by structural changes that bring about power equalization. Such conditions may be facilitative in bringing about what Galtung (1967) calls negative peace or absence of conflicts, but they do not ensure the development of positive interdependence among the members of the two groups that are ideal for ensuring a harmonious relationship and for bringing about positive peace. Un-othering should show up in the behavior of the members of the two groups developing and subscribing to new norms which are integrative, which draw from each other's culture and are based on mutual respect and recognition (DeRidder & Tripathi, 1992). It has been found that such changed terms of relationships allow the members of the two groups to become cultur-ally sensitive and develop mutuality (Tripathi et al., 2014). Most other methods of conflict resolution offered by psychologists focus more on the causes of the conflict and less on the relationship between the two groups (Böhm et al., 2020).

Gandhi approaches un-othering from a moral and spiritual perspective which draws from his religious upbringing and his philosophy of non-violence. It is an approach that is very different from the approaches that psychologists have propounded for the reduction of prejudice and estab-lishment of harmonious social relations which focus more on de-othering of the other with the purpose and hope of establishing a common in-group identity (Freter, 2017; Gaertner, 1993). Gandhi's approach of un-othering permits groups to retain their identities. Un-othering of the other focuses less on the restoration of individual rights but more on achieving commensality based on mutuality and relationships. This requires the otherer to engage in taking a reverse look at the self, rid it of the negative emotions that it carries about the other, engage in actions that allow it to view the other as a part of 'us' and not follow an 'us-they' divide. The two processes which are conjointly present in this approach that is driven by Gandhian values are self-othering along with un-othering of the other. The former results in self-purification, and the latter, in the purification of the other. The two processes act in a dialectical fashion to make it possible for the mind to develop new cognitive and affective frames that are then used for relating with the other. Other-purification dissolves the division between the self and the other and creates conditions for the enfoldment of the other with greater possibilities for positive peace.

The Gandhian Method of Un-othering

It is generally recognized that Gandhi did not distinguish between his political or social philosophy and the philosophy he used to live his own life. He believed in the essential unity of humankind which was greatly supported by his belief in Jainism and Vaishnavism, both of which believe in a unitary divinity that has many forms. His approach was simple and it drew considerably from his reading of the Bhagavad Gita which told him that purity of means is as important as the purity of goals. It requires that all '*karmas*' (deeds) should be in line with the man's '*dharma*' (his/her calling). This, however, is not possible until one learns to detach oneself from one's material and aspired goals. One must treat oneself not as an agent who is responsible for the outcome but as someone who is simply a 'hetu' (an instrument).

When such an attitude is generalized to others, it becomes possible to view events with a radically different perspective whereby the others are not attributed blame for one's or one's group's negative outcomes which enter the construction of the other. Tripathi (2016) points out that Gandhi developed a kind of dialogic politics wherein he tried to give a semiotic turn to words used to characterize the negative traits of the othered groups or coined new ones. An example of this is that he called the people belonging to the Shudra caste '*Harijan*' (Children of God) and started a newspaper called '*Harijan*' to popularize this new coinage. Gandhi's idea was to create a new social space for the Shudras among the high-caste Hindus with the specific purpose of making them reflect on their moral conscience when they discriminated against them. Rao and Paranjpe (2016) draw our attention to this Gandhian dialectic which seeks to dissolve the dichotomy between the moral and the practical aspects. They see human development as resulting from the reconciliation that takes place between the animal impulses and aspirations of the humans.

From the literal interpretation of bodily purity, Gandhi rallied for the symbolic purity of the soul. This was also reflected in the philosophy that underlay his approach to 'satyagraha' (truth-insistence). Many accounts of Gandhi mention that he resorted to indefinite fasting whenever there were moral transgressions by his own people against the British or whenever any kind of violence/riots took place. Gandhi's reaction to the burning of a police station in Chauri Chaura was an immediate suspension of the civil disobedience movement. This showed how a reflective glance on the self and those who were part of one's collective self was a necessary condition for the un-othering of the other. Gandhi further believed that when he insisted on 'truth' and resorted to fasting, his suffering, besides making him reflect on his own self, also made the wrong-doer reflect on his act. Negative emotions find expression in behavior, speech or thoughts about the other. Gandhi's 'satyagraha' displayed none of them as he took to silence (*'maun'*) and fasted. This did not result in making the other angry nor did it elicit a tit-for-tat reaction. As Gandhi's suffering increased, the moral conscience of the oppressor was awakened which led him to review his earlier action/s. In the process a new relationship was formed between the 'satyagrahi' and the erstwhile 'wrong-doer' based on love. In the process, the selves of both were transformed. The key to un-othering lies in using personal suffering for the spiritual growth of the other. Vahali and Vahali (2019) discuss several instances in support of this to show how suffering makes the self and other whole.

Self-Purification as a Way of Un-othering

The essential condition that seems critical for Gandhi's way of un-othering to succeed is the annihilation of the egos of the persons involved in othering (Rao & Paranjpe, 2016). This is possible when the positive qualities of the minds (*Sattvik*) of the parties involved in conflicts are foregrounded rather than their negative propensities (*Tamasik*) which are based on such negative emotions as false pride, anger and arrogance. Purification of the self should result in the transformation of the self. Two things are needed for that to happen. Firstly, one has to reduce one's needs and detach oneself from the material outcomes of one's efforts and, as per Bhagavad Gita's teachings, become an '*anasakt*' (detached) person. Secondly, one also needs to engage in the dissolution of one's agency beliefs around which one's ego is built. When done, these two changes prepare the ground which enables one to bring about changes in one's negative attachment to the other group.

Gandhi was able to see that individual and group-level behaviors were related. The actions of individuals also had inevitable implications at the level of the group, of which they were members. In Gandhi's case, for un-othering of the other group and also its members to happen, the purification of both the personal as well as the social selves had to take place. Also, this process of un-othering needed to move to the core of the group members' personal identities as well as their social identities. Contrary to what Leary (2007) suggests, Gandhi's self, when it was seeking its moral side, did not seek validation from anyone because it did not need it. Such validation came from within. It came from his inner voice. This is how psychologists believe it should be. Kakar (1982) suggests that the movement of the essentialized self toward the moral self does not happen outside the person but happens within the person. Thus, Gandhi's approach of un-othering was rooted in the moral grounding of humans.

For un-othering through self-purification, Gandhi relied on two methods. The first involved taking to silence (*Maun*) and the second was fasting. Gandhi saw silence as a method of spiritual disciplining but its greater use was that it allowed him to turn inwards and watch his own negative emotions which tinged his cognitions about the other group and prevented him from relating with them with love instead of anger. It was possible for him to do this because he was able to empathize with the other by seeking to understand how and why they may have acted in the manner in which they did. His inner awakening made him act in a more compassionate fashion.

The second method, namely fasting, has been seen as a weapon that is integral to Gandhi's 'satyagraha'. It appears to some that this weapon was directed by Gandhi at his adversaries. We take a different view. Fasting, when it is directed at the other to secure one's selfish ends, usually does not deliver the desired results. It cannot build bridges of peace. Fasting has to be a spiritual act of a person who already has a purified self but feels that she/he needs greater self-purification. This can occur only when she/he decides to undergo suffering and insists on the idea that only the truth should prevail, but in the process, no harm should befall the other person or members of a group. This is clear from the fact that the emotions associated with Gandhi's fast were not of hate, anger or other negative emotions. Rather, they were positive emotions. His fasts were undertaken to send the message that 'I have decided to suffer and even sacrifice my life because I care for you and want to build a stronger bond of love with you'.

Two of his fasts clearly illustrate this. The first fast that he undertook was in 1932 to oppose the Poona pact to ensure that Shudras did not lose out on their already flimsy relationship with the high caste Hindus, and the second fast was undertaken in January 1948 when riots had broken out post partition of India. It was clear to Gandhi that with the Poona pact, which sought to provide a separate electorate to the depressed groups or Shudras, the British wanted to drive a wedge between the '*savarnas*' (high-caste Hindus) and '*avarnas*' (people not within the caste hierarchy) of the Hindu society. They had done the very same thing in the case of Muslims in 1909 which many believe led to Hindu-Muslim separatism in India. The British had the support of Ambedkar in creating a separate electorate for the depressed groups. He differed from them only about the number of seats that were to be reserved for the depressed groups in the legislature. The British also saw this as an opportunity to drive a wedge between Gandhi and Ambedkar. When Gandhi's fast approached the sixth day and his health deteriorated, both the British and Ambedkar had to agree to Gandhi's proposal of a joint electorate. What followed was remarkable in the history of India. A large number of temples in the country threw open their gates to the Shudras. It was evident that Gandhi's fast had resulted in not only his self-purification but also other-purification as those Hindus who once opposed the entry of the Shudras into the temples now happily allowed them entry into their temples.

The second fast, also his last, which was undertaken by Gandhi in January 1948 for self-purification and for restoring peace between Hindus and Muslims, illustrates how Gandhi used fasting as a tool for both self-purification and other-purification. He attempted to turn negative emotions into positive emotions by trying to appeal to the moral conscience of all. He asked both groups to listen 'to the echoes in their hearts' and was confident that if they did, there would be a 'union of hearts' 'awakened by a sense of duty'. Gandhi's fast may not have achieved the kind of purification of the others as had happened in the case of his other fasts but his assassination seemingly did. Unlike what we have seen elsewhere in similar cases, no large-scale riots followed Gandhi's assassination. Even Muslims in Pakistan mourned his death. Whether it was because of the trauma that followed his assassination or because the transformation of the selves had taken place is anyone's guess. We would certainly like to believe the latter because no major Hindu-Muslim riots took place for several years after Gandhi's death.

Other-Purification as a Way of Un-othering

Purification of the self alone cannot bring about lasting peace which is the ultimate goal of un-othering. The other, too, must transform and change. Gandhi's fast as part of his 'satyagraha' was as much directed against the self as it was against the other, both internal and external others. Gandhi assumed that 'satyagraha' was an instrument that forced people to reflect on how they saw the other and felt about the other. It was this kind of reflection that made the other develop new coordinates for redefining their relationship with one's intractable other. Purification was achieved when the other not only agreed to adopt the perspective of the group of people she/he was against but also became more compassionate, trusting and helpful.

The fast undertaken by Gandhi against the Poona pact, as pointed out above, did purify the internal others, i.e., those Hindus who were opposed to the Gandhian way of inclusion of *Harijans* or the Shudras, who decided to disregard what *Manu Smriti* says in support of the '*varna*' system. But whether it had the same kind of effect on the actual oppressors, in this case the British, is a question that cannot be easily answered. What, though, is obvious is that the British did not carry the same kind of hate or anger against him as they did against their other political opponents. Gandhi's method of other-purification involved attacking the practices that reinforced day-to-day othering. One such practice was to not allow Harijans to inter-dine with high-caste people nor accept food cooked by them. Not only did Gandhi's Sevagram kitchen have Harijans as cooks, but all those living in the ashram were expected to inter-dine. They, along with Gandhi, even engaged in cleaning of latrines which, outside Sevagram, was the task of the Harijans. This method of un-othering of Harijans by Gandhi has taken root in the culture of Gujarat. More recently, it was taken forward by the Swadhyaya movement in Gujarat led by a Brahmin, Swami Athawale. Shourie (1996) provides the details of how inter-dining and offering prayers to God in a place where there were only trees but no idols resulted in the inclusion of the people belonging to the untouchable caste.

Gandhi's last fast may have achieved un-othering to a slightly greater extent. His assassination that followed his fast resulted in a tremendous outpouring of grief by Hindus and Muslims within and outside India. Gandhi's method of suffering invoked not only self-purification but also other-purification. Had the purification of the other not happened, the communal harmony that followed Gandhi's assassination would not have been possible in such troubled times. It is the perceived suffering of the 'satyagrahi' that appears common to self-purification and other-purification. It provides the cement that the relationship between the two groups, both of which are essentially human, need. The following words of Gandhi as cited in Metta Center (2006) bear this out-

> ... suffering is infinitely more powerful than the law of the jungle for converting the opponent and opening his ears, which are otherwise shut, to the voice of reason.... The appeal to reason is more to the head but the penetration of the heart comes from suffering. (*Young India*, November 5, 1931)

In Sum

Psychologists have long attempted to understand how and why humans develop relationships that are disharmonious and full of conflicts. Some theories show that groups engage in differentiation and their identities make them defend their groups, which often results in conflicts because that is the only way they can protect their positive distinctiveness and remain socially dominant (Sidanius & Pratto, 1999; Tajfel & Turner, 1979). Gandhi believed that there was more to being a human than merely being a rational creature. He, therefore, looked at the moral side of humans because he believed that all humans carry within them an element of divinity that seeks to connect with the supreme consciousness. The human mind is primed to be altruistic. It seeks relationships and abhors conflicts. For resolving a conflict all one has to do is to

create conditions that make people look beyond their narrow selves and connect with the big Self.

Acknowledgements   The authors would like to thank Shruti Narain for her help in copy-editing this chapter.

References

Bano, S., Mishra, R. C., & Tripathi, R. C. (2018). Mutual perception and relational strategies of Hindus and Muslims in India. In M. Karasawa, M. Yuki, K. Ishii, Y. Uchida, K. Sato, & W. Friedlmeier (Eds.), *Venture into cross-cultural psychology: Proceedings from the 23rd Congress of the International Association for Cross-Cultural Psychology.* https://scholarworks.gvsu.edu/iaccp_papers/155/

Benbassa, E., & Attias, J. C. (2004). *The Jew and the other.* Cornell University Press.

Bloom, P. (2016). *Against empathy: The case of rational compassion.* Ecco Press.

Böhm, R., Rusch, H., & Baron, J. (2020). The Psychology of intergroup conflict: A review of theories and measures. *Journal of Economic Behavior & Organization, 178*, 947–962.

Branan, N. (2010, January 1). Are our brains wired for categorization? *Scientific American Mind.* Retrieved May 10, 2018, from https://www.scientificamerican.com/article/wired-for-categorization/

DeRidder, R., & Tripathi, R. C. (1992). *Norm violation and intergroup relations.* Clarendon Press.

Gaertner, S. L., Dovidio, J. F., Anastasio, P. A., Bachman, B. A., & Rust, M. C. (1993). The common ingroup identity model: Recategorization and the reduction of ingroup bias. In W. Stroebe & M. Hewstone (Eds.), *European review of social psychology* (Vol. 4, pp. 1–26). Wiley.

Galtung, J. (1967). *Theory and methods of social science research.* Columbia University Press.

Gearhart, S. (1982). The future—If there is one is female. In P. McAllister (Ed.), *Reweaving the web of life: Feminism and non-violence* (pp. 266–285). New Society Publishers.

Ghosh, E. S., & Kumar, R. (1991). Hindu-Muslim intergroup relations in India: Applying socio-psychological perspectives. *Psychology and Developing Societies, 3*(1), 93–112.

Guru, G. (Ed.). (2009). *Humiliation: Claims and contexts.* Oxford University Press.

Freter, F. (2017). *De-othering the other.* Retrieved January 21, 2020, from https://www.researchgate.net/publication/323187183_De-Othering_the_Other

Kakar, S. (1982). *Shamans, mystics and doctors.* Oxford University Press.

Kapur, S. (2010). *Gandhi, Ambedkar and eradication of untouchability.* Retrieved May 56, 2021, from https://www.mkgandhi.org/articles/Gandhi-Ambedkar-and-eradication-of-Untouchability.html

King, M. E. (2015). *Gandhian nonviolent struggle and untouchability in South India: The 1924–25 Vykom Satyagraha and mechanisms of change.* Oxford University Press.

Leary, M. (2007). Motivational and emotional aspects of the self. *Annual Review of Psychology, 58,* 317–344.

Metta Center. (2006). *Law of suffering.* Retrieved April 10, 2021, from https://mettacenter.org/definitions/gloss-concepts/law-of-suffering/

Obama, B. (2020). *A promised land.* Crown.

Pettigrew, T. (1991). Normative theory of intergroup relations. *Psychology and Developing Societies, 3*(1), 3–16.

Raabe, T., & Beelmann, A. (2011). Development of ethnic, racial, and national prejudice in childhood and adolescence: A multinational meta-analysis of age differences. *Child Development, 82,* 1715–1737. https://doi.org/10.1111/j.1467-8624.2011.01668.x

Rao, R. K., & Paranjpe, A. C. (2016). *Psychology in the Indian tradition.* Springer India

Sidanius, J., & Pratto, F. (1999). *Social dominance: An intergroup theory of social hierarchy and oppression.* Cambridge University Press.

Singh, A. K. (1989). Intergroup relations and social tensions. In J. Pandey (Ed.), *Psychology in India: The state-of-the-art, Vol. 2: Basic and applied social psychology* (pp. 159–223). Sage.

Sen, R., & Wagner, W. (2009). Central mechanics of fundamentalism: Religion as ideology, divided identities and violence in post-Gandhi India. *Culture and Psychology, 15*(3), 299–326.

Shah, G., Mander, H., Thorat, S. K., Deshpande, S., & Baviskar, A. (2006). *Untouchability in rural India.* Sage.

Shourie, A. (1996, January 14). Rituals, idols, have great significance. *Pioneer*, 8.

Srinivas, M. N. (1952). *Religion and society among the Coorgs of South India.* Oxford University Press.

Tajfel, H., Billig, M., Bundy, R. P., & Flament, C. (1971). Social categorization and intergroup behaviour. *European Journal of Social Psychology, 1*(2), 149–178.

Tajfel, H., & Turner, J. C. (1979). An integrative theory of intergroup conflict. In W. G. Austin & S. Worchel (Eds.), *The social psychology of intergroup relations* (pp. 33–47). Brooks-Cole.

Tripathi, R. C. (2016). Violence and the other: Contestations in multicultural societies. In R. C. Tripathi & P. Singh (Eds.), *Perspectives on violence and othering in India* (pp. 1–28). Springer.

Tripathi, R. C. (2021). Un-othering of the other: The role of shared cultural spaces. In P. Graf & D. J. A. Dozois (Eds.), *Handbook on the state of the art in applied psychology* (pp. 361–389). Wiley-Blackwell.

Tripathi, R. C., Ghosh, E. S. K., & Kumar, R. (2014). The Hindu-Muslim divide: Building sustainable bridges. In R. C. Tripathi & Y. Sinha (Eds.), *Psychology, development and social policy* (pp. 257–284). Springer.

Vahali, H. O., & Vahali, D. O. (2019). The (im)possible embrace: A search for non-violent possibilities in the aftermath of violent uprootedness. *Psychology and Developing Societies, 31*, 139–161.

7

Gandhi's Theory of Trusteeship and Its Influence on Employee Ownership in the Twenty-First Century

Graeme Nuttall

Introduction

Gandhi predicted that his theory of trusteeship would stand the test of time. Although no widespread way of realising his trusteeship aims has been identified, two important developments show the theory's continuing relevance. The growth of employee ownership (EO) allows workers to realise their trusteeship responsibilities. And, numerous initiatives to encourage wider corporate purpose can be seen as trying to achieve trusteeship responsibilities to society. Gandhi's theory of trusteeship encourages employee-owned companies to be bolder and to integrate all of Gandhi's trusteeship responsibilities into how such businesses operate. Doing so offers a way to realise trusteeship on a widespread basis.

G. Nuttall (✉)
Institute for the Study of Employee Ownership and Profit Sharing, The Rutgers School of Management and Labor Relations,
Piscataway, NJ, USA
e-mail: graeme.nuttall@fieldfisher.com

© The Author(s), under exclusive license to Springer Nature Switzerland AG 2022
V. K. Kool and R. Agrawal (eds.), *Gandhi's Wisdom*,
https://doi.org/10.1007/978-3-030-87491-9_7

Part 1—The Lack of Progress Towards a Trusteeship Model for All Businesses

Gandhi's trusteeship theory developed from his experiments with truth. Truth was the sovereign principle for him. He was heavily influenced by a Hindu scripture, the Gita. "Words like aparigraha (non-possession) and samabhava (equability) gripped me" (Gandhi, 1927, p. 244). His training as a barrister also influenced him. When trying to make a particular decision he observed that "Snell's discussion of the maxims of Equity came to my memory. I understood more clearly in the light of the Gita teaching the implication of the word 'trustee'" (Gandhi, 1927, p. 244). From this, he understood that,

> the Gita teaching of non-possession to mean that those who desired salvation should act like the trustee who, though having control over great possessions, regards not an iota of them as his own. (Gandhi, 1927, p. 244)

Although everyone can act like a trustee, the theory resonates strongly with business owners because of their multifaceted relationships, through their business, with employees, suppliers, customers and the community. Indeed, it is hard to conceive of trusteeship working at scale unless it can be made to work in relation to businesses and business owners.

Gandhi wished to see these changes in how businesses were owned and operated because he believed capitalism had "profoundly dehumanised both workers and capitalists and lowered the level of human existence" (Parekh, 1989, p. 135). His theory of trusteeship was "intended to avoid the evils and combine the advantages of capitalism and communism" (Parekh, 1989, p. 138).

It is accepted that Gandhi's theory of trusteeship and, in particular, ideas about its practical application were never fully formed (Goyder, 1979c; Joseph et al., 2016). So trusteeship is very much a theory. As Parekh (1989) explains, Gandhi's:

theory of trusteeship is an economic extension of his philosophical concept of man as a trustee of all he had... as [Gandhi] imagined it, every industrialist ... was to look upon his industry not as his property but as a social trust. (p. 138)

Although it was primarily for entrepreneurs to uphold trusteeship, workers too had responsibilities. Gandhi said to workers,

Each of you should consider himself to be a trustee for the welfare of the rest of his fellow labourers

and that

you should treat the business of your employers as if it were your own business and give to it your honest and undivided attention. (Gandhi, 1959a, Vol. 3, pp. 101–2)

Goyder (1979a, p. 10), summed up the theory of trusteeship in a way that holds its own at any contemporary conference on corporate purpose.

The principle of trusteeship expresses the inherent responsibility of business enterprise to its consumers, workers, shareholders, suppliers, and the community and the mutual responsibilities of these to one other.

Gandhi's later iterations of his trusteeship theory are radical. One is set out in a document prepared in draft by Professor Dantwala and others, to which Gandhi made amendments (Joseph, 2016). It envisages a possibly state-regulated trusteeship, with limited private ownership of property and limits on how much the higher paid earn, under which "an individual will not be free to hold or use his wealth for selfish satisfaction or in disregard of the interests of society" (*Harijan*, 25 October 1952 cited in Gandhi, 1960, p. 27).

There have been periodic attempts to give practical expression to Gandhi's theory of trusteeship, mostly involving scaling back from its radical form, to focus on businesses and how they might adopt trusteeship. These attempts all resonate with debates around corporations needing a broader purpose beyond profit-making.

A 1965 conference in Delhi resulted in a declaration that,

> There should be increasing association of workers with the management. One way of doing this is by the sharing of profits and its reinvestment in the company through purchase of the company's shares to be held in trust or by other means which serve to identify the worker with his work and give him an interest in the company ... (Mukharji, 1969 as cited in Goyder, 1979c, p. 39)

Again it was emphasised that workers have obligations:

> Likewise, workers should recognise their obligation to do a good day's work for a good day's wage, to co-operate in increasing productivity, to come forward with suggestions and to participate responsibly in the life of the plant community. (Mukharji, 1969 as cited in Goyder, 1979c, pp. 39-40)

Draft trusteeship laws were promoted in India periodically from 1967 but never enacted (Ranjan, 2016, p. 161). A 1979 conference to review trusteeship concluded that little of significance had happened since the 1965 declaration (Goyder, 1979a). Interestingly the English law concept of an employee trust received little attention. Speakers explained the UK's "common ownership" movement. The John Lewis Partnership (JLP) was mentioned but the potential for its trust ownership structure to provide a way to make Gandhi's trusteeship work in practise seemed to have been missed. There was, instead, a general acceptance that no model of a responsible enterprise can serve for all. JLP and the charity-owned Scott Bader Group were each called a "pioneer experiment" (Goyder, 1979b). There were disparate approaches to EO in the UK at this pioneering time. It is understandable how no particular model emerged as a way of putting Gandhi's theory of trusteeship into practise.

In India, too, there are companies that have been and are still influenced by Gandhi's ideas (Jones & Sheth, 2019). However, these companies' activities have not produced a standard model for implementing

Gandhi's theory of trusteeship. It is challenging to try to encompass all aspects of Gandhi's theory of trusteeship in a business model but a step-by-step approach shows that much can be achieved. As a first step the EO business model can be assessed in relation to workers' trusteeship responsibilities.

Part 2—Workers' Trusteeship Responsibilities Achieved Through EO

Gandhi's theory of trusteeship places a fundamental responsibility on workers: to treat the business that employs them as their own. When employees own shares, directly or indirectly, in their employer's business, then, clearly the business is their own, to some extent, but does employee share ownership mean employees will treat the business as their own? The evidence strongly suggests that they do, when the company is employee-owned.

The EO business model is a tried and tested successful business model. The accounts of the UK's 50 largest employee-owned companies in May 2020 showed combined sales of £20.1 billion. Sales were up 4.3 per cent on a like-for-like basis compared to their previous year's results. They had 178,000 employees and operating profits up five per cent (Employee Ownership Association [EOA], 2020b). Admittedly these statistics include a very large business, JLP. But what is significant is how EO has grown in smaller to medium sized enterprises. EO Day 2020 celebrated the best year, yet, as far as growing the UK EO sector is concerned. There were over 100 new employee-owned companies in the 12 months to June 2020. Companies of all sizes, in numerous sectors and across the UK are now employee-owned (Employee Ownership Association, 2020c). EO clearly works. It has moved beyond the era of pioneering experiments.

What has made this difference in the UK is the employee owner-ship trust (EOT). The UK EO sector has grown by over 300 per cent since 2014, when the UK introduced the EOT (Robinson & Pendleton, 2019) and EOA (2020b). Well over 90 per cent of that growth is from companies adopting the EOT ownership model (EOA, 2020a). This is largely because selling to the trustee of an EOT is an acceptable business succession solution for many private company owners (Nuttall, 2014a). In particular, a sale to the trustee of an EOT avoids selling to a competitor and can preserve a company's ethos. The money to buy the company comes from company profits. Once the founders have been paid, profits that would previously have been paid out as dividends can be paid out as all-employee bonuses. The EOT's trustee can hold shares permanently on behalf of all the company's employees. The trustee of the EOT can protect the employees' long-term interests. A key feature is that the trustee does not have exclusive possession of the shares it holds; they are held on behalf of all employees, for the time being, as a class of beneficiaries.

It is worth emphasising the flexibility and ease of use of the EOT ownership model. Most companies converting to this model have between 10 and 49 employees but much larger and smaller companies have also adopted this model successfully (EOA, 2020a, p. 9). There are no complexities from buying and selling individual employee shareholdings with an EOT. The collective holding of shares by a trustee company works whatever the size and type of the employed workforce.

A properly established trustee company has few running costs, as evidenced by the "non-trading" or "dormant" company status of such companies at UK Companies House.

The main reason why the structure is elegant is that it is dependent for success on a readily available resource, a company's employees. A good practise is to have a paritarian board: one comprising representatives of senior management and the same number representing other employees. In this way there is parity between the interests of the two main stakeholder groups. Each group can appoint and remove "its" trustee directors and there is usually an independent chair (Nuttall, 2012, p. 61). Day-to-day management remains with the trading company's board of directors, who may include directors specifically selected or elected to represent employees. There is also likely to be an employees' council that interacts regularly with the trading company board (Pendleton & Robinson, 2015). In this way the trustee board is free to act as custodian or guardian of the company's EO ethos, in accordance with its fiduciary duties under the EOT's trust deed (its constitution). Overall, there are checks and balances to try to prevent mismanagement and to promote the success of the business for the benefit of its employees.

The EO business model and, in particular, the EOT provides a way for workers to meet their trusteeship responsibilities by encouraging and enabling them to "participate responsibly in the life of the plant community". This outcome is entirely consistent with a change in emphasis as to what EO means.

An early UK analysis of the legal and tax aspects of EO concentrated on who owned the shares in an employee-owned company (Nelson-Jones & Nuttall, 1987) (call this "EO Version 1"). Three main forms of EO were identified:

- Individual employees owning shares personally in their company;
- A trustee owning shares in an employee trust on behalf of all employees, as a class of beneficiaries of that trust; and
- A hybrid model that mixed the two.

This definition worked well when describing the legal mechanics and tax consequences of changing from one set of shareholders to another. This definition fitted in with the times. By 1984 the UK had a useful array of tax-advantaged share and share option plans, which allowed executives and other employees to acquire shares personally in their company (HM Revenue & Customs, 2020). Lobbying to promote EO was part and parcel of promoting all types of employee share ownership including executive share plans. Although tax changes were made in response to such lobbying none of these acted as the trigger to large-scale growth of EO.

In 2012 the UK Coalition Government decided to review why EO had not taken off in the private sector (U.K. Department for Business, Innovation and Skills, 2012). The initial announcement was not clearly understood by the Press. There was an assumption by some that the Government was simply going to re-examine employee share plans. The review, therefore, needed to include a clear definition of EO.

The Nuttall Review of Employee Ownership (Nuttall, 2012) defined EO in a significantly different way to EO Version 1 (call this "EO Version 2"). This new definition started with EO Version 1 by including trustee ownership as well as individual EO and hybrid models. But, importantly, the definition went beyond looking at who owned shares to requiring that the employees' shareholding underpinned genuine employee engagement. It also made it clear that share ownership by a few employees was not enough: it had to be all employees. And, it was not enough that all employees owned an insignificant percentage of a company's shares. The shareholding had to be significant so that it could underpin meaningful employee engagement (Nuttall, 2012, pp. 74–75).

This definition helped move EO from an add-on to the standard business model to a business model in its own right. This emphasis also helped move EO from being promoted by reference to the tax system to something that had strong commercial merits: it was good for business success and happier staff.

As a result of the Nuttall Review the EOT was introduced in the Finance Act 2014. The review had emphasised the benefits of the trust model of EO and argued that tax advantages should not be limited to individual EO. After discussion with HM Treasury, two key tax advantages were introduced: a capital gains tax exemption for individuals selling a controlling shareholding to the trustee of an EOT and an income tax exemption on certain cash bonuses to all the employees of an EOT controlled company, up to £3600 per employee per tax year (Nuttall, 2014b).

Sellers to an EOT usually have to wait for several years to be paid in full (Nuttall & Morris, 2018). The capital gains tax exemption is a vital part of making a sale to an EOT work in practise, as well as acting as a nudge to professional advisers to talk about EO. The income tax exemption means there is a tangible benefit to employees from this ownership model.

Although an increase in the use of the trust model was expected, it was thought that other EO models based on employees holding shares directly would also continue to be popular but the EOT has turned into the dominant type of UK EO.

In 2012 EO Version 2 changed the emphasis towards the main trigger of EO's success and to what is fundamental to achieving workers' Gandhian trusteeship responsibilities: genuine employee engagement.

Part 3—The Challenge of Making the Twenty-First Century Corporation Responsible to Society

Much has changed and changed quickly in the business world in recent years. Businesses are increasingly expected to have a role in addressing inequality, sustainability and climate change. There is greater clarity around what Gandhi's theory of trusteeship calls "the interests of society" and widespread support for addressing these interests, rather than disregarding them. Nationally and internationally there are initiatives to tackle societal and environmental problems, encompassing corporate social responsibility (CSR), environmental, social and governance (or ESG) criteria, purpose beyond profit and the like. The British Academy (2019, p. 15) provides a timeline of key developments in support of purposeful business from November 2018 to September 2019. There have been well-publicised moves by major organisations that demonstrate a major shift away from shareholder primacy, the idea that a successful company is one that maximises its profits for its shareholders.

Examining some of these initiatives helps identify what it means for a company to have a positive impact on society and the environment. It also highlights how corporations generally, notwithstanding an increased interest in ESG, have struggled to find a universal way to incorporate these elements of Gandhi's theory of trusteeship into corporate governance.

There are global initiatives such as The 2030 Agenda for Sustainable Development, adopted by all U.N. Member States, which has at its heart 17 Sustainable Development Goals, including no poverty, zero hunger, good health and well-being (U.N. General Assembly, 2015).

As another example, the U.N. supported Principles for Responsible Investment (PRI) initiative helps integrate ESG considerations into investment decision-making (PRI, 2017). In relation to environmental issues, PRI highlights climate change as well as water risk, sustainable land use, fracking, methane as a climate pollutant and plastic risks. Social issues highlighted are human rights, labour standards, employee relations and conflict zones. Governance issues highlighted are tax avoidance, executive pay, corruption, director nomination processes and cyber security risks (PRI, 2019).

There are country-specific responses. In 2014, a change to Indian company law made it mandatory for large private and public sector firms to spend at least two per cent of their net profits on CSR projects as set out in the law. This change was entirely in keeping with Gandhi's trusteeship principles. The list of possible projects in Schedule VII to the Companies Act 2013 includes, as examples, gender equality, empowering women, homes and hostels for women and orphans; old age homes and other facilities for senior citizens. By 2019, social impact spending had grown by 100 per cent in the relevant companies (KPMG, 2020). The majority of spending was on education, health and sanitation projects and was through third party agencies, rather than a company's own foundation or direct spending. In the UK certain larger companies, now, have to include a statement, known as a Section 172(1) statement, within their annual report and accounts, explaining how directors "have regard" to what are called "enlightened shareholder value" considerations (as set out in Section 172[1] of the Companies Act 2006). These statements set out company-specific actions. It is, too, early to tell the impact of this additional accountability (U.K. Department for Business, Energy & Industrial Strategy, 2019). Additional regulation may be needed to ensure reporting is done with integrity and meaning (Brydon, 2019).

Certain key issues that need to be analysed when trying to define what is needed are as follows:

- To what extent should wider corporate purpose be integral to how a business operates;
- If it is integral how should it rank compared to serving shareholders' interests;
- What mechanisms are needed for a business to work out exactly what it can do to achieve substantive positive change; and
- To what extent should achieving a wider corporate purpose be compulsory?

Making wider corporate purpose integral to how a business operates means going beyond worthwhile activities, such as ad hoc charitable donations, that are incidental to doing business. This means viewing CSR as much more than a marketing tool to increase profits. It also means more than simple compliance with the letter of relevant ESG laws. Commitment is needed to help avoid, mitigate and indeed solve societal and environmental problems.

Upholding shareholder value is what UK company law currently prescribes as the default duty on directors. This duty is caveated as mentioned above by a requirement that directors must "have regard to" various matters including the impact of the company's operations on the community and the environment. Directors of an ordinary trading company should, under UK company law, already take into account corporate interests other than maximising profits.

As to how these wider interests rank alongside, for example, making a profit and providing good work, the established position is that there needs to be flexibility. The long process culminating in the Companies Act 2006 considered changing a director's duty so it is not just a duty to shareholders but also to employees, the wider community, and the environment. A pluralist approach would have forced directors to consider the interests of each set of stakeholders. The directors would have had to weigh these interests against each other when making decisions and shareholder interests could lose out. This change was rejected because according to the House of Commons Trade and Industry Committee (2003) it would confuse decision-making and ran the risk of creating a litigious climate.

The practicalities of identifying how a business may serve these wider interests, also, highlights the need for flexibility. As seen from the above initiatives, in practice, a business has to move swiftly from concerns at a State level, to look at industry-specific concerns and business-specific concerns to answer this question. What are priorities for one company will not be the same for another. Some companies will find it harder to make a positive impact locally or globally than others. A flexible solution is needed at a corporate level.

As to compulsion, there are calls for UK companies of all types to be required to state their purpose (The British Academy, 2019). The directors' duty would then be to promote that purpose. There are renewed calls for directors' duties to have a pluralist approach such that social, environment and employee interests are on an equal footing with shareholder profit (Short, 2019). There is some momentum around these initiatives. Current law does not readily permit directors to further wider corporate interests, at the expense of shareholders, and it may not provide protection to the directors of companies that promote purposes beyond shareholder value, unless this is expressly permitted under a company's articles of association (GC100, 2018; Sales, 2019; UNEP Finance Initiative, 2005).

A UK Government report on corporate responsibility noted that "There was a near equal split between those who favoured more legislation in this field and those against it" (U.K. Department for Business, Innovation & Skills, 2014).

Transforming the governance of all corporations to include wider corporate purpose is demonstrably an ongoing debate. A more focussed approach building on the EO business model, therefore, stands out for consideration, to try to progress this policy issue.

Part 4—EO with Added Gandhian Purpose

Part 2 above shows how workers' trusteeship responsibilities are integral to EO Version 2. Under the Nuttall Review definition of EO, employees must have a genuine voice both individually and as a group in how the business is run, and, a share in its profits. Making workers owners immediately reduces the complexities of trusteeship by making owners and workers one and the same. This provides a solid starting point for trying to extend the responsibilities of the EO business model to encompass other trusteeship responsibilities. What Gandhi's theory of trusteeship encourages is to get to the position that a company is not employee-owned unless it also serves society and the environment, locally and globally, as well as its shareholders, its employees (call this EO with added Gandhian purpose or "EO Version 3").

This is unfinished business from the Nuttall Review. The Nuttall Review did consider requiring employee-owned companies to have a clear corporate mission and also to have a limit on pay differentials. Many employee-owned companies have powerful mission statements and a few have express constitutional limitations to prevent senior management being paid more than a reasonable multiple of average pay. For example, the February 2020 edition of The JLP Constitution provides that "The pay of the highest paid Partner will be no more than 75 times the average basic pay of non-management Partners, calculated on an hourly basis" (p. 20). It seems uncanny that in Gandhi's draft trusteeship formula there are references to "the character of production will be determined by social necessity and not by personal whim or greed" and also to fixing "the maximum income that would be allowed to any person in society" (*Harijan*, 25 October 1952, cited in Gandhi, 1960, p. 27). But, it is not so surprising when one of the UK examples of pioneering EO is, as already mentioned, the Scott Bader Group. This was established by Ernst Bader as an express attempt to realise Gandhi's trusteeship principles (Bader, 1997).

It is not radical in the EO sector, to suggest that an EO business supports wider corporate purpose, in that there are already employee-owned companies which are Certified B Corporations (see, for examples, Riverford Organic Farmers 2020; Paradigm Norton, 2019). This means they have had their standards of social and environmental performance, public transparency and legal accountability verified through the B Corp Certification process (B Lab [UK], 2020). They have articles of association that expressly require a company to make a positive contribution to society and the environment as well as serve shareholders. The success of the Certified B Corporation community is encouraging in formulating the proposal that EO should also involve making an overall positive contribution to society and the environment.

There are many other examples of how wider corporate purpose co-exists with EO. Public service mutuals are employee-led organisations that deliver public services (GOV.UK, 2017). These are often structured as community interest companies (Social Enterprise UK, 2018). Also, worker co-operatives have the internationally recognised objective of "creating and maintaining sustainable jobs and generating wealth, in order to improve the quality of life of the worker-members, dignify human work, allow workers' democratic self-management and promote community and local development" (CICOPA, 2005).

The Ownership Dividend report found that a majority of employee-owned companies made explicit commitments to contribute directly to their local communities, albeit with an emphasis on sustaining local jobs (Ownership Effect Inquiry, 2018). Deb Oxley, Chief Executive of the EOA further explains that "Evidence in the report the Ownership Dividend showed that employee owned businesses tend to have an approach that supports them to do well while doing good" (Nuttall, 2020).

Gandhi encouraged boldness when proposing an all-encompassing idea. Moreover, he wanted practical solutions. The EO sector can provide this.

It is unrealistic to expect every employee-owned company to become a Certified B Corporation or to adopt the detailed ownership and governance structure of the Scott Bader Group. A mission statement or equivalent document could contain these commitments to make an overall positive contribution to society and the environment, suitably adapted to the circumstances of a business. This wider corporate aim could be succinct. For example, the Useful Simple Trust is a group of companies with expertise in engineering, design, architecture and communication. Their objective is to "improve the human environment by delivering useful, simple outcomes that are beautiful and good" (Useful Simple Trust, n.d.).

The EOT offers important additional protection of these broader corporate aims. The trustee's board of directors has fiduciary duties and cannot act in its own interest. The trusteeship concept can be encapsulated in a suitable purpose clause in an EOT trust deed. This would align the aims of the EOT with that of its underlying trading company. Many EOT deeds contain as standard a "main purpose" clause that requires the company the trustee controls to have an EO ethos. That clause could also require the company it controls to take into account making an overall positive contribution to society and the environment. This helps overcome company law concerns about whether serving the interests of shareholders is compatible with wider corporate purpose.

This new definition of EO is a good fit for the EO sector because:

- Employee-owned companies are generally good corporate citizens. They already take care of their workforce and are structured so as to deliver great customer service (Lampel et al., 2018). Many are also already taking care of society and the environment;
- Employee-owned companies have good systems of governance and accountability to ensure companies will fulfil these wider purposes: systems that can be readily adapted to encompass a broader corporate purpose;
- In particular, EO offers the stability of ownership required to fulfil these purposes; and
- It mobilises a large group, employee owners, to identify the wide-ranging ideas needed to tackle societal and environmental issues.

This new definition may seem only a technical change. But, it could be part of a bigger need and that is for EO to be recognised as more than a business model. What might eventually happen is that EO is recognised as an "-ism", a distinctive belief system synonymous with good corporate citizenship. Employee owners could then say "I believe in employee ownership". And, it is M. K. Gandhi who encourages such an ambition.

Gandhi said of his theory of trusteeship that it "… is no make-shift, certainly no camouflage. I am confident that it will survive all other theories. It has the sanction of philosophy and religion behind it …" (*Harijan*, 16 December 1939 cited in Gandhi, 1960, p. 4). Gandhi encourages greater ambitions for EO.

Many accept the need for positive changes in society and our relationship with the environment. What better dynamic to make these essential changes than to channel the energies of employee owners towards finding and implementing solutions. The EO sector can become an exemplar for good corporate citizenship by embracing wider corporate purposes as part of what it means to be employee-owned.

Conclusions

Gandhi's theory of trusteeship encourages every employee-owned company to make an overall positive contribution to society and the environment, as part of promoting the success of the company, and to make this commitment in the strongest terms appropriate to its business. This would be a step on the way to a new definition of EO, one that is synonymous with good corporate citizenship. This would send a strong message to other businesses that they also need to adopt wider corporate purpose.

The proposal in this chapter has achieved widespread support from the EO community. Leading EO organisations have declared their support for EO Version 3 (Nuttall, 2020). The EOA, Employee Ownership Wales, Scotland for Employee Ownership, Irish ProShare Association and Employee Ownership Australia jointly announced in 2020 that they encourage every employee-owned company to make an overall positive contribution to society and the environment, as part of promoting the success of the business and to make this commitment in the strongest possible terms. Co-Operative Development Scotland announced it sees EO as key to a stronger, more resilient, productive and fair economy. In June 2021, the Japan Employee Ownership Association and the Southern Africa Employee Ownership Association joined in supporting this initiative (Nuttall, 2021). Graeme Nuttall first proposed this initiative in his Gandhi Foundation (UK) annual lecture in 2020 and was heartily supported by the Gandhi Foundation (Nuttall, 2020).

It is Gandhi's thought and life and, in particular, his theory of trusteeship that encourages this change to how EO is defined, so that employee-owned companies better meet the needs of society and the environment.

Another broader conclusion can be reached. If the 1979 Conference on Trusteeship was reconvened today, the EOT with added Gandhian purpose might be recognised as a model of responsible business that can serve for all. The EOT-owned company can be seen as the long sought way of realising Gandhi's theory of trusteeship on a widespread basis, and achieving this peacefully.

Boulding (1990) identifies three major categories of power: threat power, economic power and integrative power ("the stick, the carrot and the hug") (p. 10). The latter power relates to creating relationships such as love, respect, friendship and legitimacy. His thesis is that integrative power is the most significant power, in that "without legitimacy, both threat and riches are 'naked'" (p. 10). Employee ownership, and particularly EOT ownership, can be seen as creating that integrated legitimacy in businesses, bringing together all who work in the business in a way that impacts positively on society as a whole.

Gandhi was critical of capitalism, as he was of communism. He is not the obvious starting point for providing a better way to run an ordinary trading company. But, the momentum provided by owners looking for an acceptable business succession solution provides a non-confrontational way to move from exclusive possession by the few to trust ownership on behalf of the many, in a way that also benefits society. We can re-cast the first point in Gandhi's trusteeship formula, substituting "EO" for "trusteeship", such that:

> [EO] provides a means of transforming the present capitalist order of society into an egalitarian one. It gives no quarter to capitalism, but gives the present owning class a chance of reforming itself.

This realises Gandhi's vision that:

> The rich should take the initiative in dispossession with a view to a universal diffusion of the spirit of contentment. If only they keep their own property within moderate limits, the starving will be easily fed, and will learn the lesson of contentment along with the rich. (Gandhi, 1959b, p. 131)

References

B Lab (UK). (2020). *The B impact assessment and B Corp certification*. Retrieved March 17, 2021, from https://bcorporation.uk/certification

Bader, G. (1997). Trusteeship: The transforming ethic. In A. Copley & G. Paxton (Eds.), *Gandhi and the contemporary world* (pp. 159–171). Indo-British Historical Society.

Boulding, K. (1990). *Three faces of power*. Sage.

Brydon, D. (2019). *Assess, assure and inform: Improving audit quality and effectiveness*. Independent Review into the Quality and Effectiveness of Audit. Crown. www.gov.uk

CICOPA. (2005). *World declaration on worker co-operatives*. http://cicopa.coop

Employee Ownership Association. (2020a). *EOT survey 2020 results*. https://secure.toolkitfiles.co.uk/clients/32555/sitedata/files/EOT-Survey-2020-Results.pdf

Employee Ownership Association. (2020b). *The employee ownership top 50*. https://employeeownership.co.uk/wp-content/uploads/Employee-Ownership-Top-50-2020.pdf

Employee Ownership Association. (2020c). *How to build back better: Employee ownership is the answer*. [Webinar]. YouTube. https://www.youtube.com/watch?v=qQ8vKvqL91Y

Gandhi, M. K. (1927). *An autobiography or the story of my experiments with truth* (M. Desai, Trans.). Navajivan.

Gandhi, M. K. (1959a). *Economic and industrial life and relations* (V. B. Kher, Ed.) (2nd ed., Vols. 1–3). Navajivan.

Gandhi, M. K. (1959b). *All men are brothers: Life and thoughts of Mahatma Gandhi as told in his own words*. UNESCO.

Gandhi, M. K. (1960). *Trusteeship* (R. Kelkar, Ed.). Navajivan.

GC100. (2018). *Guidance on directors' duties—Section 172 and stakeholder considerations*. www.uk.practicallaw.thomsonreuters.com

GOV.UK. (2017). *Introduction to public service mutuals*. Retrieved March 17, 2021, from https://www.gov.uk/guidance/introduction-to-public-service-mutuals

Goyder, G. (1979a). Introduction. In G. Goyder (Ed.), *Trusteeship: A possible solution to problems of power, exploitation, conflict and alienation* (pp. 3–7). Leslie Sawhny.

Goyder, G. (1979b). The responsible company. In G. Goyder (Ed.), *Trusteeship: A possible solution to problems of power, exploitation, conflict and alienation* (pp. 52–57). Leslie Sawhny.

Goyder, G. (Ed.). (1979c). *Trusteeship: A possible solution to problems of power, exploitation, conflict and alienation*. Leslie Sawhny.

HM Revenue & Customs. (2020). *Tax-advantaged schemes*, ERSM300000. GOV.UK. Retrieved March 17, 2021, from https://www.gov.uk/hmrc-int ernal-manuals/employment-related-securities/ersm300000

House of Commons Trade and Industry Committee. (2003). *The White Paper on modernising company law* (2002–03, HC 439).

Jones, G., & Sheth, S. (2019). What Gandhi believed is the purpose of a corporation. *The Conversation*. https://theconversation.com/what-gandhi-believed-is-the-purpose-of-a-corporation-124470

Joseph, S. K. (2016). Gandhi's trusteeship: An alternative to capitalist and socialist systems (pp. 123–138). In S. K. Joseph, B. Mahodaya, & R. C. Pradhan (Eds.), *Trusteeship: A path less travelled*. Institute of Gandhian Studies.

Joseph, S. K., Mahodaya, B., & Pradhan, R. C. (Eds.). (2016). *Trusteeship: A path less travelled*. Institute of Gandhian Studies.

KPMG. (2020). *India's CSR reporting survey 2019*. http://assets.kpmg

Lampel, J, Banerjee, A., & Bhalla, A. (2018). *Final evidence report*. The Ownership Effect Inquiry. http://theownershipeffect.co.uk

Mukharji, P. B. (1969). *Social responsibilities of business: Report of the study group of the Calcutta seminar*. IBH.

Nelson-Jones, J., & Nuttall, G. (1987). *Employee ownership: Legal and tax aspects*. Fourmat.

Nuttall, G. (2012). *Sharing success: The Nuttall review of employee ownership*. U.K. Department for Business, Innovation & Skills.

Nuttall, G. (2014a, September). Neat. *Trusts and Estates Law & Tax Journal*, 16–20.

Nuttall, G. (2014b, October). Tried and tested. *Tax Adviser*, 43–45.

Nuttall, G. (2020). *Employee ownership: The solution to higher standards of ESG*. [Press release]. Fieldfisher. https://www.fieldfisher.com

Nuttall, G. (2021). *Renewed international call for employee ownership as a solution to higher standards of ESG*. Press release. https://www.fieldfisher.com/en/insights/renewed-international-call-for-employee-ownership

Nuttall, G., & Morris, P. (2018). *How to move to employee ownership*. [Presentation]. Employee Ownership Association Annual Conference. https://emp

loyeeownership.co.uk/wp-content/uploads/8.-How-to-move-to-employee-ownership.pdf

Paradigm Norton. (2019). *Proud to be certified 'B' corporation business*. Retrieved March 17, 2021, from https://www.paradigmnorton.co.uk

Parekh, B. (1989). *Gandhi's political philosophy: A critical examination*. Palgrave Macmillan.

Pendleton, A., & Robinson, R. (2015). *Employee ownership in Britain today*. White Rose Employee Ownership Centre. http://lubswww.leeds.ac.uk/filead min/webfiles/WREOC/WHITE_ROSE_PAPER_-_EMPLOYEE_OWN ERSHIP_IN_BRITAIN.pdf

Principles for Responsible Investment. (2017). *A blue print for responsible investment*. https://www.unpri.org

Principles for Responsible Investment. (2019). *Environmental, social and governance issues*. Retrieved March 17, 2021, from https://www.unpri.org/sustai nability-issues/environmental-social-and-governance-issues

Ranjan, S. (2016). Gandhi: Trusteeship and socialism. In S. K. Joseph, B. Mahodaya, & R. C. Pradhan (Eds.), *Trusteeship: A path less travelled* (pp. 139–150). Institute of Gandhian Studies.

Riverford Organic Farmers. (2020). *Certified B Corp*. Retrieved March 17, 2021, from https://www.riverford.co.uk/ethics-and-ethos/bcorp

Robinson, A., & Pendleton, A. (2019). *Employee ownership in Britain: Size and character*. White Rose Employee Ownership Centre https://employeeo wnership.co.uk/wp-content/uploads/White-Rose-Centre-for-employee-own ership-survey-2019-report.pdf

Sales. P. J. (2019). *Directors' duties and climate change: Keeping pace with environmental challenges*. https://law-ccli-2019.sites.olt.ubc.ca/files/2019/09/ Lord-Sales-speech.pdf

Short, S. (2019). *How do companies act? The time for change is now*. Social Enterprise Mark. https://www.socialenterprisemark.org.uk/how-do-compan ies-actthe-time-for-change-is-now/

Social Enterprise UK. (2018). *Public service mutuals: The state of the sector*. https://www.socialenterprise.org.uk

The British Academy. (2019). *Principles for purposeful business: How to deliver the framework for the future of the corporation*.

The Ownership Effect Inquiry. (2018). *The ownership dividend: The economic case for employee ownership*. LID Publishing.

U.K. Department for Business, Energy & Industrial Strategy. (2019). *Stakeholder perceptions of non-financial reporting* (Research paper 2019/027).

U.K. Department for Business, Innovation and Skills. (2012, February 8). *Graeme Nuttall appointed Government adviser on employee ownership.* [Press release].

U.K. Department for Business, Innovation & Skills. (2014). *Good for business & society: Government response to call for views on corporate responsibility.*

UNEP Finance Initiative. (2005). *A legal framework for the integration of environmental, social and governance issues into institutional investment.*

United Nations General Assembly. (2015, September 25). *Transforming our world: The 2030 agenda for sustainable development* (A/RES/70/1).

Useful Simple Trust. (n.d.). *About the trust.* Retrieved August 5, 2020, from https://www.usefulsimple.co.uk

8

Calling Orientation as Sustainability in Gandhi's Wisdom

Nachiketa Tripathi and Chayan Poddar

One of the significant characteristics of the contemporary times is the presence of organizations of different sizes across the world, private or public, which employ millions of people in varying capacities for substantial periods of their lives. Moreover, for the existence of such organizations, the resounding buzzword of these times is sustainability (Power, 2018). However, when we think of sustainability in terms of organizations, it is generally associated with economic indicators or environmental parameters such as reduction in the carbon footprint across all processes and stakeholders. Consequently, individuals working in these

N. Tripathi (✉)
Department of Humanities & Social Sciences, and School of Business, Indian Institute of Technology Guwahati, Guwahati, Assam, India
e-mail: nachi@iitg.ac.in

C. Poddar
Indian Institute of Management Shillong, Shillong, Meghalaya, India

© The Author(s), under exclusive license to Springer Nature Switzerland AG 2022
V. K. Kool and R. Agrawal (eds.), *Gandhi's Wisdom*,
https://doi.org/10.1007/978-3-030-87491-9_8

organizations get reduced to minuscule units whose sustainability is identified with financial stability. Be that as it may, we argue that financial stability is not the sole motivator of individuals working in organizations—for their continued sustenance in organizations they need to grow both psychologically and socially. This will not only impact the work they do but will also be reflected in the image of the organization. Thus, in the backdrop of organizations, it becomes essential to conceptualize individual sustainability so as to identify processes, practices, work culture, and other dimensions within organizations that may help individuals to rise to their full potential as a human.

Seeing that the twenty-first century is an epitome of competition, we have individuals pursuing better designations and organizations engaging in competition in order to attract the best of talents. At the same time, the gig economy has led to a changed scenario with employees valuing appreciation, dignity, and demonstration of new-age social values much more than their salaries (Brun & Dugas, 2008; Solnet et al., 2012). To bridge the competition on both sides, organizations need to deduce strategies to deliver these values.

While there is no doubt that employees are the most valuable asset of an organization, these employees tend to lose motivation when only a salary is received for the work done. On the other hand, when some additional perks are added to the salary, it tends to make the employees more secure with a greater sense of responsibility toward the organization. In other words, respect and value are reciprocal in nature and apply to organizations as well, irrespective of their size. Workplaces that facilitate employees' growth, helping them learn and grow, accommodating them with homeliness, and providing them a chance to perform according to their potential are some of the most sought-after places by employees. Hence, empowering employees can enable long-term value for an organization, thereby helping it to embrace sustainability (Polman & Bhattacharya, 2016; Raub & Robert, 2010; Zu, 2019). In turn, individual sustainability can contribute to organizational sustainability.

Over the past two decades, the evolving working practices and organizational development have provided increasing importance to psychological assets. Organizations now need to manage the processes of production rather than mere tangible inventories. Hence, organizations have evolved from having a particular hierarchal framework to being places that constantly modify and develop with the employees' psychological needs. Such abstract areas contain social and psychological experiences over and above financial and material resources. This, along with the ever-increasing competitive business environment, has led organizations to work on the employees' psychological needs. Although these strategies initially emerged for the elimination of negative behaviors, it has been recognized, over time, that the development of positive behaviors would result in positive outcomes for both the organizations and its employees.

The changes in outlook toward employee behavior have influenced research in psychology and organizational behavior like never before. The findings of extensive research for improvement in the quality of workplace for the employees, as well as the quest of individual improvement in an organizational setting, seems to reciprocate the ideals that Gandhi preached decades before, through the creation of a number of successful and sustainable communities of satyagrahis guided by his ultimate belief in nonviolence as fundamental for reaching the highest levels of human behavior.

In the backdrop of the above, and the contention that modern scientific psychology and nearly all of its subfields can effectively draw from satyagraha and the nonviolence ideals of Gandhi (Kool & Agrawal, 2013), it becomes essential to analyze and utilize Gandhi's wisdom for the development of individuals so as to prolong organizational sustainability. In this chapter, we discuss the various facets of applying Gandhi's idea of sustainability in the organizational context.

We have divided the chapter into the following sections: the introductory section tries to understand the concept of Calling Orientation; the second section looks into how Calling Orientation can contribute to organizational sustainability, followed by the third section delving into the comprehension of sustainability using Gandhi's perspective. The fourth section analyses good citizenry of employees in organizations as an outcome of nonviolence while the fifth section reflects on whether community feelings can be developed in organizational settings. The sixth section tries to illustrate the importance of Gandhian ideals in contemporary organizational behavior.

The Concept of Calling Orientation

The concept of Calling Orientation talks about the continuous engagement of employees to their jobs in an organization because of their love for it (Wrzesniewski, 2003). As far as employees are concerned, Calling Orientation is probably far more important than earning a salary or seeking advancement and promotion in their careers. This has been found to be related to the enhancement of productivity in the workplace as well as to the well-being of the employees, harnessing good citizenship and contributing to positive qualities at work. What has been recognized as Calling Orientation in Western research was preached by Gandhi decades ago, in the form of the practicing of nonviolence in daily behavior in the light of the unceasing evaluation of oneself, bringing in its wake, wholehearted belief in the work that they did.

In the light of neoclassical callings, the broad definition of Calling Orientation has been,

> Transcendent summons, experienced as originating beyond the self, to approach a particular life-role in a manner oriented toward demonstrating or deriving a sense of purpose or meaningfulness and that holds other-oriented values and goals as primary sources of motivation (Dik & Duffy, 2009, p. 427).

Dik and Shimizu (2019) have illustrated several characteristics of Calling Orientation, including the presence of a transcendent source or destiny which can be either God, the legacy of one's family, or an urge to perform for the greater good of society by engaging in purposeful actions and to utilize one's skills for a positive impact of the highest degree. Despite the different sources of an individual's calling, scholars have mostly agreed that Calling Orientation broadly entails attachment of purpose and meaning to one's work (Hirschi, 2011).

The concept of Calling Orientation has been carried forward in further research to include the exercise of "Job Crafting," by virtue of which an individual undertakes configuration and reconfiguration of everyday work so as to reach a higher level of fulfillment. This can be made possible through emphasizing service and craftsmanship in the pursuit of excellence for the sole purpose of reaching inner fulfillment. Thus, Calling Orientation, in itself, possesses the ability to turn any job into a dream job for an individual, even though it is becoming increasingly difficult to get into aspirational designations categorized as dream jobs since most of the times, the monetary benefit associated with such designations have been found to be the sole motivator. Thus, the attainment of Calling Orientation for employees in their workplace, in which organizational psychology has only recently started researching, is bound to have a positive impact on increasing productivity and commitment toward their work. The role of supervisors and senior management becomes important, as research has established the positive trickle-down effect of senior supervisor's Calling Orientation on their subordinate's Calling Orientation (Xie et al., 2019).

Calling Orientation and Organizational Sustainability

The competitiveness in the contemporary business world demands innovation and creativity from organizations across their entire product portfolio. In turn, the possibility of such consistent innovation and creativity demands employees being able to perform to their fullest potential. This achievement can be ensured only when employees grow psychologically as individuals. An impactful societal change can be only spearheaded by the combination of small changes within individuals. This, in turn, helps an individual to be able to collaborate with others for achieving life-affirming decisions. Thus, sustainability through joint efforts of community-driven actions results from combining determined positive value systems with everyday actions. Hence, individual sustainability, which promotes organizational sustainability, can resonate with good citizenry practices through repeated self-evaluation.

Calling Orientation has been seen to be dependent on several factors—the influence of spirituality and theology on an individual, conditions in the family, the expectations of the local society and culture as well as specific circumstances in one's life (Longman et al., 2011). However, empirical investigations on different groups of people, from medical students (Duffy et al., 2011) to musicians (Dobrow, 2013) and nursing workers (Esteves & Lopes, 2017), have found similarities in terms of a higher-order calling and an inner sense of purpose in the work that they do. Yet, further research on the contextual and relational factors leading to the development of the Calling Orientation is the need of the hour.

At the same time, it has been established that Calling Orientation arises out of intrinsic motivation and is not dependent on external reinforcements of either rewards or punishment. While several theories of motivation have influenced organizational behavior in the past decades, almost all of these have been developed in the US, raising serious questions regarding their applicability in societies with different value systems (Arnett, 2008). Further, Hofstede's findings report major differences in culture (Hofstede, 1980). It thus becomes mandatory to draw ideas from parts of the globe, other than from the US or the Western world. In this regard, can a better exemplar from the eastern parts of the world be found? Gandhi's practice of satyagraha, and the satyagrahi model of life fits the bill and provides considerable practical tenets for the achievement of sustainability at all levels of the organization.

Modern research talks about the importance of spirituality in one's inner calling (Kaufman, 2018) for associating meaning to one's work. This is totally in line with Gandhi's ideals. The first condition for someone to be a satyagrahi under Gandhi's teaching was to "listen to their inner voice and to carve their behavior through continuous self-evaluation" (Kool & Agrawal, 2013). Thus, a satyagrahi rose above menial contingencies of compensation and punishment in society and emerged as a champion of "soul force" driven by morals, justice, and conscience. The continued sustainability of satyagrahi communities and their ways of life and the failure of a similar commune of Skinner in the US, successfully illustrates the manner in which the Calling Orientation can bring about organizational sustainability.

Organizational Sustainability in the Gandhian Perspective

The dominant form of business in the twenty-first century is through conglomerates and large organizations employing millions of people in the formal sector. Gandhi, in contrast, preached the model of village-based self-sufficient economy and shunned the formation of big businesses, industries, and organizations for the sustainability of the planet. In fact, Gandhi's ideas of self-control through positive reinforcement and willful punishment acting as negative reinforcement for the betterment of the individual contributed to the diffusion of conflicts, engagement in greater pro-social behavior, and resilience of the inner self for betterment of the communal family at large.

The contemporary approach toward organizational sustainability has been regulatory in nature, either through a quota on emissions or paying a tariff on the level of pollution. It usually focuses on policy reforms to continue the process of economic growth by strategizing efficiency mechanisms to reduce pollution levels. This approach fails to develop a humane perspective to devise sustainable mechanisms in which individual morality toward ecology becomes the foundation block of sustainability. What is required is an,

> Authentic 'ecological citizenship' for a more fundamental change in the framework of moral values guiding individuals' behaviour and attitude towards the environment and their choices to live lightly on earth. (Dash, 2014, p. 27)

This is where the Gandhian paradigm, emanating out of nonviolence and ethical morality can emerge with flying colors as an alternative to the dominant approach. The moral development of the individual as opposed to a dichotomous "mean-spirited and distorted view of human nature" (Illes & Zsolnai, 2014; Mitroff, 2004), occurring as a realization of the revolution of the self to improve one's quality, can serve as a stepping stone toward a societal transformation which is free, equal, just, and peaceful.

Sustainability in an individual's context combines with a congenial, interconnected working environment and possessing abilities of thoughtful self-awareness in how one acts, values, and behaves at a higher plane. Individual growth is also cultivated by emotional, philosophical, social, physical, and intellectual abilities. In the context of the organizational setup, this helps an employee to feel motivated about the workplace and to contribute to the organization's sustenance in the long run. If we are to consider the positive trickle-down effects of higher order Calling Orientation on subordinates as mentioned above, perhaps there is a need for charismatic, transformational leaders at large in organizations to drive positive change toward sustainability based on Gandhian ideals.

The growing socio-political inequalities, changes in the pattern of weather and environment owing to climate change, as well as challenges related to financial crises and turbulences have led to tremendous instability in organizations as far as conducting business in the contemporary world is concerned (Ahmed et al., 2012; Buckley, & Carter, 2004). As such, organizations now need to design strategies for using their resources, be it natural, cultural, social, or human, prudently (Viederman, 1994) for sustainably continuing their businesses. Thus, if sustainability were to be defined as the embodiment of,

> the promise of societal evolution towards a more equitable and wealthy world in which the natural environment and our cultural achievements are preserved for generations to come (Dyllick, & Hockerts, 2002, p. 130).

Then, organizational sustainability can only be possible when an organization keeps in view all stakeholders, including the society and the environment, while designing business strategies as mentioned above.

Good Citizenry as an Outcome of Nonviolence

Employees practicing Calling Orientation have often been referred to as good citizens within an organization (Wrzesniewski, 2003; Kool & Agrawal, 2020). It can also be termed organizational commitment, which includes an eagerness to make considerable efforts on behalf of the organization, a strong belief in and affirming the goals, code of business ethics, and values of the organization as well as a strong desire to see oneself as an organization's integral member. Such aspects of organizational engagement indicate pro-social behavior. This may lead to contextual performance of employees based on one's disposition or empathy for others (Borman & Motowidlo, 1993).

All of the above qualities can be seen in Gandhi and his satyagrahi followers. The strength of fearlessness in satyagrahis which develops from the bond of love and compassion, demands wholehearted dedication attained through self-resonance. As preached by Gandhi, this selfless attitude enables the creation of capacities for treating communities as families in the first stage, and then going beyond those boundaries to consider the universe as a family or what Gandhi termed Vasudhaiva Kutumbakam. Gandhi was able to ensure the above qualities in the satyagrahis through the practice of utter self-control based on the 11 vows each and every satyagrahi had to take. These were as follows:

- The honest practicing of '*Satya*' or truth.
- The practicing of '*Ahimsa*' or nonviolence.
- The practicing of '*Brahmacharya*' or chastity.
- The control and regulation of the '*Aswad*' or taste buds to consume food in balanced proportions.
- The practicing of '*Asteya*' or non-stealing both physically and mentally.
- The practicing of '*Aparigraha*' or voluntary acceptance of poverty.
- The practicing of '*Abhay*' or fearlessness to be free from death and delusions.
- The practicing of '*Asprushyta Nivaran*' or removing the notions of untouchability.

- The practicing of '*Jatmehnat*' or voluntary labor in order to receive food.
- The practicing of '*Sarvadharmsambhav*' or acceptance of all religions.
- The practicing of '*Swadeshi*' or dutiful service for neighbors for production and consumption of goods without selfishness.

The attainment of the above principles for any individual at the micro-level, seemingly, holds the key for answering the fundamental problems that organizations, nations, and mankind as a whole face in present times—continuous economic growth with insatiable demands, practices of monopoly, appropriation of astronomical sums of profit, and environmental disasters. Gandhi's model of individual behavior posits the greatest possibility for leveraging a socioeconomic order for sustainability at all levels. Thus, the steadfast intrinsic motivation of self-resilient individuals contributed to such behavior which modern psychology identifies in the light of organizational citizenship behavior through manifestation of responsibility, judicious use of resources, commitment to the organization, and involvement in job (Cohen & Vigoda, 2000; Kaufman et al., 2001; Ingrams, 2020). The growth of interdependence among fellow employees to contribute to the organizational cause, the sharing of camaraderie and forming a greater goal above personal ambitions would, indeed, make an individual a good citizen in any organization. In the above lies the crux of Gandhi's wisdom which can be effectively harnessed for the betterment and sustainability of the organization.

Replication of Community Feeling in an Organizational Context

Numerous factors emanating from within the organization have an impact on an employee's psychology. Some of these include the work environment, peer professionals, and the authority of the senior leaders and management. The above factors also influence the commitment levels of employees for operating and finding satisfaction.

Management is characterized by the actions of a person who guides the group activities toward achieving the shared goals with a non-coercive effect (Rowden, 1999), helping employees to enhance their psychological state. Supervisors and HR administrators who are part of the management play a bridging role and have a significant responsibility in introducing new employees to the organization, retaining these individuals as well as encouraging them to engage in the job, eventually leading them to becoming attached to the organization. An employee placed in an appropriate role, presented with power and responsibility, as well as looked upon by her/his supervisor, ought to be anticipated to continually better her/his productivity with being dedicated to her/his role.

Contemporary research identifies the need for the education of the whole person to provide opportunities toward self-discovery, with the purpose of developing integrity in one's belief and conduct (Illes & Zsolnai, 2014). This is evident from the increased emphasis on the need for ethics and virtues in business education. As such, realizing the importance of one's conscience and acting accordingly helps developing character in spiritual ways, even when they are not labeled as such.

> Spiritual-based leaders respect others and are guided by the fundamental ethic: service to others comes before serving oneself. From an existential perspective, the raison d'être of organizations is to serve human needs. Really, there is no other reason for their existence. Individuals and organizations grow when they give themselves to others. Relationships improve when there is a focus on serving the other, be it at the level of the individual, the family, the organization, the community, the society or all of humanity. (Pruzan & Pruzan, 2007, p. 52)

The functioning of any group is dependent on a variety of factors, among which cohesiveness and energy level of group members are the most significant. While research suggests increased efficiency in groups with reduction in the number of members, Gandhi's followers and communities defied this finding. This was possible owing to high cohesiveness as a result of greater interdependence among members, by embedding the feeling of duty among members to contribute to the benefit of the group in some way, and the practice of '*Jatmehnat*' or food as a result of labor, that is, bread labor (Kool & Agrawal, 2020). The combination of motivated, cohesive groups of call-oriented members can indeed form communities within themselves, which would contribute to the efficiency and productivity of the group.

The effectiveness of the above is manifested in the successful rise of cooperative business models (Williams, 2007) and societies such as Self-Employed Women Associations (SEWA, Kool & Agrawal, 2020), which have helped millions of women financially and helped them rise above the veil of social stigma, functioning according to the values of Gandhi. AMUL as an organization is also based on Gandhi's ideas of "capillary action which means development from below to the grassroots" (Bansal & Bajpai, 2011).

The existence of alternative societies, such as the Kibbutz in Israel, also, deserves a special mention (Joel, 1989). Kibbutz is a way of communal life, practiced almost as a religion where everyone is treated equally. The material possession of a Kibbutz member is neither more nor less than any other member. Joel (1989) mentions, "A kibbutz member dedicates his life to the collective good of the society. Since everyone is equal, all the members rotate jobs, taking a turn at each—cleaning the chicken coop one year, running the front office the next. In return the kibbutz provides for all of the member's needs - food, clothing, shelter, medicine, education for the member's children." This type of community based on equal economic participation, democratic, collective ownership, and voluntary principles has successfully existed over a hundred years and provides an alternative to dominant discourses of economic approach. The adaptability of the Kibbutz with the rise in technology has not changed the above-mentioned four principles which continue to operate even to this day (Cheng & Sun, 2015; Leviatan, 2013).

Application of Gandhi's Wisdom in Organizational Behavior

Based on his ideas of collectivism as a social orientation, the structure of oceanic circles of power in organizations and the essence of trusteeship, Gandhi's wisdom is applicable in contemporary organizational psychology and Human Resource Management (Kool, 2013; Kool & Agrawal, 2020). We attempt to illustrate the applicability of the Gandhian model to current management practices. Organizations have been generally analyzed across three levels—individual, group, and organizational, with Gandhi's ideas being applicable in all three.

Gandhi's focus on 'service' for the attainment of truth leading to inner self-fulfillment forms the cornerstone of satyagraha. Gandhi was not only able to pursue his own calling, but to enable his followers in masses to follow their callings (Afsar et al., 2019). Nonviolence formed the standalone rubric of Calling Orientation of Gandhi.

Various theories have been used to maintain employee motivation levels for attaining organizational motivation, including those by Maslow, Skinner, Bandura, Seligman, and others, and have influenced organizational practices in the US for the last few decades. The applicability of such behaviors has been in question in countries with widely different cultures. Moreover, reinforcement and contingences without genuine identification of an individual at the community level have proven to be inadequate in value (Erikson, 1969). The paradoxes presented by Gandhi's satyagrahi followers were non-explainable through Skinner's reinforcement strategies, while Bandura (1997) has credited Gandhi as being an epitome of self-efficacy,

> Gandhi provides a striking example of self-sacrifice in the exercise of commanding personal efficacy. He spearheaded the triumph over oppressive rule through unceasing non-violent resistance and repeatedly forced concessions from ruling authorities by going on life-threatening fasts. He lived ascetically, not self-indulgently. Without a resilient sense of self, people are easily overwhelmed by adversities in their attempts to improve their group life through collective effort. (Bandura 1997, p. 32)

Gandhi has been identified as a charismatic, transformational, and servant leader who "has left behind a legacy for all those in leadership positions" (Kool & Agrawal, 2020), through practicing humility, constant learning for positive change, self-generated change, continuous persistence, believing in humanity, being humorous, and united for a common cause. By refuting discrimination and prejudice at every stage, Gandhi has provided examples for the management of inclusion and diversity.

Intezari's (2015) model on the interconnection between wisdom and sustainability talks about the requirement of "a self-transcendence approach to the human and surrounding environment as an integrated whole" (Intezari, 2015), where wisdom contributes to sustainable strategies and wise practices in the future, leading to sustainable capacity creation for organizations, calling in further wisdom (Fig. 1, Wisdom and Sustainability, Intezari, 2015). This continues as an ongoing cycle, combining the virtues of wisdom and sustainability for the development of sustainable frameworks and guidelines, contributing to holistic and integrative practices for all stakeholders. All four aspects of this cyclical model are well in line with Gandhi's ideas, a major point of which was that organizations, and for that matter, society, too, can be sustainable only by following wise practices with the entire universe being regarded as a family (Vasudhaiva Kutumbakam).

Further, Intezari (2016) provides certain fundamental questions that need to be considered for the theoretical and practical implementation of sustainable organizations of the future. These are as follows:

- "From whose point of view is our sustainability initiative sustainable?
- Does the sustainability initiative represent the internal and external realities?
- To what extent is the sustainability initiative justifiable both cognitively and affectively?
- To what extent do the senior management and leadership's presumptions toward the business and society reflect the sustainability approach?
- Is the sustainability initiative sustainable in practice?" (Intezari, 2016, p. 5)

Once again, these five questions enable us to apply the Gandhian perspective regarding sustainability. According to Gandhi, the initiative should be sustainable from the point of view of all things sentient in nature and it should be based on nonviolence, the Truth according to Gandhi, and thereby representing all types of realities. Moreover, Gandhi made every effort to reduce the cognitive and affective load of his followers through appropriate scripting and priming. The answer to the last question can be found in the resounding success of his non-violent movement praised around the globe.

Extensive research supports the need to devise human resource plans for organizations for the development and maintenance of competitive advantages and for considering aspects that are particularly different and important, context specific, aggregate, sustainable, difficult to replicate, and irreplaceable (De Saa-Perez & Garcia-Falcon, 2002). Management in organizations can take cues from Gandhi's wisdom and practice it in their everyday activities. Adopting truth as a value leads to credibility, trust, and transparency for an organization and its employees. A humanistic and harmonious workplace with less stress and exploitative methods can contribute a long way for avoiding harassment of employees in any way, and contribute to a culture of nonviolence across the organization. Welfare projects through selfless service for serving society at large can be inculcated by organizations at large.

Decentralization of hierarchy by delegating powers to lower order employees would lead to their development and contribute to their nurturance. Tolerance and punctuality are two ethos that organizations should look to inculcate in their employees. Practicing humility, equanimity, and the zeal for continuous learning will contribute to positive social change. As sustainability becomes inevitable rather than being a necessity (Intezari, 2015), sustainable practices empower practical implementation of wisdom. The interconnectedness of wisdom and sustainability calls for extensive research and practice in both academia and industry (Intezari, 2016). The manifestation of wisdom and sustainability at individual, organizational, and societal level calls for refocusing our attention to Gandhi's wisdom, and especially the development of calling-oriented individuals based on Gandhian ideals, that will advance organizational sustainability in the short run and augment societal transformation for a sustainable future.

References

Afsar, B., Umrani, W. A., & Khan, A. (2019, January 9). The impact of perceived calling on work outcomes in a nursing context: The role of career commitment and living one's calling. *Journal of Applied Behavioral Research, 24*(1), e12154. https://doi.org/10.1111/jabr.12154

Ahmed, A., Hasnain, N., & Venkatesan, M. (2012). Decision making in relation to personality types and cognitive styles of business students. *The IUP Journal of Management Research, XI*(2), 20–30.

Arnett, J. J. (2008). The neglected 95%: Why American psychology needs to become less American. *American Psychologist, 63*(7), 602–614.

Bandura, A. (1997). *Self-efficacy.* Freeman.

Bansal, I., & Bajpai, N. (2011). Gandhian values: Guidelines for managing organizations. *Journal of Human Values, 17*(2), 145–160.

Borman, W. C., & Motowidlo, S. J. (1993). Expanding the criterion domain to include elements of contextual performance. In N. Schmitt & W. C. Borman (Eds.), *Personnel selection in organizations* (pp. 71–98). Jossey-Bass.

Brun, J. P., & Dugas, N. (2008). An analysis of employee recognition: Perspectives on human resources practices. *The International Journal of Human Resource Management, 19*(4), 716–730. https://doi.org/10.1080/09585190801953723

Buckley, P. J., & Carter, M. J. (2004). A formal analysis of knowledge combination in multinational enterprises. *Journal of International Business Studies, 35*(5), 371–384.

Cheng, E., & Sun, Y. (2015). Israeli kibbutz: A successful example of collective economy. *World Review of Political Economy, 6*(2), 160–175. https://doi.org/10.13169/worlrevipoliecon.6.2.0160#metadata_info_tab_contents

Cohen, A., & Vigoda, E. (2000). Do good citizens make good organizational citizens? An empirical examination of the relationship between general citizenship and organizational citizenship behaviour in Israel. *Administration and Society, 32*(5), 596–624.

Dash, A. (2014). The moral basis of sustainable society: The Gandhian concept of ecological citizenship. *International Review of Sociology, 24*(1), 27–37. https://doi.org/10.1080/03906701.2014.894343

De Saa-Perez, P., & Garcia-Falcon, J. M. (2002). A resource-based view of human resource management and organizational capabilities development. *International Journal of Human Resource Management, 13*(1), 123–140.

Dik, B. J., & Duffy, R. D. (2009). Calling and vocation at work: Definitions and prospects for research and practice. *The Counseling Psychologist, 37*, 424–450. https://doi.org/10.1177/0011000008316430

Dik, B. J., & Shimizu, A. B. (2019). Multiple meanings of calling: Next steps for studying an evolving construct. *Journal of Career Assessment, 27*, 323–336. https://doi.org/10.1177/1069072717748676

Dobrow, S. R. (2013). Dynamics of calling: A longitudinal study of musicians. *Journal of Organizational Behavior, 34*, 431–452. https://doi.org/10.1002/job.1808

Duffy, R. D., Manuel, R. S., Borges, N. J., & Bott, E. M. (2011). Calling, vocational development, and well-being: A longitudinal study of medical students. *Journal of Vocational Behavior, 79*, 361–366. https://doi.org/10.1016/j.jvb.2011.03.023

Dyllick, T., & Hockerts, K. (2002). Beyond the business case for corporate sustainability. *Business Strategy and the Environment, 141*, 130–141.

Erikson, E. (1969). *Gandhi's truth*. Norton.

Esteves, T., & Lopes, M. P. (2017). Crafting a calling: The mediating role of calling between challenging job demands and turnover intention. *Journal of Career Development, 44*, 34–48. https://doi.org/10.1177/0894845316633789

Hirschi, A. (2011). Callings in career: A typological approach to essential and optional components. *Journal of Vocational Behavior, 79*, 60–73.

Hofstede, G. (1980). *Culture's consequences: International differences in work related values*. Sage.

Illes, K., & Zsolnai, L. (2014). The role of spirituality in business education. *Society and Business Review, 10*(1), 67–75. https://doi.org/10.1108/SBR-07-2014-0034

Ingrams, A. (2020). Organizational citizenship behaviour in the public and private sectors: A multilevel test of public service motivation and traditional antecedents. *Review of Public Personnel Administration, 40*(2), 222–244.

Intezari, A. (2015). Integrating wisdom and sustainability: Dealing with instability. *Business Strategy and the Environment, 24*(7), 617–627.

Intezari, A. (2016). Practical wisdom through sustainability: A meta-approach. In S. O. Idowu, & R. Schmidpeter (Eds.), *CSR, sustainability, wisdom & governance* (pp. 23–37). Springer.

Joel, B. (1989, March 5). Debts make Israelis rethink an ideal: The Kibbutz. *The New York Times*. https://www.nytimes.com/1989/03/05/world/debts-make-israelis-rethink-an-ideal-the-kibbutz.html

Kaufman, J. D., Stamper, C. L., & Tesluk, P. E. (2001). Do supportive organizations make for good corporate citizens? *Journal of Managerial Issues, 13*(4), 436–449.

Kaufman, S. B. (2018, May 22). *Finding your calling at work with Amy Wrzesniewski.* scottbarrykaufman.com

Kool, V. K. (2013). Application of Gandhian concepts in psychology and allied disciplines. *Indian Journal of Psychiatry, 55*(2), 235–238. https://doi.org/10.4103/0019-5545.105541

Kool, V. K., & Agrawal, R. (2013). Whither Skinner's science of behaviour, his assessment of Gandhi, and its aftermath? *Gandhi Marg Quarterly, 35*(4), 487–518.

Kool, V. K., & Agrawal, R. (2020). Gandhi's calling orientation: Applications to organizational behavior. In *Gandhi and the psychology of nonviolence* (Vol. 2). Palgrave Macmillan.

Leviatan, U. (2013). Values and organizational commitment. *International Critical Thought, 3*(3), 315–331.

Longman, K. A., Dahlvig, J., Wikkerink, R. J., Cunningham, D., & O'Connor, C. M. (2011). Conceptualization of calling: A grounded theory exploration of CCCU women leaders. *Christian Higher Education, 10*, 254–275. https://doi.org/10.1080/15363759.2011.576213

Mitroff, I. (2004). An open letter to the deans and the faculties of American business schools. *Journal of Business Ethics, 54*(2), 185–189.

Polman, P., & Bhattacharya, C. B. (2016). Engaging employees to create a sustainable business. *Stanford Social Innovation Review, 14*(4), 34–39.

Power, R. (2018, April 18). Think sustainability's a buzzword? These changes prove otherwise. *Inc.* https://www.inc.com/rhett-power/think-sustainabilitys-a-buzzword-these-changes-prove-otherwise.html

Pruzan, P., & Pruzan, M. K. (2007). *Leading with wisdom: Spiritual-based leadership in business.* Greenleaf Publishing.

Raub, S., & Robert, C. (2010). Differential effects of empowering leadership on in-role and extra-role employee behaviors: Exploring the role of psychological empowerment and power values. *Human Relations, 63*(11), 1743–1770. https://doi.org/10.1177/0018726710365092

Rowden, R. W. (1999). The relationship between charismatic leadership behaviors and organizational commitment. *The Leadership & Organization Development Journal, 21*(1), 30–35.

Solnet, D., Kralj, A., & Kandampully, J. (2012). Generation Y employees: An examination of work attitude differences. *Journal of Applied Management and Entrepreneurship, 17*(3), 36–54.

Viederman, S. (1994). *The economics of sustainability: Challenges.* Paper presented at the workshop, The Economics of Sustainability, Gundacao Joaquim Nabuco, Recife, Brazil.

Williams, R. C. (2007). *The cooperative movement: Globalization from below.* Routledge. ISBN: 978-0-7546-7038-4.

Wrzesniewski, A. (2003). Finding positive meaning in work. In K. S. Cameron, J. E. Dutton, & R. E. Quinn (Eds.), *Positive organizational scholarship* (pp. 296–308). Berrett-Koehler.

Xie, B., Xhou, W., Xia, D., & Guo, Y. (2019). What drives the trickle-down effect of calling orientation from supervisors to subordinates? The perspective of social learning theory. *Frontiers in Psychology, 10,* 905. https://doi.org/10.3389/fpsyg.2019.00905

Zu, L. (2019). Purpose-driven leadership for sustainable business: From the perspective of Taoism. *International Journal of Corporate Social Responsibility, 4*(3). https://doi.org/10.1186/s40991-019-0041-z

9

The Wisdom of Gandhi: Achieving a Sustainable Economy

Tej Prakash

Introduction

Is there a well-articulated and consistent framework of 'Gandhian economics'? How relevant is it today? These are questions that need to be answered and the present chapter attempts to discuss these and related issues.

Gandhi was not a formal 'economist' in the academic sense of our times, although, he had read and was more than familiar with the thoughts of economists such as Adam Smith and thinkers such as Karl Marx and it was while he was in prison during World War II, that he, first, read volume 1 of *Das Capital* as also the writings of Engels, Lenin, and Stalin (Tendulkar, 1953).

T. Prakash (✉)
Duke University, Durham, NC, USA

Delhi University, New Delhi, India

International Monetary Fund, Washington, DC, USA

Gandhi's social and economic thinking and philosophy evolved over time, through his social and political work in South Africa and later in India. This evolution was deeply rooted in his personal experiences and an integral part of his thinking was his approach to morality and ethics of the individual and the society and was deeply interwoven with his belief in nonviolence.

Gandhi had a holistic view of life and society. His ideal society was an economically self-reliant society, where all wealth was socially owned or owned by some as trustees for the society. In most aspects of living, his approach was to look to nature and use what it provided, whether it was in the construction of houses in the ashrams or his approach to health care. At the center of his economic philosophy were the individual and the society.

Since his time, the world has changed in ways that Gandhi could not have anticipated. It has become far more complex and interdependent than it was in the early 1900s. The advance of technology, such as the Internet, television and other technologies, globalization, and interdependence of the economies, have changed the world. It has given rise to multiple challenges, biggest and most existential among them being global warming. Globalization, for all its benefits, has also brought many challenges where bad economic policies of one country have been found to adversely affect the people in another country.

In view of the above, the Gandhian approach to modern economics has to be seen through the prism of his times, although most of his economic ideas remain relevant, even, today. His response to the economic issues of today can be fairly assessed through three fundamentals of his beliefs: truth, nonviolence, and welfare of all.

However, it cannot be said that Gandhian economics has all the answers to many of the technology-driven economic issues of the twenty-first century. It would be equally wrong to say that Gandhian was a Luddite who distrusted technology and its role in the lives of people. If anything, Gandhi was a realist and his views evolved in response to events, even as his moral universe remained unchanged. It was not accidental that Gandhi praised the sewing machine, one of the early examples of technology, and his close friends were the most well-known industrialists of the time. The only unchanging core was his moral belief and, thus, his economic philosophy cannot be understood in isolation. It is an integral part of an integrated moral and ethical view of the individual, social, and national life. For example, his views on industry or labor are a part of his vision of village economy, machination, and ethical living.

This chapter is broadly divided into two parts. The first part explores and explains the fundamentals of Gandhian economic thought. It relates his economic thinking to his overall moral vision (especially to truth and nonviolence). The second part explores how relevant these concepts are today.

Main Pillars of Gandhi's Economic Thoughts: Truth (Satya) and Nonviolence (Ahimsa)

Gandhi called his autobiography *The Story of My Experiments with Truth*. Truth for Gandhi was a complex philosophical concept. He made a distinction between 'God is truth' and 'Truth is God'. It is best explained by Gandhi himself and writes,

> I have come to the conclusion that, for myself, God is Truth. But two years ago I went a step further and said that Truth is God. You will see the distinction between the two statements, viz., that God is Truth and Truth is God. (Gandhi, *Young India*, 31 December 1931, pp. 427–428)

For him, Truth is not just an attribute of God, it *is* God. In fact, when one considers the Sanskrit root of the word Truth or Satya, it is 'Sat', which can be understood as 'that which is unchangeable' and 'universal principle'. There is, thus, a moral and ethical dimension to it and inequity or economic exploitation cannot be a part of Satya or Truth.

In the Gandhian framework nonviolence is a part of Truth. Nonviolence is the means while Truth is the end. Only through nonviolence can Truth or God be reached. At the simplest level, nonviolence does not cause harm to anyone, person, animal, or environment under any circumstances. It is not based on any religious philosophy, and it can be used for strategic purposes.

Nonviolence can be used for achieving political, social, and economic change, through rejection of violence and through civic rejection and disobedience. It can, also, be used as an economic strategy through a boycott of certain goods and commodities that have been produced through exploitation of labor and would result in hurting others. Thus, his call for the rejection of British textiles was a nonviolent way of protecting the Indian village textile industry, and rejecting the economic violence or exploitation by the British.

Gandhi believed that a nonviolent society is not consistent with the existence of wide economic inequality (Kumarappa, 1951). Every person should give to the society the best of his time, work, and talent and the society should provide him with his needs. He said: 'My ideal is equal distribution, but so far as I can see, it is not to be realized. I therefore work for equitable distribution'. The ways through which economic inequality can be overcome have been detailed below.

Property Rights and Aparigriha (Non-possession) and Sarvodaya (Welfare of All)

Right to property is a fundamental economic institution of open economies and is fundamental to modern economic theory. It is a system for the allocation of resources and it is the basis of many other social and economic institutions such as freedom of expression.

Gandhi's view of property rights was more nuanced. He held a deep belief that all wealth is ultimately given by God and should be held on God's behalf for others. His conversation with Madhav Desai (in England on 26 November 1931, reported in the *Young India* on 26 November 1931) acknowledges that a person with greater earning capacity due to their talents will have more, however, 'the bulk of his greater earnings must be used for the good of the State, just as the income of all earning sons of the father goes to the common family fund'.

He elaborates it further in the *Harijan* (3 June 1939, p. 145):

Suppose I have come by a fair amount of wealth, either by legacy or by means of trade or industry-I must know that all that wealth does not belong to me; what belongs to me is the right to an honorable livelihood. No better than that enjoyed by millions of others. The rest of my wealth belongs to the community and must be used for the welfare of the community. I enunciated this theory in respect of the possessions held by Zamindars and privileged classes.

Also,

As for the present owners of wealth, they would have to make their choice between class war and voluntarily converting themselves into trustees of their wealth. (Gandhi, *Harijan*, 31 March 1946, pp. 63–64)

'Aparigraha', non-attachment or non-possession of property is a basic concept of Gandhian economic thought. Gandhi was a believer in a verse from the Isha Upanishad: 'Covet nothing, all belongs to the God'. He was of the view that if only this verse were to be saved for generations to come, it would be enough.

Gandhi, also, believed in communal living and social organization, where 'from each according to his capacity and to each according to his need' was the defining principle. He founded the Tolstoy Ashram in South Africa along these lines. All the property was commonly held and for common good. He rejected class war and the Marxian vision of communism as being too violent. He, also, rejected materialism. Economic well-being, in his view, should lead to spiritualism.

Are these two concepts—property rights and non-possession—contradictory in nature? Gandhi's view on property is a part of his overall moral and ethical framework and cannot be viewed in isolation. In fact, it is a part of his view on environment, equity, and overall human welfare. Property rights should be fair and result in economic efficiency, and maximize human well-being. How much property should an individual own? His answer was that it should be as much as an individual requires to meet his essential needs.

So, who should own the property? This leads us to Gandhi's view on trusteeship, which is widely applicable to business, industrial, or social property. A mill or a business is held by its owner as a trustee for society and can, therefore, not be used for anything detrimental to the society. Among Gandhi's close associates were the biggest industrialists of the time, namely, Birla and Bajaj, who supported his idea of trusteeship. That the practice of 'trusteeship' today is alive and well is seen from the practices followed by the likes of Bill Gates and Warren Buffet. The COVID-19 virus has further highlighted how the globe is linked together and that 'trusteeship' of all properties, including intellectual property (such as that related to vaccines), is essential for human survival.

Capital and Labor

The next question that arises is how should one reconcile the idea of 'trusteeship' with industrial action such as workers' unions and the right to industrial strike? Gandhi believed that the value addition provided by labor was by far superior to that of capital. However, his view was that workers should invoke their right to industrial action through nonviolent action, and in ways that do not hurt production. Gandhi's view of property includes his view of self-sufficiency and village industry. Trusteeship leads to his basic principle of 'Sarvodaya' (welfare of all) while attachment to property, that is, parigriha or the opposite of aparigriha gives rise to violence. Hence, he advocated non-possession.

The following two quotations capture Gandhi's views on capital and labor that are central to modern economics.

> I have always said that my ideal is that capital and labor should supplement and help each other. They should be a great family living in unity and harmony, capital not only looking to the material welfare of the laborers, but their moral welfare also—capitalists being trustees for the welfare of the laboring classes under them. (Gandhi, *Young India*, 20 August 1925, p. 285)

> I do not think there need be any clash between capital and labor. Each is dependent on the other. What is essential today is that the capitalist should not lord it over the laborer. In my opinion, the mill-hands are

as much the proprietors of their mills as the shareholders, and when the mill-owners realize that the mill-hands are as much mill-owners as they, there will be no quarrel between them. (Gandhi, *Young India*, 4 August 1927, p. 248)

Gandhi's views on capital and labor were a part of his total vision of Sarvodaya (that is, the welfare of all) and nonviolence. He was not opposed to industry and machines and even praised sewing machines that relieved tedium and favored industry that provided employment rather than saved labor, and at the same time led to self-sufficiency. Hence, we see his advocacy of village industry and weaving.

Gandhi considered dignity of labor as supreme and demonstrated his belief by his spinning wheel and through his insistence, early in his life, of his wife (Kasturba) cleaning the toilets. Further, he was against exploitative industry and his demonstrations and satyagraha in Kheda and Champaran were specifically for the abolishment of exploitative industry.

Gandhi led a labor strike at Ahmedabad in the spring of 1918, during the First World War. Though the strike attracted little attention, it had significant long-term results and implications as an experiment in the application of Gandhian ideas to industrial relations (Anjaneyulu, 1969). His ideas however evolved along with his ideas of Trusteeship and nonviolence.

Unlike Marx, who saw the interests of workers and capitalists as irreconcilable, Gandhi sought a new convergence of interests. Marx saw labor as being handicapped as it did not own the means and tools of production; Gandhi's charkha visualized the opposite reality. A worker can and should be able to provide for his or her basic needs through his or her own tools and ability to earn a living. In other words, there need not be an inherent conflict between labor and capital, and any dispute can be resolved nonviolently.

Village Production and Decentralization of Economy

Gandhi had anticipated the decentralization of economy based on the village as the epicenter of production a long way back. He had explained his central idea of village production and village self-sufficiency, i.e., Swadeshi in *Young India* in 1921 and had said,

> The central idea is not so much to carry on a commercial war against foreign countries as to utilize the idle hours of the nation and thus by natural processes to help it get rid of her growing pauperism. (Gandhi, *Young India*, 12 August 1921)

Gandhi's insistence on the principle of simple living and high thinking confused quite a few into supposing that he cherished poverty for poverty's sake. This was not the case. While he was studying law in London, he was known for his leanings towards elite sartorial styles. But, on witnessing the conditions under which the Indians lived in South Africa, he started moving towards aparigriha. It was much later, when he returned to India and travelled far and wide and saw the utter poverty of the masses, that he discarded his normal clothes and took to wearing just a small dhoti. His goal is clear from his writings,

> My ideal is equal distribution, but so far as I can see, it is not to be realized. I therefore work for equitable distribution. (UNESCO: *All Men are Brothers*, 1959, p. 129)

Decentralization of the economy to the village level was a part of his philosophy of Swadeshi (local and country made) and self-sufficiency. He was not against industry but against industry that resulted in unemployment. Employment and dignity of labor is a part of human dignity and meaningful full employment was a central part of economic philosophy (Ghosh, 2012).

Relevance of Gandhian Economics Today

The global economy has become far more complex than during Gandhi's time. Thus, while evaluating his economic views in today's context, one has to consider the central message he was trying to convey (Ishii, 2001). We examine each of the main ideas below.

Economic Growth: Modern economics measures economic growth by growth in productivity of goods and services, quantified as Gross Domestic Production or GDP. The concept of growth is evolving and countries such as Bhutan consider human happiness as a far better measure of growth. Many countries around the world are measuring health, education, and other indicators such as infant mortality rate or nutritional status and are of the view that these are superior indicators of growth. Gandhi was, thus, ahead of his time in focusing on human welfare as a measure of growth (Diwan, 1982).

Employment: One of the main aims of current economic management is full employment and is the focus of most central banks and monetary policies. Gandhi's focus on ensuring full employment, as part of Sarvodaya, through local and village industry was way ahead of his times. Today, the call is once again 'vocal for local' made imperative with the restrictions on movement of both people and products due to lockdowns during COVID-19 times.

Economic equity: Another aspect causing grave concern to economists, today, is regarding the rising income inequity in the world, bringing in its wake, divides of various kinds, including the digital divide. At the same time, it gives rise to most economic tensions and economic deprivations. Gandhi's advocacy of aparigriha and anasakti or non-possession and non-attachment, along with the idea of 'to each according to his needs' were attempts for the correction of income inequity through nonviolent means. One does not need to become an ascetic in order to follow aparigriha. If we were all able to adopt aparigriha to some extent, it would help fulfill the needs of many. As Gandhi always posited, there is enough for every man's needs but not for his greed.

Macroeconomic ideas: Macroeconomists aim at sustainable growth measured by full employment and a stable economic environment.

Market economy plays a large role in it. However, there is an increasing realization of the importance of government regulations.

There are many other market developments that could not have been anticipated in Gandhi's time. However, his basic concepts as applied to today's economic conditions provide us a wealth of tools and means for guiding economists (Ghosh, 2012). Gandhi insisted on parsimony both in individual and social life, which at the national level, translates into fiscal prudence—spending according to needs and in an efficient manner.

Most countries are trying to reach the poorest population today. Echoing the Gandhian approach, they focus on increasing human welfare or Sarvodaya. Most economists dismiss the fragmented economic approach and take a comprehensive view, just as Gandhi did, that addresses issues such as environment, cost of conflict, and basic human needs such as education and health. The United Nations Organization is doing its bit by establishing a set of Sustainable Development Goals as part of its Agenda 2030, at the base of which is the elimination of poverty, universal education, and the fight against climate change. It is, indeed, gratifying that many of these goals have been framed taking into account the principles and practices advocated by Gandhi. In their 2020 book, *Gandhi and the Psychology of Nonviolence*, authors Kool and Agrawal spell out, in detail, the ingenious ways through which UNESCO has been working with Gandhian ideals to promote universal education.

Applied Cases of Gandhian Economic Thought

Through my career at the International Monetary Fund (IMF), I had the opportunity to experience a variety of practical applications of Gandhian economics. While it would be beyond the scope of this chapter to delve into all of them, I will focus on three initiatives that have been able to bring about widespread change at the grass-root level.

Application of Gandhian economic thought at macro-level: One of my assignments in the IMF was the assessment of public finances, including budgets of different countries where the IMF had a surveillance role. Over a period of time, I saw a shift in this role, from a clinical macro-economic examination of the economy to advice on how to manage it. In cases where a country had borrowed money from the IMF, or wanted to borrow money, this was not just an advice but it was, generally, a condition for borrowing. However, these were conditions to improve the macro-economy and make it stable. The argument was that if a country is economically stable, the benefits would flow down to the poor. However, quite frequently, the economic conditions laid down by the IMF, such as increasing taxes on certain goods, affected the poor, adversely.

I was assigned to country X, an Islamic country, in a similar mission. The country had a system of Zakat, where people were obliged to pay a certain percentage of their income to a Zakat fund (managed by the government), which used the money for the poor. However, in practice, it was merged with the budget and it was indistinguishable if it was used for charity or not.

My mission team decided to recommend that the government should reduce its expenditure by a certain percentage and increase its revenue by increasing some taxes. Following Gandhian principles, I suggested that we should protect the poor from both increase in taxes and reduction in expenditures. Recalling, Gandhi's Salt March and taxes on salt as a regressive measure, we, as a team, recommended protecting expenditures that were pro-poor.

It is gratifying to note that during my many visits to that country, over the years, I noticed that this Gandhian principle had become a part of the economic philosophy of that country, clarifying that Gandhian principles are relevant, even, today.

Gandhian economics at the village level: A second case regarding the utilization of Gandhian economic thought that I would like to point out is of a non-government organization in India called Social Work Research Center (SWRC) in Tilonia village in Rajasthan in India.

The head of SWRC is a committed Gandhian, Sanjit Roy (also called Bunker Roy). One does not often come across people who have had their education at some of the most prestigious institutes going in for active social work. But, one such person is Sanjit 'Bunker' Roy who had his schooling and college education at two of the premier institutes of learning in India.

Roy has established a rural educational center called Barefoot College, operating along the Gandhian principles of Nai Talim based on teaching through handicraft (New Education), to teach people rural crafts. SWRC has expanded its frontiers across the globe and has brought much relief to many people. Today, the Barefoot College spans four continents and is operating in 93 countries. It has demonstrated that Gandhian thoughts on labor and village industry are very relevant today and can be used as an effective means for eradicating poverty and making a community self-sufficient.

With a slogan of 'BUILDING RESILIENT COMMUNITIES: One Woman at a Time', the college has a mission aimed at creating self-sufficiency at the village level. As Gandhi envisaged and practiced, bringing children to the cities for education was creating problems of alienation when they returned to the villages. Similarly, we are seeing the ever-increasing problems of migrant workers today, not only in India but in many parts of the world. How much better it would be if we could create opportunities for economic independency at the village level itself. This is what the Barefoot College strives for. In the words of the College,

> We've designed new ways to nurture and support a journey to empowerment, one village at a time, one woman at a time. We demystify and decentralize technology and put new tools in the hands of the underserved, with the objective to spread self-sufficiency and sustainability. With a geographic focus on the Least Developed Countries, we train women worldwide as solar engineers, entrepreneurs and educators, who then return to their villages to bring light and learning to their community. (www.barefootcollege.org)

Health care at village level: The **Comprehensive Rural Health Project (CRHP)** is a NGO located in the Jamkhed district of Maharashtra, India. It was founded in 1970 by a young dedicated couple, Drs. Raj and Mabelle Arole. Soon after completing their education, they decided to dedicate their lives to the upliftment of the poor and the needy. Being medical practitioners by training, they started by trying to impart awareness regarding health, hygiene, and sanitation at the village level. But much to their woe, they realized that the villagers were not keen at all. In order to understand the link between health and poverty, they decided to live on the same amount of money that the average village family earned, averaging a bare seven dollars a month. This helped them to understand that survival and fulfillment of basic needs of food, water, and shelter were much more important to the villagers than good health and hygiene.

The mission of the organization says it all,

Health is a fundamental human right. Eliminating injustices which deny all people access to this right underlies the very essence of our work and our approach. Using the combined talents and energy of our staff and the families we work with, we strive to develop communities through a grass-roots movement. By mobilizing and building the capacity of communities all can achieve access to health care and freedom from poverty, hunger and violence. (www.jamkhedcrhp.org)

The key change agent being utilized by the organization is the Village Health Worker, who is selected by the communities and trained by the organization. These health workers, often illiterate themselves, act not only as health workers and midwives but they also help to mobilize the village resources in terms of manpower and help the community to achieve better hygiene and sanitation, family planning, and maternal and child health care. Through their help, there has been significant reduction in infectious diseases such as HIV/AIDS, and other diseases such as tuberculosis and malaria.

The CRHP model which has won accolades both in India and abroad and today, partners with a variety of organizations, has been adapted and replicated at a large number of communities worldwide. It works with the community to provide health care and improve the general standard of living through women self-help groups, adolescent programs, and even farmer clubs. To date it has treated over 800,000 patients, trained 45,000 grass-root workers, planted 5.5 million trees, has over 300 village projects, and is operating in over 100 countries.

Apart from the case studies presented above, there are countless other organizations which are operating on the cooperative business model and are not only creating wealth but also empowering people and women in particular. Examples which immediately spring to one's mind are those of Gandhian Ela Bhatt who founded SEWA (Self Employed Women's Organization), which mobilizes women to use resources within 100 miles; the Gujarat Milk Marketing Federation Limited founded in 1946 by two visionary leaders today serves the people through 3.6 million milk producing members, with *Amul* being its well-known brand of milk, ice-cream, and other dairy products and the Shri Mahila Griha Udyog Lijjat Papad founded in 1959, growing by leaps and bounds and which, by 2018, had 43,000 employees.

Conclusion

How relevant are Gandhi's economic ideas today? How would he have reacted to the COVID-19 pandemic or to the global financial meltdown of 2008? The fundamentals of his economic ideas are very relevant today (Sandel, 2020). The village economy based on ever-widening oceanic circles that he had envisaged more than a century back is tenable even in the twenty-first century, as clarified by the examples provided above.

Prasanna (2019), too, provides an answer and writes in the *Indian Express*, 'Today, more than ever before, we need Gandhi's economic wisdom'. He continues by elaborating the views of a close associate of Gandhi and eminent economist, J. C. Kumarappa on 'economy of permanence'. Such an economy can only be created by thinking more about construction of jobs rather than production and profit, thinking more about saving nature rather than exploiting nature, and thinking more about sending people from the urban hubs armed with systems of modern management and production to the villages. In other words, writes Prasanna (ibid.),

We should inspire thousands of young people, who are falling on the street side every day because of job loss, inspire them to go to the village, and work like activists of the freedom struggle. Work like Kumarappa. He was an US-trained economist. He changed his dress, threw away his salary and happily worked amongst the people, improving the systems of production of handloom, oil, soap, etc. If we sit in our comfortable chairs and criticise others, the country will collapse. Gandhiji did not just talk. He acted.

Then only will we be able to see the fruition of Gandhi's dream, so well put by Nobel Laureate poet Rabindranath Tagore (1915, pp. 27–28).

Where the mind is without fear and the head is held high;
Where knowledge is free;
Where the world has not been broken up into fragments by narrow domestic walls;
Where words come out from the depth of truth;
Where tireless striving stretches its arms towards perfection;
Where the clear stream of reason has not lost its way into the dreary desert sand of dead habit;
Where the mind is led forward by thee into ever-widening thought and action
Into that heaven of freedom, my Father, let my country awake.

References

Anjaneyulu, V. (1969). Gandhian concept of industrial relations and its influence on Indian labor policy. *Indian Journal of Industrial Relations, 5*, 123–146.
Diwan, R. (1982). The economics of love, an attempt at Gandhian economics. *Journal of Economic Issues, 16*, 413–433.
Gandhi, M. K. (1921, December 8). *Young India.*
Gandhi, M. K. (1925, August 20). *Young India* (p. 285).
Gandhi, M. K. (1927, April 8). *Young India* (p. 248).
Gandhi, M. K. (1931, November 26). *Young India.*
Gandhi, M. K. (1931, December 31). *Young India* (pp. 427–428).
Gandhi, M. K. (1939, June 3). *Harijan* (p. 145).
Gandhi, M. K. (1946, March 31). *Harijan* (pp. 63–64).

Ghosh, B. N. (2012). *Beyond Gandhian economics*. Sage.

Ishii, K. (2001). The socio economic thoughts of Gandhi as an alternative of development. *Review of Social Economy, 59*, 297–312.

Kool, V. K., & Agrawal, R. (2020). *Gandhi and the psychology of nonviolence*. Palgrave Macmillan.

Kumarappa, J. C. (1951). *Gandhian economic thought*. Vora & Company.

Prasanna. (2019, October 19). Today, more than ever before, we need Gandhi's economic wisdom. *The Indian Express*. www.indianexpress.com

Sandel, M. (2020). *The Tyranny of merit: What's become of the common good?* Farrar, Straus & Giroux.

Tagore, R. (1915). *Gitanjali (song offerings)* (pp. 27–28). The Macmillan Company.

Tendulkar, D. G. (1953). *Mahatma* (Vol. VI, p. 293).

UNESCO. (1959). *All men are brothers* (p. 129).

www.barefootcollege.org

www.jamkhedcrhp.org

10

Turing Testing and Gandhi's Wisdom in the Era of Cognitive Computing

V. K. Kool and Rita Agrawal

Would you shy away from receiving wisdom emanating from God or for that matter from any reasonable source? And, if you are offered wisdom from one of the wisest human beings of the previous century, Gandhi, as had been sought by well-known scholars and leaders such as Einstein, Tutu, King, Obama, and others as stated in Chapter 1, would you like to have him around in the form of an artifact developed by using Artificial Intelligence (AI) in the shape of a robot much like the humanoid, Sophia, who has been found to be so human-like that she has been granted citizenship by South Arabia?

Look how computer games are engaging us and becoming popular not only among kids but almost among everyone of us. We play various computer games for long periods, getting so absorbed and enmeshed in

V. K. Kool (✉)
SUNY Polytechnic Institute, Utica, NY, USA

R. Agrawal
Harish Chandra Post Graduate College, Varanasi, Uttar Pradesh, India

© The Author(s), under exclusive license to Springer Nature Switzerland AG 2022
V. K. Kool and R. Agrawal (eds.), *Gandhi's Wisdom*,
https://doi.org/10.1007/978-3-030-87491-9_10

them that we begin to feel as if they were real and that they have become a part of our lives. In this chapter, we address issues on how wisdom can enable us to manage the impact of the ever-emerging technology around us.

Let us, first, focus on how technology enters our cognition. While talking to our pet, we begin to believe that the animal is sharing the perspective expressed in our communication including our feelings and emotions. Known as anthropomorphism, this is a natural tendency that enables us to perceive and interact with the world. Almost seven decades ago, Turing (1950), in a seminal article, *Computing Machinery and Intelligence*, proposed that with interactive features, machines could also be perceived as another person with intelligence. For this purpose, he set up a criterion, now known as the Turing Test, in which if a person is not able to distinguish between the responses of a human being and that of a machine, the machine is said to have passed the test. Turing's studies laid the foundation for the growth of Artificial Intelligence (AI).

The interesting part of AI is that even when the person knows that s/he is interacting with a computer, s/he is unable to stop social interactions that would have, normally, been given while interacting with a real person. Reeves and Nass (1998) contend that it is this natural tendency, or call it a weakness of human beings, that has led to the growth of computer games in which players interact with the focal character as predesigned in the software of the system. There are many such games, for example, *Second Life, The Sims, World of Warcraft*, with new ones appearing ever so often. Before we realize, each of these become much more than a game; we tend to become not only oblivious of the surroundings but also completely immersed in it, leading to the formation of what is described as the second self (Turkle, 2011).

Technology, in some form or the other, has been with us ever since humankind became conscious of its existence and began its attempt at mastering nature and all its vagaries. While highlighting the role of technology in our lives, Heidegger has differentiated between two aspects, *hervobringen*, that is to make things and *herausforden*, that is to change nature (as cited in Kool & Agrawal, 2016). Almost all technology can be classified according to these two categories.

Gradually but surely, the role of technology became a pervasive part of our lives, so much so that it has been forcing scientists to propose that humankind is undergoing two evolutions. On the one hand, there is the *biological evolution* following the Darwinian principles of survival of the fittest and natural selection. On the other hand, there is the *technological evolution* that is much more recent in origin and different in nature as compared to biological evolution, and upon which we have barely started reflecting. Human beings seem to be caught at the crossroad between the two.

The above can be clarified using an empirical study. Based on an example reported in the classic book by Hook (1960), *Dimensions of mind*, Kool asked his engineering students at the IIT, Bombay (now Mumbai), India in the 1970s to choose between a biological and a robotic spouse, with both having exactly the same mental and physical characteristics. Almost all of the students expressed their preference for a biological spouse. On the contrary, in the case of a prosthetic support, older people tended to prefer their mechanical limb as against the natural limb chosen by their younger counterparts. Almost 50 years later, it is clear that technology reigns on us. Yet, should its deployment not be rooted in our wisdom?

This dilemma is further exacerbated by the fact that these two evolutions, biological and technological, now seem to be undergoing a rather amazing twist. Biological evolution leads to the growth of cognition, which in turn, is the source of all technological development. However, over the course of years, technological evolution is altering the course of biological evolution through genetic engineering, internal prostheses, neurological implants, and other similar technologies. We seem to be caught in the proverbial chicken and hen puzzle—do biological forces lead to the advancement of technology or is it vice versa?

It would, perhaps, be better to think of biological forces on the one hand and technological forces on the other. Sandwiched between the two is a *third force, namely, human cognition*, which may be considered either as a byproduct of biological evolution, say, as in the school of thought known as behaviorism in psychology, or as an extension of the self, as argued by Turkle, in the domain of technological artifacts. In fact, all three are interdependent, making the entire set of relationships circular in nature (see Fig. 10.1).

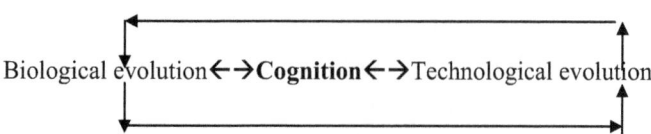

Fig. 10.1 Interdependence between biological evolution, technological evolution, and cognition

Beyond Darwin: Exaptation and Gandhi

When Gandhi was asked about his views on technology, he stated that he considered his own body to be a machine, thereby, amplifying the intertwined coexistence of the biological and technological forces. At the same time, he cautioned us that these two forces, that create and flourish us, might destroy us if we fail to carve and manage the third force, namely, cognition. With the ever-demanding, selfish genes of the biological system, the need to focus on survival takes precedence over all else and we tend to maximize the benefits of the resources around us for our children and for in-group members. In doing so, we, unwittingly, create "us–them" dichotomies and consequently, face competition, aggression, or even annihilation.

On the other hand, with wisdom, accumulated through folklores, mores, traditions, symbols, and language, we can maintain, practice, and improvise upon the treasures of our heritage and seek to harmonize them with the people and environment around us.

In the 1990s, researchers elaborated upon the ways in which the human brain, especially the cortex, grows and changes during the course of evolutionary natural selection processes (Buss et al., 1998; Gould & Vrba, 1982). In order to house new capabilities, new folds appear in the cortex, creating neurological space for the newly acquired capabilities required by the ever-changing environmental pressures. While these spaces are specifically created, other areas appear as by-products. The new spaces were called exaptations while the by-products of such exaptations were named spandrels, taking the analogy from the open areas under the pillars of a bridge which can then be used for purposes very different from that for which the bridge was constructed. Such exaptations and spandrels go a long way in enhancing our fitness for survival and adaptation (Buss et al., 1998; Gould & Vrba, 1982).

Exaptations, such as the above, occur not just in the brain but also in our very behavior. Originally, certain behaviors become part of our repertoire because they are necessary for survival but almost before we realize, they take on new unrelated purposes, often in utter disregard of the habitat and environment around us. Some examples are the enormous housing projects, originally needed to house the homeless, but which, over time, take on ugly, gargantuan proportions or, the creation of unlimited lethal weapons of mass destruction far more than that which is required for purposes of security.

It is a well-known fact that in order to fulfill our greed, we have abused technology in myriad ways, though purportedly, for some dubious consolations. For instance, while the construction of a bridge served the useful purpose of transportation to the other side of a river, the spaces under the bridge have also accorded homeless people with shelter, though in reality, they are still homeless!

Gandhi, more than a century ago, was deeply aware of the dangers of loosening the reins on human cognition and demonstrated empirically and scientifically through his experiments with truth, how our cognition must remain focused and allow for deep self-reflection working hand in glove with the context of social good. Then only would we be able to balance our behavioral exaptations as we navigate through both of the abovementioned evolutions. As Gandhi stated,

> What I object to is craze for machinery, not machinery as such. (Gandhi, 1924, p. 378)

Gandhi, further, established that only if human cognition is grounded in nonviolence, that is, if nonviolence forms the core of human cognition, will it help us in maximizing the coexistence of humankind with all forms sentient in the universe. He suggested that for peaceful coexistence, we need to continually build and reassess the third force mentioned above, that of cognition.

Leading us on, he proved through his satyagrahas that cognition can be fed by nonviolent schemas (or, mental plans, as discussed in Chapter 2) and scripts which then become amenable to priming, boosting, and nudging. The analogy that can be drawn is that of a computer system that needs to be consistently updated, so as to make it virus-free. Similarly, our cognition needs to be updated, clearing it from the virus of, and contamination from, violence.

If exaptation is the source of serendipity leading to new avenues of human wisdom, Gandhi anticipated its effects and led us in navigating the course of human cognition to forge a balance between the ruthlessness of biological evolution, on the one hand, and the consummation of technological evolution, on the other hand. Both are useful but it would need human endeavor, based on wisdom, to seek balance in our survival and well-being.

Cognizing Gandhi's Wisdom in Psychology of Technology

For any machine or robot to pass the Turing Test, especially in the context of Gandhi's wisdom, as reflected in his self-evaluation and correction in thinking, judgment, and behavior, we need to consider several criteria. These have been detailed below.

Relationship between cognition, biological evolution, and technological evolution: Probably, the most important aspect which requires consideration is regarding the relationship between cognition and the two evolutions, namely, biological evolution and technological evolution. Figure 10.1 depicts the status of cognition and its interconnectedness with organic sources and artifacts around it. As the reader can decipher, cognition remains the driver of both biological and technological forces, for, the biological aspect would be lost in the absence of human behavior, so necessary to feed the selfish genes. On the other hand, enhancing adaptation in the absence of technology would be unrealistic, as exemplified by communities such as the Amish, who, though known for their active avoidance of technology, have been unable to abandon it totally and have been forced to incorporate some technological artifacts into their lives.

Philosophy of technology and Gandhi: A second important aspect is the philosophy behind the technology. Before thinkers and scientists present any form of knowledge, they require a sound philosophy which should be well known to all concerned and should be firmly established. Every discipline is grounded in a philosophy which serves as the guiding post and enables decisions regarding the trajectory of its future development.

While the philosophy of science has been there for years together, forming the basis of all natural and social sciences including psychology, the emergence, and growth of the philosophy of technology has its roots only in the latter part of the previous century and is far less formidable than the philosophy of science (see Fig. 10.2 and the discussion on this topic in our book, *Psychology of Technology*, Kool & Agrawal, 2016). In the absence of a philosophy of technology, it is difficult, and even questionable, to define the applications of an intervention. For example, in developing an instructional technology using the Socrates' method, are we creating problems for a competing method (the Confucius method popular in the East) and is the former commensurate with the culture of members of other communities that engage in different ways of learning (Reeves & Nass, 1998)? This problem arises even when we offer Gandhi as a model for the trajectory for the advancement of technology. In the face of the lack of a robust philosophy of technology, certain questions could be raised—for example—why take Gandhi as an exemplar and not someone who has supported both violence and nonviolence?

Predictability: A third criterion for judging any technology is its predictability, since, the strength of any science is judged by the range of its predictability. Any alliance between scientific reasoning and its applied technological form is an invitation to its vulnerability because, in addition to a weak or almost non-existent philosophy of technology, the predictability of technology is extremely low and virtually impossible to gauge, both in terms of time and its substance. This has been corroborated by the findings of the National Science Foundation, USA, which is of the view that, at best, the future of any technology can be predicted

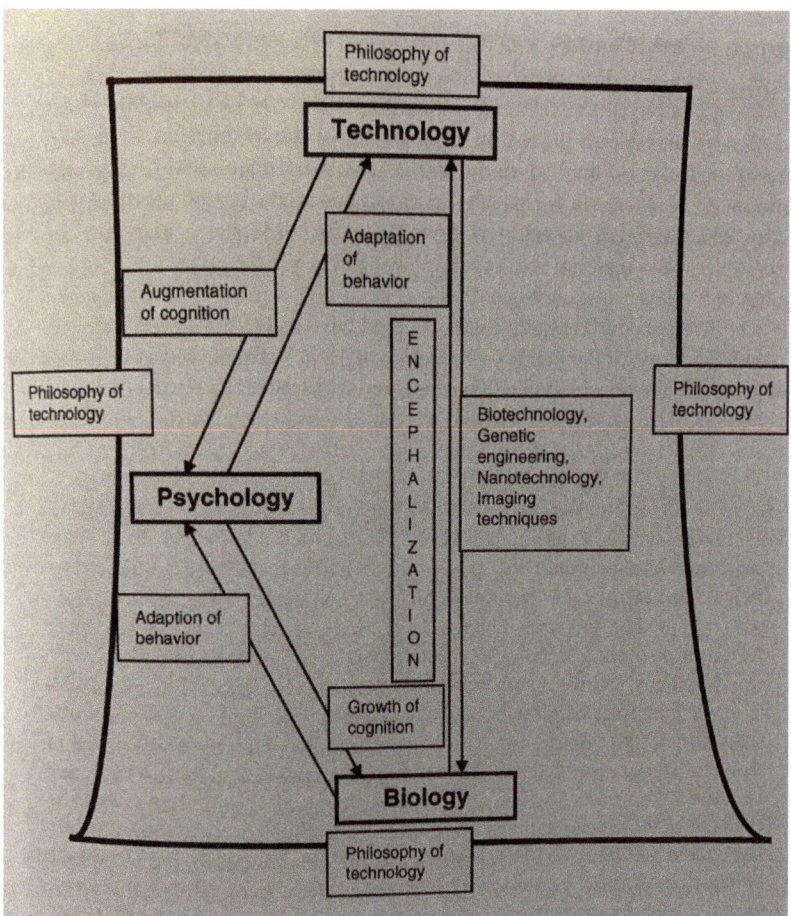

Fig. 10.2 A conceptual framework of psychology of technology (*Source* Kool & Agrawal [2016], *Psychology of Technology*. Switzerland: Springer, p. 31)

for about 20 years, with even these predictions failing to be completely reliable.

The above begs a question regarding the development of technological applications and the effectiveness of interventions sought through technology. In psychology, behavior modification, in the form of a popular and commonly used technique of behavioral technology, has been around us for quite some time. Undoubtedly, it helps, but at the same time, it also raises questions of ethicality (for example, the use of teaching machines developed by Skinner or the attempts of projecting Gandhi in a computerized form). Technocrats are of the opinion that, while Gandhi is still alive through almost 5000 books written on him in addition to several films, the use of interactive tools and Gandhi-type robots would bring about a rejuvenated interest in Gandhi and help us in the more effective dissemination of his message. Apparently, through the computerized iteration of Gandhi they are seeking advantages accruing from the Turkle's second self.

Incorporeality: Moving further, the question of the artificiality of AI raises another core issue in terms of incorporeality. Kompridis (2009) argues that technology is likely to disturb our normative ways of living, the ways through which we had inherited our culture. Basically, the application of technology raises a substantive issue regarding our very existence and engages us in attempts at deciphering between, "having a body and being a body, between what is born and what is made, between organic and manufactured life" (p. 25). This argument, drawn on phenomenological grounds, causes us to engage in apocalyptical thinking by asking if by deploying machines we would become unrecognizable as human beings. One thing is certain, that the deployment of machines for enhancing our capabilities would lead to asking ourselves what it means to be human.

At the same time, it is undeniably true that AI has become an integral part of our lives and is here to stay. While the use of technology in explaining Gandhi would be welcome, owing to its fundamental approach of seeking coexistence, the desirability of substituting or embodying Gandhi as "artificial" in AI is problematic since such efforts might appear as manipulations that offer affordance of Gandhi without any trace of the genuineness of the source or the messenger. Gandhi would, probably, not agree to the above, as he was always skeptical of those goals that were not in line with the purity of means embedded in truth and realized through the creed of nonviolence. As Bilgrami (2003) argues, desirability becomes the sine qua non when bridging the gap between theory and practice and for this purpose, the nomenclature "artificial" is certainly not helpful. In 1936, in reply to a Japanese corre-spondent who asked Gandhi as to whether he was against the machine age, he replied,

> To say that is to caricature my views. I am not against machinery as such, but I am totally opposed to it when it masters us. (Gandhi, *Harijan*, 1937)

Further, by presenting Gandhi in automated or semi-automated ways, for example, as a cyborg or as a zombie or by using super technologies to have him genetically engineered, would point directly to the source or authority initiating the creation and implementation of such technolo-gies. Have they lived and found Gandhi within themselves? And, if this is so, then to what extent have they succeeded in doing so? With things as they stand at present, the second self or the modified self, as offered by technology appears almost inevitable and calls for a philosophy of tech-nology rooted in nonviolence with Gandhi as a genuine exemplar; else, a technologically created Gandhi is likely to appear more distant and unrealistic than what we find him today.

William James, the founding father of modern psychology, was so correct in identifying the dangers of the conflict caused by the divided self of an individual facing a conflict—that between the self which knows what ought to be done and at the same time acknowledges its inability to do it or as St. Paul remarked, "The good I would, I do not, and that I would not, that I do." The use of technology is likely to reinforce this dilemma, if its creators fail to follow certain scruples. A good example of such a scenario would be that of a utility knife, which can be employed to butter a toast or for any other purposes, including our proneness to harm people or objects around us.

On the Applications of Converging Technologies and Cognitive Computing

The current trend in automation is that of incorporating features resembling those of humans, for example, emotions and feelings, and is certainly a welcome one. As discussed in the preceding paragraphs, the connotation of the word "artificial" in artificial intelligence has stood in the way of offering a unified perception of human–machine alliances. The "us–them" distinction bolstered by the selfish genes of our biological heritage also leads to questions about the incorporeality of technology as a second or modified self. The word "artificial" in AI or for that matter, in any type of automation, raises issues of "fusion with technology versus keeping our free will" or "living as technology determined versus naturally determined" and exacerbates the problem of the "us–them" dichotomy, and as such, calls for a replacement.

Some attempts have been made to tackle the abovementioned difficulties, one consequence of which is the development of technology that helps us to synchronize and interconnect all the gadgets we use. Such technologies have been called the Internet of Things (IoT). However, to be truly interactive, the machine must be intelligent, a limitation that has been mitigated through a paradigm called cognitive computing or CIoT, claiming to offer far more sophistication than the earlier efforts at unifying human–machine interaction.

Basically, cognitive computing, in its current form of usability and service, involves predicting results obtained from machines and deciding whether humans or machines should be used to accomplish the tasks. Machine intelligence in the domain of cognitive computing has been identified at four levels, Fig. 10.3:

1. *Mechanical*: involving learning and adaption with precision and consistency.
2. *Analytical*: involving rule learning as in the computerized version of a chess player.
3. *Intuitive*: involving artificial neural networks, hard thinking, and statistical models, as is done by a poker player.

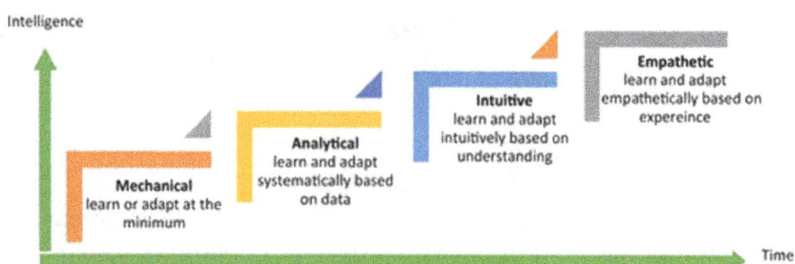

Fig. 10.3 Four levels of cognitive computing

4. *Empathetic*: incorporating emotions in decision-making, for example, as embodied in Sophia, a humanoid robot that was granted citizenship by the government of South Arabia.

The last level of intelligence, #4, reflects the most advanced level in the hierarchy and is geared toward the generation of self-learning and connectivity (Huang & Rust, 2018). Additionally, the developments in cognitive computing have sparked interdisciplinary research blurring the boundary between physical, digital, and biological spheres, as contended in the thesis of the Fourth Industrial Revolution and posited by Krause Schwab (2017), following mechanization, mass production, and electronic booms constituting industrial revolutions of the first, second, and third order. This fourth revolution is expected to create rules, norms, and incentives that would reshape the ways of not only communication and entertainment but also interpersonal relationships and, additionally and most importantly, our conception of human beings.

In general, by increasing the levels of predictability and continuously augmenting and mimicking, the machines appear to be behaving very much like human beings, with technologists finding some consolation from the Turing Test. The above has been put very succinctly by Huang and Rust (2018):

> However, just as in the Turing test, as long as AI "demonstrates" emotions, for the purpose of service provision, it may not matter how they achieve that. The debate about the nature of empathetic AI employs arguments similar to those the debate about whether intuitive AI can think like humans.

Did you notice the phrase "...it may not matter how they achieve that" in the quote above? From the sentence, it is clear that ends seem to be more relevant than the means used to achieve those ends, an issue totally discredited by Gandhi, whose emphasis was on means, not ends. Throughout his life, Gandhi taught us to focus on the clarity, genuineness, and purity of means before embarking on the journey for the achievement of certain ends. According to veteran Gandhi scholar Raghavan Iyer (1983), for Gandhi, any accomplishment of goals was futile if the desirability of the means did not emanate from our conscience and failed to be tested in terms of the appropriate means around us.

Perspectives in Living with Humanoid Gandhi

From the above discussion, it is clear that, so far, the efforts in cognitive computing are confined to the development and demonstration of human intelligence in machine operation. However, psychologists have, now, argued that wisdom, not intelligence, is needed to deal with the problems of the present-day world. Huang and Rust (2018) put the same issue in the form of a question by asking whether we would ever be able to develop collective intelligence. While Droid's "collective commons," obtained through pooling the best solutions from the minds of people on our planet and seeking an innovation that would be reduced to minutes or even less as compared to our decades of waiting to occur, might sound doable and optimistic, the wisdom of machines does not appear to be in the menu of cognitive computer experts.

In the absence of wisdom, robots around us might create a scenario similar to that witnessed in Pierre Boyle's novel, *In the Planet of Apes*, in which creatures, with intelligence resembling that of humans, create a wide variety of problems related to survival. In fact, as and when robots do exceed human intelligence, will they have enough wisdom and how would they be set up to coexist with other human beings or are we building them to learn to coexist with other human beings as a substitute or even as a partner?

The above scenarios bring us back to the point from where we had started, that is, if intelligence is not considered enough to solve world problems and has led psychologists to focus on wisdom, the current status of interdisciplinary research in cognitive computing puts us at the same crossroad where psychology was in the not too distant past. While we do not aim to be pessimistic, yet, attempts to seek real reality in the use of artificial intelligence begs a question regarding the future of human beings. Do we need more company than what we already have in addition to other living beings and natural things around us?

Also, are we, genuinely, curious to interact with a new phenomenon based on technology, albeit exceeding our capabilities and intelligence and at the same time, let it govern and dictate us? While we do face this very same dilemma at the biological level allowing our children to excel in ways that they intend to, but do we also seek such a course in developing technologies? While the philosophy of life is deeply rooted in survival and the raising of our offsprings, will it also apply to mechanical artifacts like robots around us?

When prominent behavioral psychologist Skinner was asked if he would prefer his books to be saved over his children, he remarked that between his books and his children, he would prefer his books to be saved. Paraphrasing the same scenario, one could ask whether humanoids should be saved in preference to actual human beings. After South Arabia granted citizenship to the humanoid, Sophia, should such humanoids be entitled to the same rights, privileges, and other affordances that humans currently enjoy?

For Gandhi, the central issue was how nonviolence should be designed and implanted in the architecture of our brain. Unlike eminent psychologist Skinner, he was opposed to violence toward anything, including Skinner's books or his children. He was even opposed to the killing of a snake at his ashrams (his residence). He had no problem with any technology in as much as the sanctity of life was preserved, peaceful means remain rooted in using technology, and the goals, in conjunction with or without technology, did not take precedence over any peaceful means. He clearly distinguished between modernization and modernity, realizing that while human beings have thrived with the use of technology, its unlimited and uncontrolled use was against wisdom rooted in survival.

Further, wisdom clarified that survival could be best achieved through principles of nonviolence, for "an eye for an eye would leave the whole world blind" (reference to our interview with Justice Dharmadhikari, a close associate of Gandhi, on February 2017 in Mumbai, India and reported in our book, *Gandhi and the Psychology of Nonviolence, Volumes 1 and 2*, Kool & Agrawal, 2020).

Research Trajectory for Studying Gandhi's Wisdom

Following British philosopher Bertrand Russel's pragmatism highlighting the fact that what is useful is useful and the usefulness of any useful approach must be pursued to assess the outcomes, it is contended here that digitizing Gandhi is a welcome move and one that is gaining ground in several continents and growing with the support of the UNESCO. However, such efforts need to be rooted in a sound philosophy of technology. So long as they operate with the objective of helping us to remember and emulate, it is similar to creating another new medium just as we moved from writing symbols on stones to writing on paper and then on to printing and announcing on radios and finally, presenting it through multimedia. Creating Gandhi in computerized forms might have its own value, but for now, neither can Gandhi's intelligence nor his wisdom be tracked, cognized, or wired through a humanoid form, even more so, in the absence of a well-defined philosophy of technology. What we have are snapshots of Gandhi and in such scenarios, as Easwaran (1983), another leading scholar on Gandhi, contended, Gandhi would be difficult, or even impossible, to understand with fragmentation of his holistically configured life rooted in the context of the wisdom of nonviolence.

For psychology, convergent technologies offer a silver lining, since cognition is among its four core components, the other three being Nanotechnology, Biotechnology, and Information Technology, as reported by the National Science Foundation's project report on converging technologies (depicted as a tetrahedron, Fig. 10.4). In its report, it is stated,

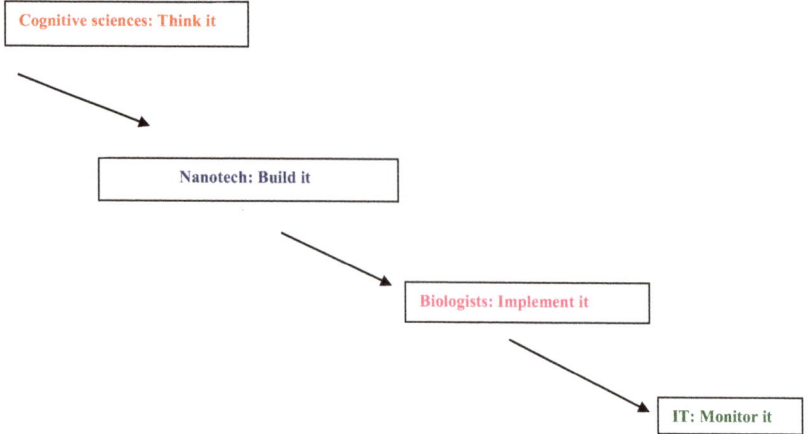

Fig. 10.4 Convergent technologies NBIC (Nano-Bio-Info-Cog) (*Source* Adapted from Kool & Agrawal, 2016)

"Allow us for the first time to understand the natural world and cognition in terms of complex, hierarchical systems." (p. 3) and, "Each scientific and engineering field has much to contribute to enhancing human abilities, to solving the pressing problems of the twenty-first century; but combined, their potential contribution is vast." (p. 4)

One problem with the growth of psychology is that during its inception it leaned heavily on the developments in the field of biology, including comparative biology, sought its growth through studies of pathological forms of behavior and is, now, leaning on converging technologies for the understanding of human behavior. This poses an existential threat to psychology which can be overcome through the ripening of the discipline, evolving in the form of a dynamic interface in which the user utilizes "the computer as a tool that frames its appropriate forms" (Glassman, 2012, p. 311). The good news is that with the current focus on wisdom in psychology, the imminent threat posed by the current wave of cognitive computing and machines attempting to regulate and control the level #4 functions will be afforded some respite.

As mentioned above, human intelligence has offered only limited support to the understanding of human problems (Sternberg et al., 2019) and as machines become ready to substitute intelligence, we reiterate that, with the collapse of psychology of wisdom, the thinness of human cognition would increase. The core of nonviolence, as revealed and expanded in the context of studying and developing cognition, whether emanating from any of the sources, biological, technological, or mixed as in the second self, would need wisdom for recognizing ourselves as human beings.

So, if psychology is to find its niche by shifting gears in the study of behaviors ranging from its pathological roots to finding its positive forms and more recently, by employing computer models, it needs to embark deeply and extensively in the field of psychology of nonviolence (Kool, 2008). This subfield of psychology is vital as it affords opportunities for the coexistence of all things sentient. Scholars, for example, Professor Michael Nagler (1990) of UC-Berkeley, have been arguing for the development of a science of nonviolence (please also refer to his article in this book and to our two-volume book on *Gandhi and the Psychology of Nonviolence*, Kool & Agrawal, 2020). Further, Murray et al. (2014) summarize in their chapter, *Toward a Psychology of Nonviolence*:

> Although there have been some efforts to develop a psychology of nonviolence (e.g., Kool, 2008), and the APA has had a division of peace psychology since 1988, the potential for contributions of psychology to the study and practice of nonviolence has been largely untapped. The possibilities, however, are exciting. We have only enough space to make a few suggestions. Kool (2008) gives a far more extensive discussion. (p. 179)

With a focus on psychology of nonviolence, we propose that it will be prudent to pursue research on wisdom in two ways. First, in consonance with a computer analogy-based information processing approach to study human cognition or its variant alternative as in humanoids, nonsocial objects need to be tested and their relevance be determined in having and augmenting human cognition. In the absence of a philosophy of technology, the curiosity in developing such artifacts is handy and could be useful, but it is certainly not fully ready, at least for now. Many abuses of technology are not known until they reach some catastrophic levels, as we are witnessing during the current COVID-19 pandemic. For now, forget applications to human cognition. The service industry, according to Huang and Rust (2018), is reluctant to reap the benefits of cognitive computing for reasons ranging from security to labor issues. Simply put, the intelligence developed through such intelligent products does not see wisdom in the deployment of such artifacts (Box 10.1).

In short, deep learning algorithms have helped the machines in building and operating machines intelligently at the level #4, but they have limited use in unpredictable, novel situations as compared to human beings who use commonsense to understand and deal with the way the world works in general. For example, if an unknown baby falls down, we use our attributions and intent to take decisions regarding helping her but it could be very specific to the wisdom rooted in a culture, as child-rearing practices differ from culture to culture.

Box 10.1 The Future of Wisdom: On Creating a Machine That We Cannot Control

Gandhi's wisdom is best understood in the context of our ability to exercise self-control leading to the optimizing of survival. While he set a number of examples to demonstrate this remarkable ability of controlling himself, he was also very successful in inspiring millions of people to join him in cultivating this cardinal virtue (Kool & Agrawal, 2018). Can we teach this virtue to super-intelligent machines?

Unfortunately, machines cannot always be controlled, contend Alfonseca and his team of researchers (2021), because the algorithms developed to simulate AI working do not in any way guarantee that it will not lead to any harm. In other words, out of Asimov's three laws of robotics, the one that is geared to express no harm or injury is unsustainable in the context of what we know now about the state of affairs in the realm of AI. Nick Bostrom of the Future of Humanity Institute, Oxford University, contends that with super-intelligent robots around, humans may not be able to train and manage them. His thesis is based on two issues related to controls: one, what AI can do, and the other, what it intends to do. Summarizing Bostrom's argument, Charles Choi (2021), stated,

The problem with the former is that Bostrom thought a super-smart machine could probably break free from any bonds we could make. With the latter, he essentially feared that humans might not be smart enough to train a super-intelligent AI.

Gandhi was right again (as stated by Stricker, 2000). He was always in favor of technology and supported its role in human life. At the same time, he warned us about its detrimental effects, including the ways in which it would ruin human dignity and survival. For more details, see our book, *Psychology of Technology* (Kool & Agrawal, 2016) and Chapter 3, Gandhi and the psychology of technology, in Volume 2, *Gandhi and the Psychology of Nonviolence*, by Kool and Agrawal (2020).

There is nothing to lose in studying Gandhi's wisdom in the context of modern psychological science of behavior that is significantly engaged in finding an alternate to intelligence in order to address global problems. Gandhi's wisdom, attested by luminaries such as Einstein, grew because, to a very great extent, it was rooted in at least three continents of the globe. Pick his macro behavior, such as satyagraha that taught millions of people to practice self-control and many other forms showing empathy, compassion, and more, or his micro behavior, rooted in fasting and silence, and you will find plenty of wisdom out there, waiting to be cognized and demonstrated for social and personal good (Kool, 2013; Kool & Agrawal, 2013). Whether Gandhi's wisdom is found in those humans trying to emulate Gandhi, as one of the most prominent scholars on human intelligence Howard Gardner, of Harvard University, who actually wishes to be like him, or is taught by a robot, it's a win–win situation to learn wisdom from one of the wisest human beings of the previous century. However, the ultimate decision regarding the preference between the two sources of wisdom will rest in the wisdom of the user.

Gandhi said that there was nothing new in his nonviolence, for nonviolence is as old as the hills, and so is wisdom with its roots in nonviolence. His wisdom in the use of technology has its own universal appeal and offers help to its developers in seeking a genuine philosophy for their discipline. Therefore, we need a philosophy of technology before we embark further on the road to technological advancement. Technology must take into account our responsibilities toward one another and afford self-realization so as to make a positive impact on our identity, community, and political system. More than 70 years ago, Erikson (1969), in his classic book, *Gandhi's Truth*, had warned about genuine messages of Gandhi being lost in the "images, impulses and ritualizations" with the passage of time. The possibility of this is even more so with the Fourth Industrial Revolution that was nonexistent at the time of Erikson. In addition to the converging technologies and the tetrahedron of the National Foundation of Science, the call of the hour is the sharing of converging goals and means. We end by quoting Erikson, "…indeed, only faith gives back to man the dignity of nature" (p. 435).

References

Alfonseca, M., Cebrian, M., Anta, A. F., Coviello, L., Abeliuk, A., & Rahwan, I. (2021). Superintelligence cannot be contained: Lessons from computability theory. *Journal of Artificial Intelligence Research, 70,* 65. https://doi.org/10.1613/jair.1.12202

Bilgrami, A. (2003). Gandhi the philosopher. *Economic and Political Weekly,* pp. 38–39.

Buss, D. M., Haselton, M. G., Shackelford, T. K., Bleske, A. L., & Wakefield, J. C. (1998). Adaptations, exaptations, and spandrels. *American Psychologist, 53,* 533–548.

Choi, C. Q. (2021, January 18). Superintelligent AI may be impossible to control: That's the good news. *IEEE Spectrum.* Spectrum.ieee.org

Easwaran, E. (1983). *Gandhi the man.* Random House.

Erikson, E. (1969). *Gandhi's truth.* Norton.

Gandhi, M. K. (1924, June 26). *Young India.*

Gandhi, M. K. (1937, February 27). *Harijan,* p. 18.

Glassman, M. (2012). An era of webs: Technique, technology and the new cognitive (r)evolution. *New Ideas in Psychology, 30,* 308–318.

Gould, S. J., & Vrba, E. S. (1982). Exaptation—A missing term in the science of form. *Paleobiology, 8,* 4–15.

Hook, S. (1960). *Dimensions of mind.* New York University Press.

Huang, M., & Rust, R. T. (2018). Artificial intelligence in service. *Journal of Service Research, 21*(2), 155–172. https://doi.org/10.1177/109467051775 2459

Iyer, R. (1983). *The moral and political thought of Mahatma Gandhi*. The Concord Group of Press.

Kompridis, N. (2009). Technology's challenge to democracy: What of the human. *Parrhesia, 8*, 22–33.

Kool, V. K. (2008). *The psychology of nonviolence and aggression*. Palgrave Macmillan.

Kool, V. K. (2013). Applications of Gandhian concepts in psychology and allied disciplines. *Indian Journal of Psychiatry, 55*, 235–238.

Kool, V. K., & Agrawal, R. (2013). Whither Skinner's science of behavior, his assessment of Gandhi, and its aftermath? *Gandhi Marg, 35*, 487–518.

Kool, V. K., & Agrawal, R. (2016). *Psychology of technology*. Springer.

Kool, V. K., & Agrawal, R. (2018). Gandhian philosophy for living in the modern world: Lessons from the psychology of satyagraha. In S. Fernando & R. Moodley (Eds.), *Global psychologies: Mental health and the global south*. Palgrave Macmillan.

Kool, V. K., & Agrawal, R. (2020). *Gandhi and the psychology of nonviolence, Volumes 1 and 2*. Palgrave Macmillan.

Murray, H., Lyubansky, M., Miller, K., & Ortega, L. (2014). Toward a psychology of nonviolence. In E. Mustakova-Possardt, M. Lyubanski, et al. (Eds.), *Toward socially responsible psychology for a global era* (pp. 151–182). Springer.

Nagler, M. N. (1990). Nonviolence as new science. In V. K. Kool (Ed.), *Perspectives on nonviolence* (pp. 131–139). Springer.

Reeves, B., & Nass, C. (1998). *The media equation: How people treat computers, television, and mass media like real people and places*. Cambridge University Press.

Schwab, K. (2017). *The fourth industrial revolution*. Crown Business/Random House Penguin.

Sternberg, R. J., Nusbaum, H. C., & Gluck, J. (2019). *Applying wisdom to contemporary problems*. Palgrave Macmillan.

Stricker, G. (2000). The scientist practitioner model: Gandhi was right again. *American Psychologist, 55*, 254.

Turing, A. M. (1950). Computing machinery and intelligence. *Mind, 49*, 433–460.

Turkle, S. (2011). *Alone together: Why we expect more from technology and less from each other*. Basic Books.

11

Situated Moral Practice: Resisting Authority in Stanley Milgram's "Obedience" Experiment

Jason Turowetz and Matthew M. Hollander

There is perhaps no better exemplar of civil disobedience to immoral authority than Mohandas Gandhi. By the time his decades-long campaign for Indian independence succeeded in 1947, Gandhi had been practicing, refining, and teaching his methods of nonviolent resistance (*satyagraha*) for many years, first in South Africa (1906–1915) and subsequently in his native India (1915–1948). His steadfast commitment to nonviolence proved revolutionary and required tremendous discipline and self-restraint. More than once, his followers erupted in violence against their British colonial oppressors, as when a crowd in the town of Chauri Chaura surrounded and killed 21 policemen. Gandhi responded to that episode by canceling his campaign in the region and denouncing

J. Turowetz (✉)
University of Siegen, Siegen, Germany

M. M. Hollander
Marion Technical College, Marion, OH, USA
e-mail: hollanderm@mtc.edu

© The Author(s), under exclusive license to Springer Nature
Switzerland AG 2022
V. K. Kool and R. Agrawal (eds.), *Gandhi's Wisdom*,
https://doi.org/10.1007/978-3-030-87491-9_11

the violence, though he was eventually sentenced to prison for six years on a charge of sedition (Gardner, 2008/1997, p. 106). Setbacks like this could easily have deterred Gandhi or made him question his strategy of passive resistance. Instead, he treated them as learning opportunities, failed experiments that called for new ways of performing nonviolent resistance rather than its abandonment. His unwavering commitment to doing what is morally right, even in the face of unanticipated consequences and failures, became a key model for future generations of antiracism and anticolonialism leaders such as Martin Luther King Jr., in the United States, who took to heart Gandhi's view that obedience to immoral authority goes against the wisdom of co-survival.

Likewise, Stanley Milgram (1933–1984) refers to Gandhi in his 1974 book on the most famous (and controversial) social psychological lab experiment (1961–1962) of the twentieth century: obedience to authority. As readers will recall, Milgram's cover story had research participants ("Teachers") delivering seemingly lethal electroshocks to an unwilling peer (the confederate "Learner") at the behest of a scientist authority figure (the confederate "Experimenter") conducting a "learning and memory experiment" at Yale University (Milgram, 1974; Perry, 2013). This chapter contributes to the ongoing renaissance of interest in Milgram (Gibson, 2019) by connecting his work to recent research on morality (Hollander & Turowetz, forthcoming). We treat Milgram's lab as a sociological case study of situated moral practice in social interaction, highlighting connections between moral action and power. Though morality and power—topics often overlooked by Milgram scholarship—are not always so intertwined in everyday life, the experiment tightly coupled them by forcing participants to make morally charged decisions that entailed the exercise of power: either *over* the Learner or *against* the Experimenter. Below, we first say more about morality and power in Milgram's lab, then introduce our data and methods. Second, we examine directive-response conversational sequences in the experiment, which formed the local environment for participant resistance. Third, we show how acts of resistance and compliance occurred in a context of competing sequential relevancies (stopping vs. continuing) by which Milgram's experimental design restricted participants' actions. Finally, we discuss implications of our study of Milgram and morality for research on Gandhi, civil disobedience, and social movements.

Situated Moral Practice in Milgram's Lab

When Milgram's participants entered the lab, they believed they were participating in a study of learning and memory. As the experiment progressed, however, they found themselves being asked to shock a fellow participant, the Learner, against his will. What began as an ordinary experiment gradually developed into a tense standoff between a Learner who refused to go on with the experiment and an Experimenter who insisted that they continue. Teachers (i.e., participants) found themselves caught between two incompatible sets of demands: the Learner's demands they stop the experiment, and the Experimenter's directives to continue shocking him. The participants had a moral obligation not to harm a fellow human being. But they also had an institutional obligation to comply with the Experimenter's instructions, as he was the authority figure in charge and they had agreed to participate (on the distinction between *moral* obligations that regulate interaction and *normative* obligations created by institutions, see Rawls, 1987).

Although in hindsight we see the participants facing a stark moral dilemma, the situation was less clear for those who experienced it. The Experimenter asserted that the experiment was an ordinary study of learning and memory, and that while the shocks may be painful, the Learner would not suffer any permanent harm. By contrast, the Learner insisted he was in pain, worried out loud about his health, and demanded release. Should the participant trust the Experimenter—who seemed to be an expert at a prestigious university—or question his dismissal of the Learner's wishes?

Our methodology of conversation analysis (CA; see below) posits social actions as simultaneously context-shaped and context-renewing (Heritage, 1984). An action depends on a context of immediately prior actions for its intelligibility while also renewing that context and the local meanings it embeds. Context is an ongoing achievement by and for social actors, who must constantly renew its relevancies. But meanings are ever subject to revision: instead of simply renewing a given context, actors could challenge it, retrospectively altering the meaning of prior actions and prospectively projecting new contextual relevancies for themselves and their co-actors. When Milgram's participants *complied* with the Experimenter's directives, they renewed the context he proposed and its definition as a benign study of learning and memory. In Goffman's (1959, pp. 9–10) terms, they were renewing a *working consensus* whereby "the definitions of the situation projected by the several different participants" were "sufficiently attuned to one another so that open contradiction will not occur," and doing so despite any private misgivings they may have felt. Conversely, by *resisting* the Experimenter's directives, participants constituted themselves as defiant, at least momentarily threatening the prevailing working consensus and raising the possibility that the experiment was not benign after all. Among other things, this could potentially call into question the Experimenter's competence to assess the Learner's condition, along with his situated authority.

By challenging the local working consensus, participant defiance frequently brought a previously invisible moral dilemma to the surface. In our data, we see Milgram's Teachers orienting to possible moral violations well before they performed explicit resistance. In everyday interaction, participants are expected to protect the selves projected by others and expect that others will do the same for them in return (Goffman, 1955; Rawls, 1987, p. 142). This is not just a practical matter, but a *moral* one: self is a social object that depends for its achievement on recognition from others. If such recognition and the involvement obligations that go along with it are not respected, social order and the identities it supports cannot exist (Rawls, 1987, pp. 139–140). It follows that moral obligations are endogenous to society and everyday affairs, rather than being grafted onto them from without. As Garfinkel (1967, p. 35) observed: "A society's members encounter and know the moral order as perceived normal courses of action—familiar scenes of everyday affairs, the world of daily life known in common with others and with others taken for granted." That is, the social order is also a moral order (Turowetz & Maynard, 2010).

When Teachers first hear the Learner cry out in pain and hesitate to continue the experiment, halting its progress for even a few seconds, they perform silent resistance that orients, at least tacitly, to a potential moral violation. But such resistance is only implicit until participants start to explicitly push back against the Experimenter. In the end, what distinguished the "obedient"-outcome participants from the "disobedient" ones was not resistance—almost all participants showed at least minimal resistance—but the ability to *sustain* that resistance over time, refusing to renew the relevance of the Experimenter's directives unless he first honored his moral obligations to the Learner (e.g., by remedying his complaints).

We follow Bergmann (1998) in distinguishing between the morality of interaction and morality in interaction (see also Turowetz & Maynard, 2010). Morality *of* interaction describes the tacit moral order of everyday life, the set of unspoken expectations to which members of society adhere as a matter of course. By contrast, morality *in* interaction refers to actions that make implicit moral assumptions explicit, as actors invoke rights, responsibilities, and blame in their dealings with one another. Whereas morality of interaction operates at a tacit level, morality in interaction is explicitly observable in social actions—such as accounting for one's conduct (Garfinkel, 1967)—and can become a topic for members in its own right.

In Milgram's lab, acts of inexplicit resistance displayed awareness of the tacit moral order of everyday life by registering that a potential violation had occurred. However, such resistance remained subterranean and indirect unless and until it was upgraded through an overt orientation to moral accountability *in* interaction. And this was something defiant-outcome participants did more often, and more successfully, that their obedient-outcome counterparts.

Moral Resistance and Power

Because all participants resisted, all were defiant on at least some occasions. Similarly, all participants obeyed the Experimenter to some degree, making them obedient at least some of the time. The dialectic of resistance and compliance suggests the pervasiveness of power dynamics in Milgram's lab. As the experiment progressed, participants were repeatedly confronted with the choice of cooperating with the Experimenter to exercise power *over* the Learner, or alternatively resisting and exercising power *against* the Experimenter. This dialectic was intimately connected to participants' moral and institutional obligations: fulfilling their moral obligations to the Learner necessitated exercising power against the Experimenter, while fulfilling their institutional obligations to the Experimenter meant exercising power over the Learner. Though morality and power are not always so intertwined in everyday life, Milgram's experiment tightly coupled them by design.

In sociology, modern theories of power stress its multidimensionality (e.g., Foucault, 2012/1975; Lukes, 2004/1974; Mann, 2012/1986; Reed, 2013). But although power is certainly multidimensional, theories of power generally neglect its interactional dimension. This is a problem, because while power is encoded in symbols and built into hierarchies, it lives in the details of interaction, in the practices and orientations of actors assembling meanings and identities on a turn-by-turn basis. Even the most firmly entrenched power relations are situated accomplishments dependent on the sequential organization of social action. The achieved character of power, however, is often invisible (Rawls & Duck, 2020). Like other routine phenomena, when everything runs smoothly, power dynamics operate in the background of social life, forming the taken for granted, seen but unnoticed backdrop (Garfinkel, 1967) against which people carry on their ordinary affairs. When interactional troubles arise, however, what is ordinarily hidden in plain view comes into focus, frequently in the form of bald commands, reprimands, sanctions, punishments, and resistance.

This is precisely what happened in Milgram's lab. Beyond a certain point in the experiment, participants were recurrently pressured to exercise power, and in the process constitute themselves as compliant or defiant. These situated identities were in turn reflexively tied to the local working consensus: by engaging in acts of compliance, participants renewed the official definition of the situation and tacitly affirmed the Experimenter's competence and authority, whereas through acts of defiance, they threatened that consensus and its assumption that the experiment was benign. In constituting themselves as compliant or defiant, therefore, participants simultaneously supported or challenged the official definition of the situation, which then fed back into their situated identities. Accordingly, the Milgram setting and its inhabitants were very much moving targets: fluid entities only fixed in place, so to speak, through the retrospective application of categories and classifications.

In our empirical analysis below, we examine power and moral action as Milgram's participants worked them out in real time. In particular, we show how participants' acts of resistance and compliance, both small and large, contributed to outcomes that Milgram could categorize as "obedient" or "disobedient."

Data and Methods

Our data are 117 audio-recorded sessions from the Milgram Obedience Experiment obtained from the Milgram Archive at Yale University. In addition to the sessions themselves, the recordings also include debriefing interviews that Milgram's Experimenter conducted with participants immediately after each session ended. The recordings are drawn from five of Milgram's 24 experimental conditions: 2 and 3 ("Voice-feedback" and "Proximity"), 20 ("Women as subjects"), 23 ("Bridgeport": downtown office building location rather than Yale), and 24 ("Bring a friend": participants had a preexisting relationship). 64 of our recordings have an "obedient" outcome; the remaining 53 are "defiant" (Table 11.1).

We analyzed the data using conversation analysis (CA), which works with audio and video recordings of naturally occurring interactions to identify tacit rules and procedures actors use to assemble and organize social actions (Schegloff, 2007). Because these actions are organized at a level of detail often invisible to researchers, conversation analysts create

Table 11.1 Corpus of transcripts

Condition	2	3	20	23	24	Total
obedient outcome	25	6	22	9	2	64
disobedient outcome	15	15	15	5	3	53
Total	40	21	37	14	5	117

specialized transcripts capturing such nuances as silences (in tenths of a second), vocal emphasis, pitch, loudness, and overlapping talk.

The Sequential Context of Resistance: Directive-Response Sequences

CA research has shown that many social actions are organized as "adjacency pairs." This is a sequence of two paired actions where the first pair part makes a specific second pair part the conditionally relevant next action (Schegloff & Sacks, 1973). Examples include question–answer, offer-acceptance/declination, assessment-agreement/disagreement, blame-apology, invitation-acceptance/declination, complaint-remedy, and request-granting/denial. First pair parts are said to *structurally prefer* certain second part responses and disprefer others—for example, offers prefer acceptances, complaints prefer remedies, requests prefer granting, assessments prefer agreement, and so forth. We say "structurally" prefer to distinguish our use of preference from the more common psychological usage, which refers to private mental states. For conversation analysts, preference is built into the social order properties of interaction and preferred actions have distinctive features: they are produced immediately, without hesitation, and perform the action projected by the first pair part. Dispreferred actions, by contrast, are frequently delayed and accompanied by hesitation, disfluency, accounts, and palliatives (Heritage, 1984).

In the Milgram setting, the most pervasive adjacency pair is directive-response. In a basic sense, directives can be characterized as "utterances designed to get someone to do something" (Goodwin, 2006, p. 517). In directive-response sequences, compliance is structurally preferred and resistance is dispreferred. Through such interactional sequences, Teacher, Learner, and Experimenter constitute the setting as an experiment, specifically a study of "learning and memory." The three parties draw upon their everyday competencies for coping with directives. For example, in the following exchange, the Experimenter (E) indicates to a participant that he is to start the practice lesson (preceding the experiment itself) by announcing the scripted directive "Begin":

(1) [0322 obed, practice 0V, 1]
1 E: Ready,=Begin.
2   (1.9)
3 T: Str:ong, (0.6) ar:m. (1.7) bla:ck (0.8) curtain, ...

Like many participants, this Teacher (T) starts reading the list of word pairs after some delay (line 2). Given the institutional context (the experiment) to which T attends, such delay is not necessarily structurally dispreferred. Participants may be getting comfortable in the chair, reviewing the sheet of word pairs on the desk, trying to remember what E has instructed them to do, etc.

So long as the Teacher provides preferred responses to the Experimenter's directives by complying—performing tasks as prescribed and without "undue" delay—the Experimenter does not talk after this initial directive until the Learner starts to demand release (typically at 150 volts), and then again when he declares that he will not answer further questions (270 volts). In most conditions (and in all five in our collection), the Experimenter sits at a desk behind and to the right of the Teacher, observing and taking notes. As the Teacher participates in directive-response sequences, he continually renews the relevance of the Experimenter's directives and the context of their production. It is against this background that delays, hesitations, and protests appear as resistive and threaten the progress of the experiment.

Resistance to Continuation

The experiment runs smoothly until the Learner first cries out in pain at 75 volts. Here, most participants at least hesitate before continuing the experiment. In doing so, they halt its progression, however briefly, and orient to a potential moral violation. As they go on, the Learner's resistance becomes more pronounced and insistent, creating a possible dilemma for the Teacher, who cannot produce one sequentially relevant next action (i.e., comply with the Experimenter versus remedy the Learner's complaint) without failing to perform the other.

Finding themselves in such a situation, some participants display virtually no reluctance to continue. They appear to experience little difficulty in delivering the shocks again and again, despite the Learner's complaints, protests, screams, and in some of the experimental conditions, final ominous silence. Others, by contrast, take relatively early and firm steps to successfully effect discontinuation. Most Teachers fall somewhere between these extremes, and the overall picture of how resistance to continuation works is complex. Most "obedient" participants display at some point disapproval of what's happening and make some effort to discontinue. But it's equally true that many "disobedient" Teachers prove willing to continue the experiment to the level of 270 volts and beyond (23/53, or 43%). Resistance, then, like displays of distress (these are overlapping categories), is commonplace among *both* categories of participants, and does not by the fact of its occurrence alone tell us how the "disobedient" group eventually succeeds in a situation in which the "obedient" one fails.

To answer that question, we perform detailed analyses of situated moral practice—resistance—in its original interactional, sequential, and institutional context. We use "resistance" as an analytical term to respecify Milgram's experimental outcome categories of "obedient" and "disobedient" (or "defiant") in terms of concrete and detailed action (Atkinson & Heritage, 1984). Here, "resistance" means *problems with continuation of the experiment: action that threatens its progressivity.* Schegloff (2007) uses the term "progressivity" to refer to "action responses that further the project underway" (p. 58). Participants can resist by deferring such actions and/or by pursuing discontinuation. Of primary interest, of course, are the recurrent forms and sequential context of the Teacher's resistance, but it is important to recognize that the Learner's scripted negative reactions to the shocks—ranging from cries of pain to shouted refusals to continue—also resist continuation. Indeed, Milgram seems to have designed the Learner's script as a "model" of resistance consisting of exemplars of opposition, phrases that participants could draw on to construct their own opposition. And a number of participants do in fact appear to resist, in part, by adopting expressions that L had used earlier in the session (e.g., "I refuse"). Such repetitions appear to be a way some participants express solidarity with L in his struggle against E.

Competing Sequential Relevancies

In Milgram's lab, as Darley (1995) notes, "the attention is exactly on how the teacher copes with contraindications—the protests of the learner—discovered during the administration of the punishment sequence" (p. 151). This chapter has been respecifying Darley's point, one commonly made in the Milgram literature, in terms of sequence organization (Schegloff, 2007). The situation consists of three-party interaction: the Experimenter and Learner project competitive and opposing courses of action, with the Teacher choosing to align with one or the other. As the experiment progresses, the sequential environment increasingly becomes one of *opposing and competing relevant next actions*: continuation or discontinuation.

By 150 volts, only two participants in our collection have successfully stopped the experiment. These earliest discontinuations are at 105 volts (session 0311) and 135 volts (session 0239). In addition to *early timing* of resistance, these participants mobilize and sustain *a variety* of forms of resistance. Subject 0239 displays practices for resisting the Experimenter illustrating this variety. (In this and subsequent transcripts, underlines indicate vocal emphasis, capital letters indicate louder volume, numbers in parentheses indicate timing in tenths of a second, .hh indicates an in-breath, and colons indicate elongated syllables.)

(2) [0239, disobed, 135V, 55]
1   T: You'll receive a hundred and thirty five volt level
2   (.)
3 ((buzz))
4   L: OOH:::!
5   (1.1)
6   T: .hh ((←sniff))
7   (0.6)
8   T: I won't give any more of the:se.
9 (0.6)

10 T: .hh ((←sniff))
11   (1.1)
12 T: Just refu:se to.
13   (0.4)
14 T: .h ((←sniff))
15   (1.5)
16 E: The experiment requires that you go o:n.
17   (0.5)
18 T: Well I realize this but I mean (you want) the strongshock
19now, .hh ('an we were) up to N:, an' we hafta go all the way down
20ta Y:,=I don't wanna be responsible for anything.
21   (0.5)
22 T: I'd rather not.
23(0.6)
24 T: In fact I'd just as soon (0.2) relinquish the four fifty.
25   (0.5)
26 T: .h ((←sniff))
27   (1.1)
28 T: It doesn't mean that much ta me.
29   (2.0)
30 E: It's absolutely essential that you continue.
31 T: I'd rather not sir.
32   (1.0)
33 T: I'd rather not.
34   (3.9)
35 E: As I said before although these shocks may be quite painful
36   there is nopermanent tissue damage.
37   (0.3)
38 E: So please continue.
39   (.)
40 T: I'd rather not.
41   (0.2)
42 T: I really wouldn't- Ijust don' wanna,- I would not wanna be
43   responsible=I:- believe in- (0.2) .hhhhh (0.7) probably meting some
44   punishment out forlearning but uh: I think there is a:- (0.9)
45   point of uh return.

Here, T uses multiple practices to resist E's directives. These range from
silence and delay (e.g., lines 5, 17, 37) and what may be exhibits of

unease (e.g., the sniffing at lines 6, 10) to staunch refusal (line 12) and accounts for discontinuation (lines 18–21, 42–45). In the process, we see T orienting both to the tacit moral order *of* interaction and morality *in* interaction—as when he invokes matters of responsibility and blame (e.g., lines 20, 42–43). A little later on (not shown), he empathizes with L by reporting that he (T) found the 45-volt sample shock he received painful, and so can understand the pain L must be experiencing (to heighten experimental realism, E gave all participants a real but mild sample shock before the session began. Here, T is comparing the low-voltage shock he received to the one he imagines L is getting). Such empathy is consistent with the "Golden Rule" ("do unto others…"), a core element of many global ethical traditions.

The transcript also shows E intensifying his directives, pressuring T to cooperate with him and continue shocking L. T in turn resists, resulting in a dialectic of directive-resistance that embodies power dynamics in real time. T is refusing to go along with the experiment as though everything is basically fine. Instead, he rejects E's projected definition of the situation, wherein the shocks are okay because they cause "no permanent tissue damage" (lines 35–36), voicing doubts about L's safety (e.g., the "point of no return" beyond which "some punishment" becomes excessive: lines 42–45).

Given the rarity of discontinuation before 150 volts, it's clear that the Learner's scripted resistance at this shock level proved a catalyst that made an impact on many participants: 17 of the 52 "disobedient" participants who reached 150 volts go no further (33%; this figure includes a "disobedient" participant from Milgram's *Obedience* film). Of these 17 participants, 41% (7/17) are displaying non-silent resistance (i.e., doing more than remaining silent at points where continuation is due) for the first time. Moreover, 18 of the 65 "obedient" participants display their first non-silent resistance at 150 volts (28%; including an "obedient" participant from Milgram's *Obedience* film). Case 2021 provides an example of such resistance by an "obedient"-outcome participant. (Vertically aligned square parentheses indicate the onset and end of overlapping speech.)

(3) [2021, obedient, 150V, 22]

1   T: Wrong. (.) hundred fifty volts.
2   (.)
3   ((buzz))
4(.)
5   L:OW::!
6(0.9)
7   T: White (.) horse.
8(0.3)
9   L: That's all! get me out of here!
10(.)
11 L: I told you I had heart trouble my heart's starting to bother me now!
12(.)
13 L: Get me out of here please!
14(.)
15 E: Conti[nue please.
16 L: [my heart's starting to bother me! I refuse to go
17[on! let me   ] out!
18 E: [Go right on.]
19   (1.1)
20 T: I'm supposedto.=hm?
21(0.3)
22 E: I beg your pardon,
23(0.3)
24 T: Okay:,
25 (0.2)
26 E: Alright.
27 (0.3)
28 T: I'll be cleared of anything,
29 (0.8)
30 E: Mhm
31 (1.0)
32 T: Sad. (.) face (.) music (.) clown (.) girl…

As with participant 0239 in excerpt 2, this participant orients to interactional trouble, performing light resistance at various points as she waits to see what will happen next. When E takes no remedial action but instead ignores L's complaints and directs T to continue (lines 15, 18), T starts to ask a question about what she is "supposed" to do (line 20), only to abandon it and ask if she will be "cleared of anything" (line 28), to which E then responds in the affirmative ("Mhm," line 30). Here, T orients a breach to the moral order of interaction in legalistic terms—she seems concerned about whether she will be held legally responsible for following E's directives, rather than the ethics of compliance per se. E's response gives her permission to continue cooperating with E in spite of her misgivings and L's resistance, and thereby renews the working consensus E is proposing, according to which the experiment is essentially benign—and, if it should later turn out that E miscalculated, T is assured that she won't be held accountable for E's error. T's exchange with E illustrates one way in which obedient-outcome participants resolved the dilemma they experienced, paving the way for continued compliance with E's commands.

By 150 volts, competing sequential relevancies have become a crucial feature of the interactional environment. As one participant remarks at this point in the experiment, referring to the pressure on him to choose sides and align either with the Experimenter and his push for continuation or with the Learner and his wish to discontinue, "((sigh)) I'm in the middle here right" (0306 disobed, 150 V, 187). Nevertheless, despite the Learner's strong resistance at 150 volts, 35 of the 52 "disobedient" participants, or 67%, continued past this shock level—as do, of course, all the "obedient" ones.

Beyond 150 volts, the Learner's script calls for further summons to the Experimenter, demands to be released, and refusals to go on. At 270 volts, the Teacher reaches the end of the word list and the Experimenter directs him/her to go back to the top of the page and perform the teaching sequence again for each word pair. Meanwhile, the Learner is now declaring he will no longer answer the questions. In such cases, the Experimenter directs the Teacher to modify the teaching sequence by treating an absent answer as a wrong answer. Of the 53 "disobedient" participants, 32 go no further than 270 volts; that is, 21 of the 53 (or 40%) *do* go on. Past this voltage level, the script calls for the Learner to intensify his pain cries into screams (or to play back recorded screams) and to protest angrily after being shocked ("I told you I'm no longer part of the experiment!"). Almost all of the remaining 21 "disobedient" participants successfully discontinue no higher than 360 volts, a shock delivered by two of them (0232, 2437). In some of the experimental conditions in which the Learner is seated in an adjoining room, he is to suddenly stop playing the recorded screams and cease all protest around 420 volts. The implication, which some participants who reach this shock level in these conditions verbalize, is that the Learner is unconscious or dead. Past 360 volts, all participants go on to end as obedient except two (2026, 2036), who snatched victory from the jaws of defeat by discontinuing after the first of the three 450-volt shocks that Milgram required for an obedient outcome.

Such evidence from our collection corroborates a well-known point in the Milgram literature: the longer it takes participants to mobilize resistance, the less likely they are to succeed (Blass, 2009, p. 44). The graduated shock levels are said to create a social psychological "binding effect" which makes it increasingly unlikely that, as the session progresses, any particular instance of T's resistance will be successful (Gilbert, 1981). However, our data allow us to refine this finding in the following way. As just seen, discontinuation in our collection tends not to occur prior to 150 volts. So, when "disobedient" participants stop, they tend to do so (31/53, or 58%) in a *middle range* between 150 and 285 volts. Almost all of the remaining discontinuations then occur by 345 volts.

In sum, what participants do in this middle range of shocks appears to be decisive. And it is here that the tacit moral order of interaction is most often made explicit, as participants repeatedly find themselves confronted with two incompatible sequential trajectories, forcing them to align either with the Experimenter, to whom they have institutional and contractual obligations, or the Learner, to whom they (and the Experimenter, for that matter) have moral obligations. In general, "disobedient" participants do not distinguish themselves from "obedient" ones until they hear the Learner strongly resist at 150 volts. By the time of the Learner's declaration at 270 volts that he will no longer answer questions, 61% of disobedient participants have stopped. And by 345 volts, after punishing the Learner one to five times for refusing to answer, 93% have stopped. In the end, participants whom Milgram classified as disobedient tended to mobilize a more varied repertoire of resistive practices than obedient ones, sustaining resistance to the

Experimenter's directives and ultimately refusing to renew the working consensus of the experiment.

Discussion

This chapter has examined situated moral practice in the Milgram experiment. Morality and power are central to the tension participants experienced between their moral obligations to the Learner and their institutional obligations to the Experimenter. Caught between two competing sets of sequential relevancies, participants were forced to choose between exercising power over the Learner or against the Experimenter. However, to speak of *a* choice to comply or resist is misleading: many such choices were made over the course of the experiment. That the choices culminated in outcomes which Milgram dichotomized as "obedient" and "disobedient" can all too easily lead observers down the circular path of explaining the actions that led to these outcomes in terms of the outcomes themselves: that is, obedient participants complied "because they were obedient" and disobedient ones resisted "because they were disobedient."

Our position, by contrast, is that participants only came to be classifiable as obedient or disobedient because of the many acts of resistance and/or compliance they performed in the course of the experiment. These local acts of resistance and compliance require explanation in terms of the situated particulars of their achievement. In other words, rather than take for granted obedience and disobedience, our approach is to treat them as social objects and ask how they are accomplished and made accountable in real time.

Similar questions could be asked about civil disobedience, and political resistance more generally. In retrospect, historians largely agree that Gandhi is an outstanding example of "doing the right thing" when confronted with immoral (British colonial) authority. The rightness of his actions seems a foregone conclusion. Yet for Gandhi and those who followed him during the long years of the 1920s–1940s, things were not always so clear. Amid the many setbacks, disappointments, episodes of violence, and small victories they experienced, they would have been compelled to constantly reevaluate their situation, itself a moving target that was changing in response to their actions and transforming the meaning of those actions in turn. Like Milgram's participants, they would have found themselves choosing to renew their acts of disobedience or compliance time and again, with no guarantee that their actions would have the effects they desired or anticipated.

Gandhi himself described his efforts as "experiments with truth" (quoted in Gardner, 2008/1997, p. 121) from which he was constantly learning. As he put it, "I have found by experience that man makes his plans to be often upset by God, but at the same time when the ultimate goal is the search of truth, no matter how a man's plans are frustrated, the issue is never injurious and often better than anticipated" (ibid.). Ever a fallibilist, Gandhi was always willing to revise his definition of the situation in light of what he learned, even as he remained committed to the principle of nonviolent protest: *satyagraha*. We think there is an important analogy to be drawn between such principled fallibilism and the actions of Milgram's "disobedient" participants. Whereas the "obedient" participants were willing to preserve the working consensus projected by the Experimenter despite their misgivings, the "defiant "participants challenged that consensus, rejecting the Experimenter's claims that everything was basically okay and demanding that the Learner's complaints be remedied. In other words, they revised their understanding of the situation as the experiment progressed and refused to accept the Experimenter's insistence that what *appeared* problematic was *not really* so.

The Milgram experiment, as we have analyzed it, should also call the attention of historians and social movements scholars to interrelationship of identity and context, and how neither is static but always potentially in flux, even from moment to moment. That identity and context are often "the same" over long stretches of time is in actuality an ongoing achievement by members of a collectivity, the result of constantly renewing self and setting "for 'another first time'" (Garfinkel, 1967). Accordingly, rather than appeal to such vague concepts as "charisma" and "moral authority" to explain sociohistorical processes, studies could respecify such concepts as detailed practices of social interaction, as the accomplishments of actors looking backward and forward as they work to make sense of their circumstances and produce order from contingency.

References

Atkinson, J. M., & Heritage, J. (Eds.). (1984). *Structures of social action.* Cambridge University Press.

Bergmann, J. R. (1998). Introduction: Morality in discourse. *Research on Language & Social Interaction, 31*(3–4), 279–294.

Blass, T. (2009). From New Haven to Santa Clara: A historical perspective on the Milgram obedience experiments. *American Psychologist, 64*(1), 37.

Darley, J. M. (1995). Constructive and destructive obedience: A taxonomy of principal–agent relationships. *Journal of Social Issues, 51*(3), 125–154.

Foucault, M. (2012/1975). *Discipline and punish: The birth of the prison.* Vintage.

Gardner, H. E. (2008/1997). *Extraordinary minds: Portraits of 4 exceptional individuals and an examination of our own extraordinariness.* Basic Books.

Garfinkel, H. (1967). *Studies in ethnomethodology.* Prentice Hall.

Gibson, S. (2019). *Arguing, obeying and defying: A rhetorical perspective on Stanley Milgram's obedience experiments.* Cambridge University Press.

Gilbert, S. J. (1981). Another look at the Milgram obedience studies: The role of the gradated series of shocks. *Personality and Social Psychology Bulletin, 7*(4), 690–695.

Goffman, E. (1955). On face-work: An analysis of ritual elements in social interaction. *Psychiatry, 18*(3), 213–231.

Goffman, E. (1959). *The presentation of self in everyday life.* Double Day.

Goodwin, M. H. (2006). Participation, affect, and trajectory in family directive/response sequences. *Text & Talk, 26*(4–5), 515–543.

Heritage, J. (1984). *Garfinkel and ethnomethodology.* Polity Press.

Hoffman, E., Myerberg, N. R., & Morawski, J. G. (2015). Acting otherwise: Resistance, agency, and subjectivities in Milgram's studies of obedience. *Theory & Psychology, 25*(5), 670–689.

Hollander, M. M., & Turowetz, J. (forthcoming). *Justice in the making: Stanley Milgram's 'obedience' experiment and the new science of morality.* Oxford University Press.

Lukes, S. (2004/1974). *Power: A radical view.* Macmillan International Higher Education.

Mann, M. (2012/1986). *The sources of social power: Volume 1, a history of power from the beginning to AD 1760* (Vol. 1). Cambridge University Press.

Milgram, S. (1974). *Obedience to authority: An experimental view.* Harper & Row.

Perry, G. (2013). *Behind the shock machine: The untold story of the notorious Milgram psychology experiments.* The New Press.

Rawls, A. W. (1987). The interaction order sui generis: Goffman's contribution to social theory. *Sociological Theory, 5*(2), 136–149.

Rawls, A. W., & Duck, W. (2020). *Tacit racism.* University of Chicago Press.

Reed, I. A. (2013). Power: Relational, discursive, and performative dimensions. *Sociological Theory, 31*(3), 193–218.

Schegloff, E. A. (2007). *Sequence organization in interaction: A primer in conversation analysis I* (Vol. 1). Cambridge University Press.

Schegloff, E. A., & Sacks, H. (1973). Opening closings. *Semiotica, 8*(4), 289–327.

Turowetz, J. J., & Maynard, D. W. (2010). Morality in the social interactional and discursive world of everyday life. *Handbook of the sociology of morality* (pp. 503–526). Springer.

12

The Primacy of Intention and the Duty to Truth: A Gandhi-Inspired Argument for Retranslating *Hiṃsā* and *Ahiṃsā*

Todd Davies

Reading Gandhi: My Context

I must begin with humility. I am a cognitive scientist by training, with research interests in digital technology and democratic communication. I am not a scholar of Gandhi, India, Sanskrit, nonviolence, or civil resistance. I do have a personal history, over the past three decades, of being trained for and participating in "nonviolent direct action" and other forms of civil resistance. Since 1992, I have been an active participant in social movements for human rights. The activist tradition with which I am most familiar has its roots in the anti-nuclear movement in the U.S. during the 1970s and 80s, building on earlier work by SNCC (Carson, 1995), the May Day Tribe (Kauffman, 2002), and the Movement for a New Society (Cornell, 2011), among many others.

T. Davies (✉)
Stanford University, Stanford, CA, USA
e-mail: davies@stanford.edu

© The Author(s), under exclusive license to Springer Nature
Switzerland AG 2022
V. K. Kool and R. Agrawal (eds.), *Gandhi's Wisdom*,
https://doi.org/10.1007/978-3-030-87491-9_12

I say the above both to acknowledge my limitations and to situate my interest in Gandhi. In this chapter, I will be drawing on the work of scholars much more learned than I am on these topics, as well as on writings by Gandhi himself, together with some linguistic data. My method in writing this essay has been to focus on two Sanskrit words—*hiṃsā* and *ahiṃsā*—to which Gandhi constantly referred. My aim is to understand better what has happened in my own time, and to offer a small contribution to answering the question posed by Martin Luther King, Jr.: Where do we go from here? (King, 1967).[1]

Twenty-First Century Challenges for Advocates of Nonviolence

Among Gandhi's legacies is a vast number of people around the world who have adopted "nonviolent" methods of resistance. I write "nonviolent" (in quotes), because, even among adherents, there is broad disagreement about what this word means, who can claim it, the circumstances in which "nonviolent action" (or "civil resistance") is effective, and on what principles it depends. Although "nonviolent action" and "civil resistance" were used by Gandhi to refer to his Sanskrit neologism *satyāgraha* (roughly translated as truth-force or soul-force), later usage by Gene Sharp (1973) and others has altered the interpretation of these words away from Gandhi's original meaning. Thomas Weber (2003) wrote that this has resulted in "two approaches to nonviolence," one "principled," and the other "pragmatic." I will say more about this division in section "Where Does This Leave Us?."

Gandhi's focus was on resistance by oppressed and colonized peoples, in the context of which he argued that nonviolence provided the most effective and long-lasting potential for true liberation. However, there have been persistent negative attitudes toward nonviolence among people in struggle—ever since the legislative victories that were won by the U.S. civil rights movement in the 1960s. The kinds of principled nonviolence advocated by Gandhi and by Martin Luther King, Jr., as they are understood by most activists in the U.S., have not been the predominant tendencies within social movements since 1965. Beginning primarily with activists of color in the mid-60s, and extending to majority-White anarchist movements who imported the black bloc idea from Europe in the late 1980s, and also to prominent voices associated with the Black Lives Matter movement today, many influential voices in North American protest movements have argued for a "diversity of tactics" that includes actions outside of those generally allowed under nonviolence guidelines (Bray, 2017; Churchill, 1986; Garza, 2015; Gelderloos, 2015; Malcolm, 1964). During this period, nonviolent approaches have also been staunchly and ably defended against these critiques (see e.g., Chenoweth, 2021; Deming, 1968; King, 2018; Lakey, 2001; Wasow, 2020).

If we understand "violence" and "nonviolence" in conventional ways, my assessment is that strict nonviolence is harder to argue for today than is a more nuanced view, which (a) acknowledges the forms of social good achieved in the past through violent means and through mixed tactics; (b) carefully studies both the success of civil resistance, especially for people facing heavily armed, non-democratic governments (Chenoweth, 2021; Chenoweth & Stephan, 2011) and also the limitations of such analyses (Anisin, 2020; Chabot & Sharifi, 2013; Chabot & Vinthagen, 2015); and (c) acknowledges the apparent necessity of other factors—including support among elites and those with access to weapons, the potential for visible oppression of nonviolent activists, and critical levels of popular support—for achieving nonviolent victories (Feldstein, 2018; Ginsberg, 2013).

The meanings we attach to the terms "violence" and "nonviolence" are crucial to arriving at this conclusion, however. In what follows, I will argue that if we replace these words with ones that come closer to the meanings that Gandhi attached to *hiṃsā* and *ahiṃsā*, we can recover key insights in Gandhi's thinking that can be applied to contemporary debates about social transformation—without denying the advances in understanding that make a *simple* reading of Gandhi's pronouncements on "violence" and "nonviolence" look somewhat outmoded in today's world.

Hiṃsā and "Violence"

According to multiple Sanskrit-English dictionaries, *hiṃsā* means injury, harm, hurt, mischief, or wrong (Monier-Williams, 1899; see other entries under "Sanskrit dictionary" at https://www.wisdomlib.org/defini tion/himsa). Gandhi primarily translated *hiṃsā* as "violence," but wrote, "To say or write a distasteful word is surely not violent especially when the speaker believes it to be true. The essence of violence is that there must be a violent intention behind a thought, word, or act, i.e. an intention to do harm to the opponent, so-called" (Gandhi, 2001, p. 91). Thus, for Gandhi, "violence" necessarily refers to a mental state, first and foremost. The English word "violence," on the other hand, is rooted not in human motivation, but rather in observable effects. It derives from the Latin *violentus* ("full of force"—see "Origin of violence" at https://www.dictionary.com/browse/violence, and "Origin of violent" at https://www.dictionary.com/browse/violent), and specifically from *violentia* ("vehemence, impetuosity") (Online Etymology Dictionary, https://www.ety monline.com/search?q=violence).

Many scholars of peace and justice studies and social justice activists have more recently adopted usages of the word "violence" that appear to make it synonymous with "harm" or "injustice." The East Point Peace Academy of Oakland, California—an organization dedicated to Kingian nonviolence—defines "violence" as "physical or emotional harm" ("Violence," https://www.eastpointpeace.org/knvviolence). Peace studies founder Johan Galtung has written, "violence is present when human beings are being influenced so that their actual somatic and mental realizations are below their potential realizations" (Galtung, 1969). These definitions represent a shift away from the historical meaning of "violence" in at least two senses. First, the association of "violence" with sudden and destructive force gives it an emotional power that "harm" and "injustice" lack. Secondly, because their shared root refers to intense force, "violence" and "violent" can refer to events that do not result in harm to anyone, e.g., "the violence of a storm" or "violent thrashing of the arms."

Peace and justice scholars have, in recent decades, embraced definitions of "violence" that make it unnecessary—e.g., Michael Nagler

(2001) who calls violence "an unnecessary evil" (p. 49). Attendees at a talk I gave at the Peace and Justice Studies Association's 2016 Annual Conference appeared to agree. Twelve out of 13 (I did not participate) said they agreed with the statement, "We are never going to live in a conflict free world. But it is possible to live in a violence free world." However, Gandhi did not share the belief that violence is unnecessary. On the contrary, he wrote, "There is violence at the root of every act of living" (quoted in Rajmohan, 1996, p. 27).

Figure 12.1 shows occurrences of "violence" in English-language books published from 1800 through 2019, plotted with various synonyms and related words for comparison, using the Google Ngram tool. In the period since WWI, when all of the words except "aggression" were more common than "violence," occurrences of the latter have skyrocketed to make it the easy winner for mentions among this group. When we further consider that the term "violence" was at its low ebb (among all words—not just this group) during and between the two World Wars of the Twentieth Century, there seems to be a paradox in word usage that calls for an explanation. The psychologist Steven Pinker (2011) may be right that violence has declined since WWII. But "violence," it appears, has not.

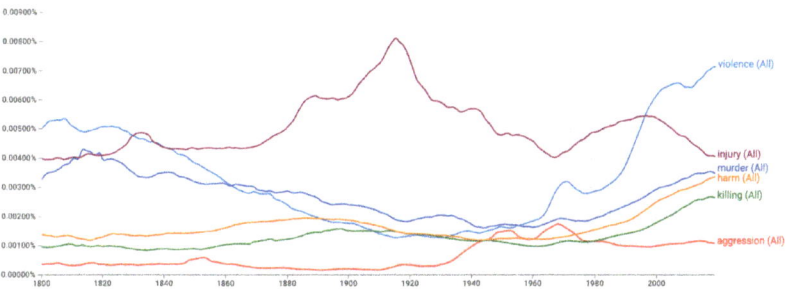

Fig. 12.1 Ngram plot for "violence" and five other related words (*Note* The Ngram plots in this chapter are each for case-insensitive queries of all English language books, with smoothing level 3 applied. More info at https://books.goo gle.com/ngrams)

Ahiṃsā and "Nonviolence"

The opposite of *hiṃsā* in Sanskrit is *ahiṃsā*, whose dictionary translation is "not injuring anything, harmlessness" or "security, safeness" (Monier-Williams, 1899). Other translations include "benevolence" (see section "Alternative Translations" below). Gandhi's main translation was "nonviolence," and, as with "violence," he described it as a "mental attitude," concerning "the feelings in our heart" (quoted in Rajmohan, 1996, p. 28). Nonviolence, for Gandhi, did not entail renouncing all killing. He wrote of a situation in which a mad man is on a killing spree: "Anyone who despatches this lunatic will earn the gratitude of the community and be regarded as a benevolent man"; and he also saw mercy killing as consistent with nonviolence (Gandhi, 2001, pp. 83–84).

"Nonviolence" is an antonym of "violence." In English usage, the two words appear to function as *ungraded* antonyms (Schmitt & Schmitt, 2020). To test this, I asked attendees of PJSA 2016, "Does this sentence make sense, or is it odd?" for the following four sentences:

1. The protest was somewhat violent. [8–3]
2. The protest was somewhat nonviolent. [0–13]
3. The verdict was somewhat unjust. [6–9]
4. The verdict was somewhat just. [6–8]

The numbers in brackets at the end of each sentence are those among the varying numbers of attendees who raised their hands to say that the sentence made sense, followed by a dash, and then the number who said it is odd.

Those who responded to (2) unanimously thought the phrase "somewhat nonviolent" is odd, which shows that while a majority thought that "violent" is a graded concept, all apparently thought that "nonviolent" is not. Situations appear to be judged as either nonviolent or violent, but not both. "Just" and "unjust," by contrast, were judged by at least some as graded antonyms, with six respondents for each word saying it is graded. Further support for this difference is found in Google Ngram data for the same pairs of words. Occurrences were found for both "somewhat just" and "somewhat unjust" between the years 1800 and 2019. But while there were many occurrences of "somewhat violent," there were none for "somewhat nonviolent" (https://books.google.com/ngrams). Similar results occur for the modifiers "partially," "a bit of," and "a lot of," *mutatis mutandis*.

Gandhi did not appear to regard *ahiṃsā* as ungraded, as he wrote "Perfect nonviolence is impossible…" (Gandhi, 2001, p. 83). *Ahiṃsā*, according to Nagler (2001), differs from the most common understanding of "nonviolence" in two other ways. First, *ahiṃsā* prioritizes "the mental dimension" in a way that "nonviolence" (like "violence") does not. If "nonviolence" is taken to imply "not violent," then it can simply mean "harmlessness," with no requirement on intentions. But if, as Gandhi states, *hiṃsā* must involve intention, then *ahiṃsā*, as Nagler writes, would mean "the absence of the desire, or intention, to harm." Even this is an inadequate translation, for as Nagler writes, there is a second way in which *ahiṃsā* differs from the straightforward understanding of "nonviolence," namely, it is not merely a negation, or absence, but "is a positive force that holds the solution to most of our personal, social, and global problems." Nagler concludes that "nonviolence" is a "misleading" translation of *ahiṃsā* (Nagler, 2001, pp. 59–60).

Words as Windows into Moral Accountability

As the preceding sections argue, contemporary meanings of "violence" and "nonviolence" do not really parallel Gandhi's *hiṃsā* and *ahiṃsā*. But in the English-speaking world, it is the English terms that are mostly used. In this section, I consider both the consequences of our use of the terms "violence" and "nonviolence," and what their popularity relative to other, related words reveals about moral accountability. Moral accountability has been studied by psychologists, religious studies scholars, and ethicists, among others (e.g., Bersoff & Miller, 1993; Bird, 1979; Oshana, 2004).

Section "*Hiṃsā* and 'Violence'" ended with a paradox: Why has usage of the word "violence" (Fig. 12.1) increased so dramatically since its low point during the World Wars of the Twentieth Century—the most violent period in modern history? A full answer would require analysis beyond the scope of this chapter, but we can begin by looking at the usage of other words in the same conceptual space. Part of the explanation may be that more specific words, such as "injury," were used instead of the more generic "violence" during that period. Indeed, "injury" peaked during WWI, not surprisingly. "Killing" also ebbed during the wars, however, and it would be difficult to produce a plausible theory that would predict both what we see in Fig. 12.1 and the results of queries yet to be done.

Whatever the explanation for the low usage of "violence" during Gandhi's time, we still need to account for the steep rise in its occurrences, particularly since about 1980. One possibility is a change in scope, with "violence" now referring to a much wider range of phenomena than it did before. We noted above how contemporary justice discourse treats "violence" as synonymous with "injustice" and "harm." The term "structural violence" (Galtung, 1969) modifies "violence" in a way consistent with the definition we saw in section "*Hiṃsā* and 'Violence'," as well as a later one: "avoidable insults to basic human needs" (Galtung, 1990, p. 292). Figure 12.2 shows usage growth among a set of modifiers for "violence," including "structural," "cultural," and "psychological," which mirror the general increase in the word "violence" during this period, up to recent peaks for each. Some evidence that this expanded scope is responsible for the steep rise in usage for "violence" comes from comparisons with the word "violent," which

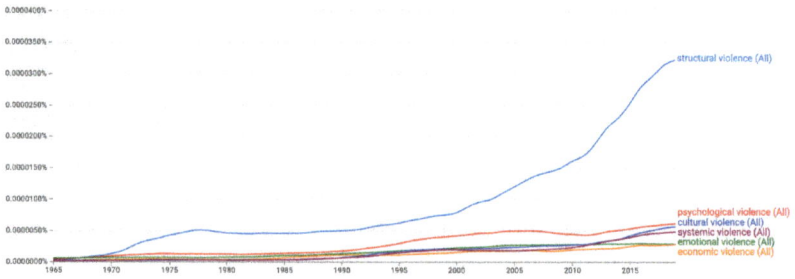

Fig. 12.2 Ngram for modifiers of the word "violence" in use since the late 1960s

does not exhibit such a dramatic increase. An Ngram query of "structural violence" and "structurally violent" shows very little relative usage for the latter, suggesting that the noun form "violence" has become a popular term for system-level injustice that requires political and cultural remedies (see Google Ngram for these comparisons).

An increase in the scope of the word "violence" has important consequences for moral accountability, if the standard is "nonviolence." What Galtung calls "structural violence" becomes personal in slogans like "Silence is violence" which make individuals accountable for acts of omission as well as commission ("Silence is Violence," https://knowyo urmeme.com/memes/silence-is-violence). If we view violence as any kind of harm, it is difficult to avoid the conclusion that we have moved from a belief that we are being nonviolent most of the time (Kool, 2008, p. 1) to an understanding that virtually *everything* we do or do not do is, in some way, violent.

The problem, however, lies deep in the language we have inherited. People do seem to regard "nonviolence" as an all-or-nothing concept, based on the evidence presented above—more than they do for other concepts like "justice." That may be why nonviolent approaches have lost some of their effectiveness in recent years (Feldstein, 2018), as authorities have become more sophisticated about combating them and exploiting their vulnerabilities—in particular by making it more difficult for movements to remain nonviolent and to be perceived as such.

Today, with omnipresent recording and the Internet, our daily actions are much more observable than ever before. This has amplified a longer term trend, away from religious authority exerted on individuals, and toward secular authority—a version of which has been called "neosecularization" (Yamane, 1997). The combination of turns toward the secular and the observable I would like to call the *political turn* in moral accountability.[2] This turn has been underway for well over a century, but in our time it manifests in standards that are (a) almost exclusively based on what can be observed by others, and (b) constantly being negotiated publicly through communication media. In this reality, what an individual has in their heart—what they intend—is increasingly irrelevant. What matters is the effect our actions have on others, and everyone's ability to monitor those actions. Interestingly, Bird (1979) found that adherents of a diverse set of new religious movements were drawn to them in part because the movements reduced adherents' feelings of moral accountability.

One effect of this grand political turn is visible in the word usage patterns plotted in Fig. 12.3. Over the past 200 years, "violence" has become a more widely used word than "sin." We discussed in section "*Hiṃsā* and 'Violence'" how "violence" in English is a highly visual, actional concept. Sharp (2012) emphasized this when he wrote that "nonviolent action" is defined "on the basis of observed behavior, not on the basis of belief, motive, attitude, or self-description" (p. 193). "Sin," on the other hand, has little place in contemporary social justice movements. It is a matter between an individual and their God—knowable to the priest mostly by confession, and to the sinner by introspection.

Sharp's decision to define "nonviolent action" solely on the basis of observable behavior is perhaps his most important departure from Gandhi, who wrote: "For abstention from mere bodily violence not to be injurious, it is at least necessary not to entertain hatred if we cannot generate active love" (Gandhi, 2001, p. 86). The importance Gandhi placed on intention is explained by his view of the goal: "It is the acid test of nonviolence that in a nonviolent conflict there is no rancour left behind, and in the end the enemies are converted into friends" (Gandhi, 2001, p. 88).

As we saw in section "*Ahiṃsā* and 'Nonviolence'," Gandhi saw violence and nonviolence as "mental attitudes." That indicates that he

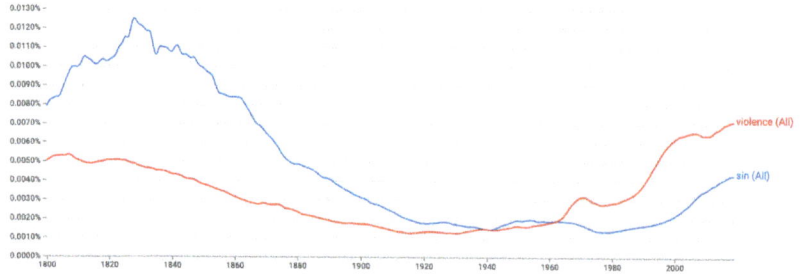

Fig. 12.3 Ngram comparison for "violence" versus "sin," showing the impact of the political turn in moral accountability

understood *hiṃsā* as a linguistic desiderative, which "means not the act but the *desire* or intention to do the act, in this case, injure" (Nagler, 2001, p. 47). Gandhi's use of phrases like "mere bodily violence," on the other hand, shows that he understood the word "violence" (and, by extension, "nonviolence") as not necessarily implying a mental state. So, when Gandhi wrote, "The essence of violence is that there must be a violent intention…" (quoted in section "*Hiṃsā* and 'Violence'"), he was, I think, attempting to import the intention implied by *hiṃsā* into "violence." But even Gandhi cannot change how English speakers understand such a well-established word. Sharp's rejection of intention as a component of "nonviolent action" is, therefore, both defensible given the traditional meanings of "violence," and important for understanding how contemporary usage of "violence" and of "nonviolence" differ from Gandhi's.

Our current *Zeitgeist* combines an increasing emphasis on violence as observable harm for which people and systems should be held accountable, on one hand, with the realization that violence cannot be completely avoided. The result is a relabeling of traditional questions about justice and values that inherently involve tradeoffs. "Violence" has become a more compelling way to say "harm" or "injustice," and its expanded scope and our increasing awareness have destroyed the illusion that we can live in a violence-free world. This, in turn, has made it harder to credibly characterize people and actions as truly "nonviolent."

Alternative Translations

Our current discourse around "violence" and "nonviolence" is Gandhi's legacy, but it does not represent what Gandhi thought. Grasping Gandhi's message requires understanding his core concepts, which are obscured rather than revealed in contemporary times by the English words he chose as their translations.

Can we improve on "nonviolence" as a translation of *ahiṃsā*? After reading many definitions of *ahiṃsā*, as well as what Gandhi and other scholars have written about it, I propose the English word "beneficence" ("Doing good, the manifestation of benevolence or kindly feeling, active kindness"—OED def. 1) as a strong candidate. "Benevolence" is sometimes listed as a translation in Sanskrit-English dictionaries. But "benevolence" also corresponds to other words in Sanskrit. And while "benevolence" conveys the intention to do good, it lacks the sense of manifestation that "beneficence" implies. There appears to be no closer word to "beneficence" in Sanskrit than *ahiṃsā*.

Gandhi wrote the following, which provides some guidance:

> whilst it is true that mental attitude is the crucial test of *ahiṃsā*, it is not the sole test… A reference to both intent and deed is thus necessary in order finally to decide whether a particular act of abstention can be classed as *ahiṃsā*. (Gandhi, 1999, pp. 109–110)

Unlike "benevolence," which means "Disposition to do good, desire to promote the happiness of others, kindness, generosity, charitable feeling (as a general state or disposition toward mankind at large)" (OED—def. 1), "beneficence" captures both the intent and its manifestation in action that corresponds with Gandhi's understanding of *ahiṃsā*.

With this choice, a natural translation of *hiṃsā* is "maleficence." "Malice" is sometimes mentioned in definitions, but, like "benevolence," it lacks the clear implication that action (even if it is a deed of thought) is involved. "Maleficence" has an archaic meaning related to "evildoing" (OED—def. 1), but its contemporary meaning is "harmful maliciousness" (see "maleficence" and "maleficent" at https://www.dictionary.com). There appears to be no closer word in Sanskrit to "maleficence" than *hiṃsā*.

"Maleficence" (particularly) and "beneficence" are not widely used in English, although they were more common before the political turn described above. Figure 12.4 shows the historical relationship between "beneficent" and "nonviolent," and Fig. 12.5 plots both "maleficence" and "beneficence," together with related words, since 1800. In recent times, one of the most important uses of "beneficence" was in the "Belmont Report" on the protection of human subjects in research (National Commission…, 1979), in which "beneficence" names the second of three principles. But I see the current unpopularity of these two words as an attractive feature in this context. They are perfectly good expressions, signifying concepts we appear to have lost sight of. I think they are ready to be revived.

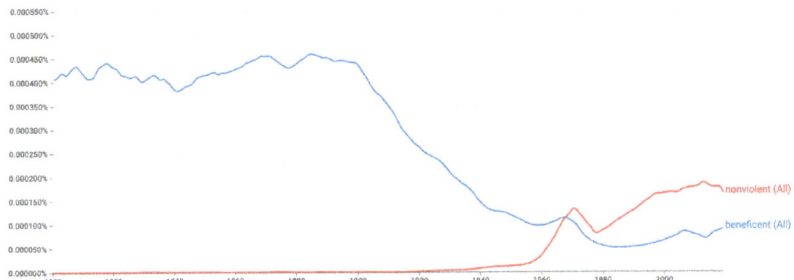

Fig. 12.4 Ngram showing that usage of "beneficent" and "nonviolent" mirrors the political turn described in section "Words as Windows into Moral Accountability"

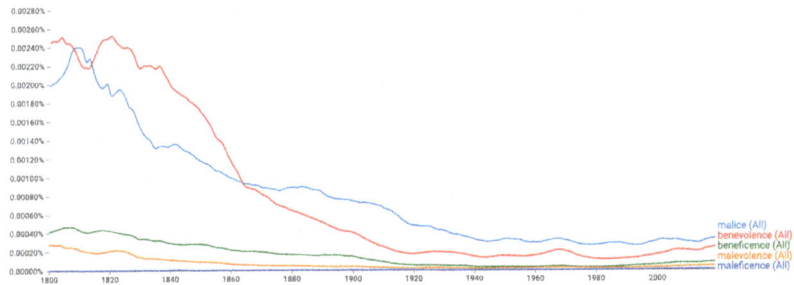

Fig. 12.5 Ngram showing the decline in usage of "maleficence," "beneficence," and related words since 1800

With these translations, we can remedy the three main problems with "violence" and "nonviolence" identified above. "Maleficence" and "beneficence" are graded antonyms, capable of being used in combination to describe mixed motives. Both words depend on and describe mental dispositions—for ill or good, respectively. And the two words are symmetric—neither is defined as just the negation of the other, with "beneficence" carrying a clear, positive meaning. I would not claim they are perfect, but the case seems strong that "maleficence" and "beneficence" are superior alternatives to "violence" and "nonviolence" as translations of *hiṃsā* and *ahiṃsā*, at least as we understand "violence" and "nonviolence" today.

Where Does This Leave Us?

What would happen if we could effect a word usage shift from "violence" to "maleficence," and from "nonviolence" to "beneficence"? And would such a shift better reflect Gandhi's overall vision? Let's consider the split between advocates of "principled" and "pragmatic" (or "strategic") nonviolence that was mentioned in section "Twenty-First Century Challenges for Advocates of Nonviolence." If we replace "nonviolence" with "beneficence," the debate no longer makes sense. Beneficence can be fleeting or permanent, universal or particular, but it cannot be just pragmatic. To suit the name "beneficence," action must be motivated by goodwill, period. A group of people blocking a bridge might be described as engaged in "nonviolent action," depending on one's definition and the circumstances, but it is their intentions, not just the effects of their actions, that define it as beneficent or not. So, in this case, the word shift removes a conflict. The two sides in the debate need not fight over words, because they would not, I think, disagree about the meaning of "beneficent" as they do about "nonviolent."

We have developed a flat understanding of violence and nonviolence that places everything associated with harm in the category of "violence." That makes perfect sense given what the word "violence" has come to mean in English. But Gandhi placed great importance on our motivations. In this way, his thinking is an antidote for the excesses of what I have called the "political turn." Gandhi should be understood, in our time, as a voice for the importance of intention in a world that is increasingly telling people their intentions do not matter (Bloom, 2021).

Another issue that was discussed in section "Twenty-First Century Challenges for Advocates of Nonviolence" is the rejection of "nonviolence," as that term has come to be understood, by many activists in North America since the victories of the civil rights movement of the early 1960s. My interpretation of this rejection is, in part, that the ungraded antonymy and lack of focus on the mental dimension in the words "violence" and "nonviolence," as documented in sections "*Hiṃsā* and 'Violence'" and "*Ahiṃsā* and 'Nonviolence'," have pushed many activists to a standard for nonviolence that demands perfection. This is a logical consequence of the ungradedness of "nonviolence," which was demonstrated through linguistic data in section *"Ahiṃsā* and 'Nonviolence'." The expectation of perfection is reinforced in concepts such as "Nagler's Law," which argues that "even a small amount of violence vitiates the effect of a nonviolent action" (Nagler, 2020, p. 154), and in similar arguments made by Moyer et al. (2001). Section "Words as Windows into Moral Accountability" ended with the conclusion that it has become harder over time to convincingly characterize people and actions as "nonviolent," because the scope of what is meant by "violence" has expanded through concepts such as "structural violence," and because the word "violence" facilitates a focus on what can be observed, independent of what is knowingly intended. The political turn in moral accountability has exacerbated these tendencies.

As quoted in section *"Ahiṃsā* and 'Nonviolence'," Gandhi regarded "perfect nonviolence" as impossible. This view is compatible with an understanding of *ahiṃsā* and of "beneficence" as concepts that admit imperfection, but is counteracted by the ungraded nature of "nonviolence" as it appears to be used by contemporary English speakers. The word "nonviolence," as Nagler (2001) has acknowledged in calling it "misleading," has therefore become an unfortunate obstacle to understanding Gandhi's wisdom.

Much in Gandhi's writing resonates with me as a social scientist, for it is clear that he had a scientific outlook. In a passage declaring "There is no such thing as Gandhism," he wrote:

> The opinions I have formed and the conclusions I have arrived at are not final. I may change them tomorrow. I have nothing new to teach the world. Truth and nonviolence are as old as the hills. All I have done is to try experiments in both, on as vast a scale as I could do. In doing so, I have sometimes erred, and learnt by my errors. Life and its problems have thus become to me so many experiments in truth and nonviolence. By instinct, I have been truthful, but not nonviolent. (Gandhi, 2001, p. 42)

The above statement poses a challenge for understanding strong positions expressed by Gandhi that have led some scholars to conclude he was an "absolutist" (Bauer, 2013). For example, while he regarded intention as essential to the definition of *ahiṃsā*, Gandhi also wrote:

> However much I may sympathize with and admire worthy motives, I am an uncompromising opponent of violent methods even to serve the noblest of causes… For experience convinces me that permanent good can never be the outcome of untruth and violence. Even if my belief is a fond delusion, it will be admitted that it is a fascinating delusion. (*Young India*, 11 December 1924, excerpted in Gandhi, 2001, p. 74)

The passage above represents both a personal and a provisional commitment. Gandhi's supreme devotion to truth made him open to changing his mind about the effectiveness of methods, and his willingness to embrace violence in certain situations somewhat contradicts the passage above. It is clear that Gandhi believed a votary of *ahiṃsā* and *satyā* cannot willfully and avoidably cause harm. The difficulties lie in knowing all the effects of one's actions, and just when harm is truly (un)avoidable. But the presumption against violence creates a strong burden of proof for anyone who claims that beneficence and violence are compatible in a given situation.

Having spent significant time within activist circles descended from Gandhi, I know that we owe him a huge debt, which can only be repaid by spreading truth and *ahiṃsā*. But a painful truth is that principled adherence to "nonviolence" is being rejected—more today than in my youth—by a majority of today's most thoughtful and committed activists. We need new approaches—ones that go beyond what Gandhi himself provided—if we are to recover his wisdom and achieve the rightful measure of influence for his ideas that our times deserve.

Gandhi's perspective offers much wisdom for clarifying and moving beyond current debates. A greater understanding of what Gandhi actually did, thought, and wrote, can dispel counterproductive myths that both divide activists and get in the way of effective long-term strategizing. It also gives us a shared base of principles—the primacy of intention and the responsibility to form our intentions based on truth as best we can—that may help us as we seek to expand democracy, human rights, peace, and justice.

Postscript: Training in Beneficence

For the word "beneficence" to become useful as a translation of *ahiṃsā*, we will need a way to put it into practice. What would training in beneficence look like? I can only begin to sketch an answer here, but I hope to pursue these ideas more with like-minded people in the years ahead.

Beneficence training would, as Gandhi said of nonviolence, "begin with the mind" (Gandhi, 2001, p. 86). It would teach us how to become detached from our egos, and what it means to love universally. Gandhi wrote, "When doing anything, one must ask oneself this question: 'Is my action inspired by egoistic attachment?' If there is no such attachment, then there is no violence" (quoted in Rajmohan, 1996, p. 33). In teaching about beneficence, we can apply lessons from the psychology of human motivation, and from the personal qualities of beneficent heroes (Kool, 2008, ch. 4–5).

Finally, training in beneficence would be rooted in what is true, honest, and genuine (*satyā*). Gandhi wrote: "I was capable of sacrificing nonviolence for the sake of the truth," but also that it was through "pursuit of truth that I discovered nonviolence" (Gandhi, 2001, p. 43). Gandhi-inspired "experiments with truth" are the corrective to our good intentions becoming disconnected from reality. The beneficent must be devoted to truth.

Notes

1. I thank Prof. Kool for inviting this chapter, having hosted and learned from him as a speaker at the 2016 conference at Stanford titled "Ways to Justice: Perspectives on Nonviolence, Civil Resistance, and Self-Defense." I am grateful also to Dr. Linda Hess for inspiring me to explore this topic, and for sharing her thoughts on a draft of this essay. The views expressed herein are mine, however, and the flaws that remain are entirely my responsibility.
2. The phrase "political turn" has appeared in a number of articles, most often in relation to ethics and philosophy (e.g., Freeden, 2014). I just mean a shift toward grounding accountability in public/political processes as opposed to private and religious ones.

References

Anisin, A. (2020). Debunking the myths behind nonviolent civil resistance. *Critical Sociology, 46*(7–8), 1121–1139.

Bauer, J. N. (2013). *The normative ethics of Gandhian nonviolence.* M.Hum. thesis, Wright State University.

Bersoff, D. M., & Miller, J. G. (1993). Culture, context, and the development of moral accountability judgments. *Developmental Psychology, 29*(4), 664.

Bird, F. (1979). The pursuit of innocence: New religious movements and moral accountability. *Sociological Analysis, 40*(4), 335–346.

Bloom, P. (2021, March 12). When intentions don't matter. *The Wall Street Journal.*

Bray, M. (2017). *Antifa: The anti-fascist handbook.* Melville House.

Carson, C. (1995). *In struggle: SNCC and the Black awakening of the 1960s, with a new introduction and epilogue by the author.* Harvard University Press.

Chabot, S., & Sharifi, M. (2013). The violence of nonviolence: Problematizing nonviolent resistance in Iran and Egypt. *Societies Without Borders, 8*(2), 205–232.

Chabot, S., & Vinthagen, S. (2015). Decolonizing civil resistance. *Mobilization: An International Quarterly, 20*(4), 517–532.

Chenoweth, E. (2021). *Civil resistance: What everyone needs to know.* Oxford University Press.

Chenoweth, E., & Stephan, M. (2011). *Why civil resistance works: The strategic logic of nonviolent conflict.* Columbia University Press.

Churchill, W. (1986). Pacifism as pathology: Notes on an American pseudo-praxis: I. *Issues in Radical Therapy.*

Cornell, A. (2011). *Oppose and propose! Lessons from Movement for a New Society.* AK Press.

Deming, B. (1968, February). On revolution and equilibrium. *Liberation.*

Feldstein, S. (2018, March 12). Rethinking Antifa. *The Blue Review.*

Freeden, M. (2014). Editorial: The political turn in political theory. *Journal of Political Ideologies, 19*(1), 1–14.

Galtung, J. (1969). Violence, peace, and peace research. *Journal of Peace Research, 6*(3), 167–191.

Galtung, J. (1990). Cultural violence. *Journal of Peace Research, 27*(3), 291–305.

Gandhi, M. (1999). *The collected works of Mahatma Gandhi, Vol. 43 (electronic version)*. Publications Division, Government of India. https://www.gandhi ashramsevagram.org/gandhi-literature/collected-works-of-mahatma-gandhi-volume-1-to-98.php

Gandhi, M. (2001). *All men are brothers: Autobiographical reflections* (K. Kripalani, Ed.). Continuum Publishing Company.

Garza, A. (2015). Black love—Resistance and liberation. *Race, Poverty & the Environment, 20*(2), 21–25.

Gelderloos, P. (2015). *The failure of nonviolence*. Left Bank Books.

Ginsberg, B. (2013, August 12). Why violence works. *The Chronicle of Higher Education*.

Kauffman, L. A. (2002). Ending a war, inventing a movement: Mayday 1971. *Radical Society: A Review of Culture and Politics, 29*(December), 29–49.

King, M. E. (2018). The ethics and "realism" of nonviolent action. In C. Brown & B. Eckersley (Eds.), *The Oxford handbook of international political theory* (pp. 273–288).

King, M. L., Jr. (1967). *Where do we go from here: Chaos or community?* Harper & Row.

Kool, V. K. (2008). *The psychology of nonviolence and aggression*. Palgrave Macmillan.

Lakey, G. (2001). *The sword that heals: Challenging Ward Churchill's "Pacifism as pathology"*. Training for Change.

Malcolm, X. (1964). Speech at the founding rally of the Organization of Afro-American Unity. In *By any means necessary: Speeches, interviews, and a letter by Malcolm X* (pp. 33–67).

Monier-Williams, M. (1899). *A Sanskrit-English dictionary: Etymologically and philologically arranged with special reference to cognate Indo-European languages*. The Clarendon Press.

Moyer, B., MacAllister, J., Finley, M. L., & Soifer, S. (2001). *Doing democracy: The MAP model for organizing social movements*. New Society Publishers.

Nagler, M. N. (2001). *Is there no other way?* Berkeley Hills Books.

Nagler, M. N. (2020). *The third harmony: Nonviolence and the new story of human nature*. Berrett-Koehler Publishers Inc.

National Commission for the Protection of Human Subjects of Biomedical and Behavioral Research. (1979, April 18). Belmont report: Ethical principles and guidelines for the protection of human subjects of research. *Federal Register*.

Pinker, S. (2011). *The better angels of our nature: Why violence has declined*. Viking Books.

Rajmohan, R. (1996). Gandhi on violence. *Peace Research*, 27–38.

Schmitt, N., & Schmitt, D. (2020). *Vocabulary in language teaching*. Cambridge University Press.

Shana, M. (2004). Moral accountability. *Philosophical Topics, 32*(1/2), 255–274.

Sharp, G. (1973). *The politics of nonviolent action*. Porter Sargent.

Sharp, G. (2012). *Sharp's dictionary of power and struggle* (M. Finkelstein, Ed.). Oxford University Press.

Wasow, O. (2020). Agenda seeding: How 1960s black protests moved elites, public opinion and voting. *American Political Science Review, 114*(3), 638–659.

Weber, T. (2003). Nonviolence is who? Gene Sharp and Gandhi. *Peace & Change, 28*(2), 250–270.

Yamane, D. (1997). Secularization on trial: In defense of a neosecularization paradigm. *Journal for the Scientific Study of Religion*, 109–122.

Part III

On Living as Gandhi

13

My Journey to Gandhi

Michael Nagler

The First Noble Sound

ONE SPRING DAY, it must have been 1959, I was sitting on my motor-cycle outside a popular coffee shop in the heart of Greenwich Village. Parked in front of me was a convertible with the top-down and the radio playing. It was a civil rights rally going on somewhere in the South. I had been feeling vaguely guilty for not going there myself, and was listening closely as one of the participants fired a challenge at the orga-nizer: "They're beating up on us: why don't we beat some of *them*?" "Because," he answered quietly, "that's not who we *are*." I was stunned: that was my first glimpse of the truth that nonviolence was not just a thing you did, it's who you are as a human being.

Years earlier, at the conclusion of WWII, the Second Army had sent around to high schools like mine captured footage of the horrors of the

M. Nagler (✉)
University of California, Berkeley, CA, USA

© The Author(s), under exclusive license to Springer Nature Switzerland AG 2022
V. K. Kool and R. Agrawal (eds.), *Gandhi's Wisdom*,
https://doi.org/10.1007/978-3-030-87491-9_13

German persecution of Jews. By coincidence (if you believe in them), I was on the "VA squad" (visual aids) of my high school, so I got to show those films over and over. The Army's intention was to justify, if not glorify, America's role in the war; but it certainly backfired with me. I was horrified. I left with a revulsion against violence and war that was to set the direction of my life.

In those days, one learned nothing whatsoever about Gandhi, in school or out (just as we learned nothing about quantum theory, which had upended the prevailing vision of reality half a century ago). My only recollection of the Mahatma, who would become a guiding light for me, is a photo on the cover of *Life* magazine showing the outpouring of grief around the cremation of his body at Raj Ghat, and like most depictions of developing countries at that time, it was probably designed to give an impression of weirdness which, I'm afraid, probably did land on me. Even at the time of my later epiphany in the Village, I knew nothing about how Bayard Rustin, Glenn Smiley, and others had brought the message of Gandhi to the Civil Rights movement, not to mention what that remark from the rally organizer really meant.

If we call this my awakening, the next steps were the needed education.

The Journey Begins

In the fall of 1966, now a just minted assistant professor at Berkeley, having been through and disappointed by the Free Speech movement, I did what quite a number of people of my outlook were doing in Berkeley in the sixties—I took to meditation. My teacher, who by another "coincidence" was introducing his meditation system about a hundred yards from my office (Passage Meditation, cf. bmcm.org), was Sri Eknath Easwaran, a former professor himself, who had met and been deeply influenced by Gandhi, and from him, I began to learn the true significance of the man. The paradox that unfolded was how Gandhi was infinitely greater than I had imagined but at the same time infinitely more relevant, even accessible. And meditation was an avenue.

The next step: by the early seventies I was already something of a maverick in the academic world (even Berkeley, which is actually not as liberal as you may think) and fell in with a group of colleagues from various disciplines who were very excited about a now-famous book by the historian of science, Thomas Kuhn (1962), called *The Structure of Scientific Revolutions*. This group was passing around mimeographed papers talking about the "prevailing paradigm" of dehumanizing materialism and what they optimistically called the "emerging paradigm" of a world of peace and justice. Recently, I have come to see the significance of Gandhi for that still-awaited emergence—the subject of this chapter.

Gandhi's "spiritual reference book," the Bhagavad Gita, contains a stark warning: "Those who hold wrong views … become the destroyers of the world" (xvi: 9). If ever there were people holding wrong views, today's conspiracy theorists qualify—and the dangers they pose, as became evident on January 6, 2021, is real. These delusions are no longer the preserve of a lunatic fringe, moreover, but have taken in large numbers of otherwise ordinary people.

The same verse also says that in the process of destroying the world these people become *naṣṭ-ātmānaḥ*, destroyers of themselves. The word actually means more: *ātman* is not just (one)self but "the Self" (think of Emerson's Oversoul), and so the text implies that the harm inflicted by such people, if we do not find a way to bring them around, is existential.

The Thirst for Meaning

Journalist Ruth Graham (2021) pointed out recently that self-described "prophets" have proliferated under Trump's umbrella, constituting now the fastest-growing phenomenon in the Christian fold. They are the antipodes of Christian spirituality (which is also growing). These "prophets" claim that they can channel supernatural powers—and they are likely to promote political conspiracy theories. No separation of church and state in this "religion!" Nor is the phenomenon restricted to nominally Christian believers. As researcher Charlotte Ward has revealed, a set of "New Age" individuals also espouse fantastical and right-wing narratives which, however childish they appear to others, are equally dangerous (Karlis, 2021). Whatever we may think of these delusional beliefs, they have certainly become a religion to their followers in the sense that they rouse the greatest passions and are impervious to reason.

That new-agers, right-wing extremists, and many in between are buying into a delusional reality speaks to some kind of widespread unmet need in our society; while the delusions have political consequences, they must be arising from something deeper. Writer Kaitlyn Tiffany (2020) identifies this in an article that was reprinted after the shocking January 6th attack, titled "This will change your life: Why the grandiose promises of multilevel marketing and QAnon conspiracy theories go hand in hand":

> As with much conspiracy thinking, the spread of QAnon in these networks is not just dangerous, but also deeply sad. The grandiose promises of the QAnon worldview are mirrored and illuminated by the similar promises of multilevel marketing: equally false, and equally predicated on **a desperate search for meaning and stability**. (para. 23)

The resonance between pyramid marketing schemes and conspiracy theories points again to a common origin that lies deeper, and clearly Tiffany identifies it: a desperate lack of meaning. Meaning is a human need (Frankl, 1946). Nothing supplies meaning more effectively than a religious belief system. That it's a false meaning in this case, and that it sidetracks the very legitimate search for meaning all human beings must engage in, does not matter to people who feel insecure and helpless. But do we all not recognize this lack to a degree? Virtually all of us are under the influence to one degree or other of a fundamentally "wrong view" that is slowly giving way, to be sure, but as yet without a clear alternative to replace it. Some writers call this wrong view the "old story"; the view that has dominated since the industrial revolution that the universe is a random collection of material particles (Nagler, 2020). That the bottom was knocked out of this view over a century ago by the astonishing discoveries of quantum theory does not seem to have loosened its grip on the popular imagination. That is because the fundamental propositions of the new science are counterintuitive; they do not easily explain how we live and experience the world of other beings and things around us. They *do* provide a framework for things like love, the meaning of life, the need for purpose and to be of some help to others. But we tend to take such things for granted, and have not noticed that they are much more to home in the quantum world than the world of Newtonian mechanics.

All this was indirectly described by Thomas Kuhn, who introduced the notion of the "paradigm shift." History does not proceed smoothly, he showed—the history of science in his case—but by the piling up of various "anomalies" that cannot be explained in the prevailing model that in time leads to the loss of confidence in that model ("paradigm break-down") and its eventual supplanting by an entirely new one ("paradigm shift"). The gap between the breakdown of one system and the installation of a new one, when the "old story" is losing its grip but a new one has yet to catch on, can be extremely disquieting, especially when it threatens to upset the belief system that's holding your society together—think of Galileo, not to mention Socrates. We need *some* story we can believe in, and to be between stories is therefore to be in a rootless void. What makes the problem more difficult to resolve is that very few people caught in this situation today understand what's happening to them. Nothing in our educational system, much less in popular culture, encourages us to think of *anything* at this depth. Thus, the breakdown of the materialist worldview, which could have heralded a new era of possibility, has instead led to a season of despair, demoralization, and violence. We are still far from the possibility envisioned by quantum physicist Henry Stapp (1989):

> The assimilation of this quantum conception of man into the cultural environment of the twenty-first century must inevitably produce a shift in values conducive to human survival. The quantum conception gives an enlarged sense of self [from which] must flow lofty values that extend far beyond the confines of narrow personal self-interest. (p. 13)

The revolution begun by the discovery of the quantum nature of nature over a century ago is showing up in the failure of many of our basic institutions and in a widespread feeling of demoralization felt by nearly everyone—except, that is, by those who have given up this empty model that only creates alienation from the rest of life and would welcome a "new" story that would actually be a rediscovery of human unity, dignity, and purpose.

Fortunately, while the intricacies of quantum theory are far beyond the capacities of most people (including the present writer), it is not hard to understand the fundamental propositions of the emerging new model of reality, and quite a few writers have already explained them (Nagler, 2020, p. 217f.). This gives at least the scientific foundation for a better narrative of reality. What can make it real for the non-scientific majority?

Enter Gandhi. That Gandhi made significant, not to say revolutionary contributions to so many fields—politics, hygiene, religion, economics health care, etc.,—should make us wonder how any one person in one lifetime could have had such a broad, not to say universal impact. To ask this question actually leads to his most significant, if yet undeveloped contribution. This is not his contribution to this field or that, but the overarching mental construct or narrative in which all those fields are embedded. Gandhi's (1999c) vision was holographic; as he explains:

> My life is an indivisible whole, and all my attitudes run into one another; and they all have their rise in my insatiable love for mankind. Seeking to realize oneness of life in practice, I cannot be happy if I see communities quarrelling with one another or men suppressing fellowmen. (vol. 60, p. 206).

The kind of love he bears witness to here would seem to be qualitatively different from the love any of us feels for those dear to us. It would seem to arise from a different vision of humanity in which humanity, as he indicates, is a single whole. In other words, the vision of the mystics. Responding to someone's claim that Gandhi was a saint, Lord Mountbatten, who nonetheless admired him no end, confidently declared that "Gandhi was certainly not a saint." Because, you see, his kaleidoscopic characteristics were "all wrapped up in a puckish sense of humor" (BBC, 1969). We may happily concede that he was not a "saint" by Mountbatten's definition! What he *was* can be gathered from another statement he himself delivered in 1931, when, fresh from the success of the Salt campaign, Gandhi used the opportunity of his visit to London to broadcast his "spiritual message" to America:

> I do dimly perceive that whilst everything around me is ever changing, ever dying, there is underlying all that change a living Power that is changeless, that holds all together, that creates, dissolves and recreates. That informing Power or Spirit is God. And since nothing else I see merely through the senses can or will persist, He alone is. And is this Power benevolent or malevolent? I see It as purely benevolent. For I can see that in the midst of death life persists, in the midst of untruth, truth persists, in the midst of darkness light persists. Hence I gather that God is Life, Truth, Light. He is Love. He is the supreme Good. (Gandhi, 1999d, vol. 23, p. 96)

Gandhi, in this way as in many others, invites comparison to the Buddha, of whom E.A. Burtt (1955) has said, "[his] very shapelessness enables him to assume any shape, his very separation from the world places him in the midst of it" (p. 226).

Call him what you will—and few Indians or the day would have failed to recognize this vision—Gandhi saw an "informing power or spirit" underlying all phenomena that was especially manifest in life, and was life's unity. I am not saying anything surprising here, perhaps, but something we can take to a less familiar conclusion: Whatever we call him, Gandhi was a messenger of the "new story." Here "new" really has to be in quotes, because in fact this story is immemorial, and far from limited to India, though in India, it was preserved in a relatively articulate and available form commonly called the Vedanta, with which Gandhi was certainly intimately familiar from childhood. What he achieved by much inner struggle was to make that vision his own, and give it a modern interpretation.

While his inner struggle was certainly on a larger-than-life scale, he insisted that what he had to teach can be grasped by anyone. While not remotely comparing myself with him, for example, I have verified the validity of those principles on many occasions, as when I was confronted during an earlier time of racial tension by four men clearly intent on attacking me and I displayed no sign of fear or anger but calmly walked through them. (Note "displayed:" not that I didn't feel any fear!) More than such isolated incidents as may have occurred, my entire career has become a dedication to sharing what I believe I've understood of Gandhi's legacy—for which we founded the Metta Center for Nonviolence.

Who would not welcome the message, after all, that the universe is not a bunch of material particles, and human life is not locked into a framework of separateness, competition, and violence. Life is, or is meant to be, a dramatic adventure of discovery of meaning and unity. A little of this awareness would go a long way toward protecting people from conspiratorial fantasies.

While Gandhi was in this sense universal, he never departed from his dedication to the principle of *svadeshi*, operating from one's own resources, one's own personal "coign of vantage" and local environment. Act well there, as his spectacular career illustrates, and one's circle would expand organically and could even have, as did his, a world-changing effect. Thus, in his 1936 interview with the delegation headed by Howard Thurman, a well-known figure of the Harlem Renaissance, he regrettably demurred to Ms. Thurman's appeal that he come to America: "How I wish I could, but I would have nothing to give you unless I had given an ocular demonstration here of all that I have been saying. I must make good the message here, before I bring it to you." Then he mused, prophetically, "Well ... it may be through the Negroes that the unadulterated message of non-violence is delivered to the world" (Gandhi, 1999b, vol. 68, p. 237). Martin Luther King was then seven years old.

Svadeshi explains the absurd misunderstanding that Gandhi was racist because he didn't try to help the indigenous Africans (on this and other misunderstandings, Lal, 2020). Ms. Thurman in fact asked if the Negroes had helped him at that time and he replied:

No, I purposely did not invite them. It would have endangered their cause. They would not have understood the technique of our struggle nor could they have seen the purpose or utility of non-violence. (Gandhi, 1999b, vol. 68, p. 235)

That he could not possibly have considered them racially incapable of understanding nonviolence is, of course, proved by the prophetic statement about African Americans and the insight I encountered in Greenwich Village, that nonviolence was "the badge of the human species." But though nonviolence can therefore be learned by anyone, to engage it on a large scale is difficult without a supportive culture, which at that time was not there for the indigenous Africans. Happily, Mandela was to overcome that disadvantage, as were King and others here in the West.

Our Challenge

Of course, despite the astonishing variety of his fields of activity, Gandhi did not directly address all the problems that have become critical to us, nor did his immediate followers like Vinoba Bhave. That is *our* challenge. There are at least three areas we need to address that await application of his principles.

The first to consider is **culture**, because of its determining influence on worldview. For example, a major cause of the regime of untruth we have fallen into today can be laid at the door of modern advertising. God spared Gandhi television, and of course the internet. It is through these powerful tools that the art of advertising, along with the "art" of propaganda, has become the pernicious influence it is today, largely thanks to one person, Edward Bernays (Curtis, 2005). We speak of "truth in advertising," but in reality, *all* advertising is untruth insofar as it creates a false picture of the human being as without inner resources and inures people to being incessantly exposed to untruth—according to some studies, at the rate of 3–5000 commercial messages a day. When we hear messages like "scientific studies prove …" we know perfectly well that there were no such studies: but we have ceased to care. The vast majority of people have little protection from the basic function of advertising, which is to rouse negative drives and harness them to some kind of consumption. When consumption (inevitably) fails to satisfy us, instead of realizing that we have an "anomaly" here and should look for another worldview, most people succumb to what Bernays' uncle, Sigmund Freud, called the "repetition compulsion." It is again noteworthy, as Kaitlyn Tiffany (2020) pointed out, that now commercial practices parallel those of violence: multilevel marketing is to QAnon what Bernays' advertising is to his propaganda. The first uses untruth for money and the second for power.

Truth, of course, was twinned with nonviolence as the core of Gandhi's life and teaching. The two words appear side by side shortly before the Gita verse cited above (xvi: 9) and he not only cited them together but even gave truth a slight edge in priority. But what he did not refer to in so many words was the mother of all untruths: that we are separate fragments in a meaningless universe. This untruth, now slowly being unraveled by science and elsewhere is what enables the twin superstitions that we can only be fulfilled by consumption and only be secure by dominating others. If we could unseat it we would be able to alleviate superstitions like that, and protect people from violent conspiracy theories.

The Environment: Living simply and care for all life were second nature for Gandhi; his lifestyle spoke volumes about simple living and vegetarianism (Akers, 2000). As Divan and Lutz (1985) point out, an acquisitive society has "powerful tendencies toward the degradation of the total environment" (p. 80). Gandhi's needs-based economy of trusteeship and localism would do the opposite. While he did not seem to foresee the level of destruction that is such a looming threat today, when activists work on protecting the environment and its living beings without yielding to hatred against those who may be less aware; when they adopt the kind of lifestyle and the kind of economy that preserves the planet, they are being Gandhian in spirit.

Gandhi's influence has been more directly felt in another threatening area.

War: Gandhi never accepted that nonviolence could not be applied to the most extreme form of violence, large-scale armed conflicts. Given his principles, he did not try to prevent those who had not reached his level of faith in nonviolence from participating in war (Brock, 1981). Much less would he ever condemn them for doing so. He held that he could "show them a better way"; and though he had his hands full

dislodging the British Raj, he did perforce confront the imminent possibility of a devastating war on his own country. Here his recommendation
repays quoting at length as it brings out the core principle of nonviolent
resistance—separating the person from the deed—as well as show how
nonviolence can be applied in extreme circumstances. (This is important
because people often argue, not very cogently, that since nonviolence
"wouldn't have worked against Hitler" it is not worth pursuing):

Japan is knocking at our gates. What are we to do in a non-violent way? **If
we were a free country**, things could be done non-violently to prevent
the Japanese from entering the country. As it is, non-violent resistance
could commence the moment the Japanese effect a landing. Thus, nonviolent resisters would refuse them any help, even water. For it is no part
of their duty to help anyone to steal their country. But if a Japanese had
missed his way and was dying of thirst and sought help as a human being,
a non-violent resister, who may not regard anyone as his enemy, would
give water to the thirsty one. Suppose the Japanese compel resisters to give
them water, the resisters must die in the act of resistance. It is conceiv-
able that they will exterminate all resisters. The underlying belief in such
non-violent resistance is that the aggressor will in time be mentally and
even physically tired of killing non-violent resisters. He will begin to
search what this new (for him) force is which refuses co-operation without
seeking to hurt, and will probably desist from further slaughter.

But resisters may find the Japanese utterly heartless, and that they do
not care how many they kill. "Nonviolent resisters will have won the day
inasmuch as they will have preferred extermination to submission.… this
is the hour to live up to our faith. If the Japanese invaded India, I would
not encourage our people to fight with arms. Neither would I suffer them
to make a pact with aggressors.Our struggle will be hard, but **it will bring
out the best in us**. (*Harijan*, 1942)

This was an impending conflict at the most advanced stage and the
widest scale, but we see nothing here that is not familiar from the principles of classic nonviolence. It may call for greater sacrifice because
the conflict is already far advanced, but the dynamics are the same:
the consciousness-raising impact of the "new" force, the way nonviolent
resistors mobilize that force by refusing to identify the aggressor with his

malevolent intention (the sin is not the sinner), and finally that success in nonviolence is primarily spiritual and long term rather than visible and immediate. These are all familiar landmarks of nonviolence, and each of these principles has been known to work. That much is history. So is, as Gandhi pointed out in the so-called Thermopylae speech ten years earlier, the possibility of self-sacrificing courage on a grand scale. The impressive thing is the boldness of imagination, Gandhi's signature: the audacity to make such a scheme public in all seriousness, as though every one of us was capable of so much more than we realize: "it will bring out the best in us."

We might also note the other phrase I've emphasized "If we were a free country." Those who think the extreme sacrifice he's calling for here shows the impracticality of nonviolence ignore the fact that he had had no time to prepare people for a safer response, having been jailed much of that time (on principle he did not engage in political action from behind bars).

Since his time, some fifty organizations have adapted an institution based on his concept of a Shanti Sena (peace army) that does not rule out what's called "interpositioning" between armed groups in active conflict, but concentrates on things that can be done to reduce the likelihood of such a confrontation, and protect non-combatants when it does: Unarmed Civilian Protection, or Unarmed Civilian Peacekeeping (UCP). Here is a dramatic example of what it can achieve.

Courage Against Violence

Derek Oakley and his team leader, Andres Gutierrez, were having an average day at the UN camp for refugees from the war. It was April 17, 2015, in Bor State, South Sudan, a country with over two million internally displaced refugees. The attack came without warning. First stones, then gunshots; a heavily armed militia broke through the camp's defense perimeter. The two internationals wore conspicuous khaki vests and the logo of the Nonviolent Peaceforce, emblems of their training and mission: to protect civilian lives. Derek and Andres started to run, then they remembered their training: you can't outrun bullets. They herded some women and children into the nearest tent. Before long, the flaps flew open and militiamen armed with axes, AK-47s, and sharpened sticks poured in. Momentarily startled to see two non-Sudanese, they soon recovered from the shock and ordered the two men out. But they were in for a bigger shock. "I'm sorry," said Derek, showing their badges. "We're international protection officers. We're not leaving." Astoundingly (if you don't know nonviolence), the would-be killers looked at each other in consternation and backed out. This happened at least twice more before the deadly attack was over, each time with the same result. Outside the tent, fifty-nine people were massacred and three hundred injured in about twenty minutes. It is interesting that a conventional protection system was in place—UN troops—that proved useless. As Andres pointed out, "If we had had a weapon, we would have been killed." And Derek added, "We had another weapon."

No one in the nonviolence community, much less any other community, believes that we will have a world without conflict in any foreseeable future. Nonviolence advocates don't even wish for that, because when properly handled, conflict is an opportunity for real growth. But we can imagine a world without *violence*. When we speak of a nonviolent future we're talking about a world where conflict is rare because justice prevails in a life-supporting culture, and robust systems are in place—like Restorative Justice and UCP—in which people can negotiate solutions to such conflicts as still do occur.

In the field of nonviolence, which is expanding dramatically in both scholarship and activism, there has traditionally been a division between "strategic" and "principled" nonviolence (hereafter SNV and PNV). The former sees nonviolence as primarily, if not exclusively, a set of tactics; the latter as an underlying capacity of human nature that is expressed as, among other things, an "informing power or spirit." As Gandhi said, "Satyagraha is an attribute of the spirit within" (Gandhi, 1999a, vol. 25, p. 489). Even as a set of tactics, nonviolence is impressive; but the dramatic successes of PNV constitute what Kuhn called an "anomaly" to the material paradigm. SNV is that aspect of nonviolence seen through the lens of the old story. PNV and its uncanny success is one of the strongest proofs that that story is wrong.

A perverse indication that this assertion is valid is seen in the way Gandhi detractors are emerging now not only in India but around the world (see the interview with Prof. Faisal Devji in *The Wire*, 2021). Gandhi is much more than the moral challenge posed by his self-sacrifice; he is the existential challenge posed by his global vision. Otherwise how to explain the vehemence of some of these detractors, who sound as if they would do to him, if they could, what their kind did to Socrates. Better a failing paradigm than none at all, they apparently feel; better flat denial than confronting despair.

But this very resistance points to the ultimate, practical value of Gandhi's legacy. Properly understood, nonviolence can be a Trojan horse for the new paradigm. Once we see deeper into it, and see that people are not motivated solely by self-interest, and that there are no cases where nonviolence "doesn't work," we are bound to be more and more impressed by nonviolence and want to understand it (Nagler, 2004). If we follow the trail of that curiosity far enough, we will, as I myself finally did, find ourselves face to face with the new story. There is no other way to understand, for example, how "unearned suffering" can be "redemptive," as King said by making a direct appeal to the empathic nature hidden within an opponent. Or to understand more generally what's often called "the power of vulnerability." These well-documented phenomena are counterintuitive in the old paradigm of separateness (which is why they are little known to the general public), but perfectly logical in the "new" story of interconnectedness.

There are three major resources available to help bring about this cultural awakening.

1. The Wisdom Tradition: The vision of the human person as an evolving spiritual being in a meaningful and deeply interconnected universe is no more eastern than it is new. It is a common thread running throughout widely different cultures, which the late Huston Smith called the "wisdom tradition." The most articulate source of the tradition, to my knowledge, is the one Gandhi inherited, that developed over the course of three or possibly more millennia in oral and then written tradition, and most importantly, in practice. To mention just one example from another branch of the wisdom tradition that shows its direct connection to nonviolence, the Jewish pacifist, Aaron Samuel

Tamaret (1968), who was born the same year as Gandhi, 1869, came up with colorful ways of describing what Einstein mockingly called "spooky actions at a distance" and modern scientists, who can no longer dismiss the phenomenon, call spiritual energy:

> Good actions set good waves moving in the air, and a man performing good acts soon purifies the air which surrounds him.… Were the eye able to perceive it, we should see that when a man raises his fist against another man the air surrounding him is filled with waving fists; that when a man raises a foot to kick another man, the air registers feet raised high and aimed at him. (p. 208)

Since Tamaret, like Gandhi, sensed the potential for violence in the cry for a Jewish homeland, we find him arguing that "for. . . the Jewish people, . . .the kingdom of the spirit is our state territory." We are slowly beginning to recognize that we all inhabit that kingdom. We hear quantum physicists use phrases like the "fundamentally mental nature of reality" and say the universe is "more like a thought than a thing."

2. Nonviolence: It becomes hard to ignore that the material model of reality cannot account for the kind of nonviolence that Gandhi and King modelled. As we have seen, verifiable principles like the "power of vulnerability" are otherwise hard to explain: why should one separate object care about another? The fact that this kind of nonviolence *does* work directs attention, if we're alert, to an entirely different model in which we are conscious beings with some degree of awareness of our interconnectedness such that one cannot inflict suffering on another without undergoing suffering oneself—what the military now calls "moral injury." When King maintained that we are all embraced in a "single garment of destiny," or that he found "hate was too great a burden to bear" he was offering an explanation for that form of injury that is actually driving military servicemen and women to suicide. When he challenged us to "rapidly begin the shift from a thing-oriented civilization to a person-oriented civilization" or a "revolution of values," he was in fact calling for exactly the kind of change that Thomas Kuhn called a paradigm shift.

3. New Science: It would be hard to overstate the significance of the new direction that has emerged from the discovery of the quantum nature of reality a little over a century ago. Religion, insofar as it can keep in play its spiritual underpinnings, is no longer at odds with the "knowledge-validating system" of our civilization, as the late Willis Harman often called science. This new direction, spreading from physics to biology, evolution, human psychology, and other fields, has given us a universe where "consciousness is fundamental," as Max Planck himself declared, so it is perfectly possible to imagine how the mental state of one person can directly influence the mental state of another. Neuroscientists have recently discovered the "mirror neurons" that mediate such influences (Iacoboni, 2008). We know now that cooperation was a more important driver of evolution than competition. Einstein's brilliant but ultimately failed attempt to disprove his "spooky actions" has proven, as far as science can prove anything, that Gandhi's "informing power or spirit" is a scientific reality (Grinberg-Zylberbaum (1994), H.P. Stapp (n.d.)". Gandhi was entirely scientific in his outlook and leaned on the science of his day to back up his vision that consciousness pervades existence and all life is thus an interconnected whole. We can only imagine how he would have welcomed—as we can—these new advances.

The vast majority of the nonviolent movements and episodes going on around the world are strategic in character. In terms of effectiveness, especially long-term, this is any day better than armed struggle, in everything from its democratizing effects to its general human uplift, however, hard it may be to document the latter (Chenoweth & Stephan, 2012). However, strategic nonviolence as such will not change the story. The early researchers, pre-eminently Gene Sharp, drawing on the earlier work of Étienne de la Boétie, were content with a negative conception of the power of nonviolence: its power lay in withholding consent from an unjust government. They missed the chance to overcome the misleading negativity of the term, nonviolence (sometimes better hyphenated, "non-violence" in this connection). It is only later scholars and activists who have begun to think in terms of a "field" or feel comfortable speaking of "love in action," as an equivalent to nonviolence from a principled or Gandhian perspective.

Materialism has led to unheard-of progress by human being. What we need now, however, is progress *of* the human being. Principled nonviolence *and* the vision it implies can help us use the fruits of this progress to build a world of cooperation instead of competition, nonviolence instead of exploitation and violence. As Gandhi said: "I do want growth, I do want self-determination, I do want freedom, but I want all these for the soul. . . It is the evolution of the soul to which the intellect and all our faculties have to be devoted" (Divan & Lutz, 1985, p. 47).

Box 13.1 The Metta Center for Nonviolence

The Metta Center for Nonviolence is a nonprofit organization whose mission is to promote nonviolence worldwide. We work at the intersection of the new science and ancient wisdom to share a new story about human nature and our capacity for nonviolence. Learn more about our work and programs at mettacenter.org

---

References

Akers, K. (2000). *The lost religion of Jesus: Simple living and nonviolence in early Christianity*. Lantern Books.

British Broadcasting Corporation & Time-Life Films. (1969). *Gandhi's India*. BBC-TV.

Brock, P. (1981). Gandhi's nonviolence and his war service. *Peace and Change, 7*(1–2), 71–84.

Burtt, E. (1955). *The teachings of the compassionate Buddha*. New American Library.

Chenoweth, E., & Stephan, M. J. (2012). *Why civil resistance works: The strategic logic of nonviolent conflict*. Columbia University Press.

Curtis, A. (Director). (2005). *Century of self* [Motion Picture].

Divan, R., & Lutz, M. (1985). *Essays in Gandhian economics.* Intermediate Technology Development Group.

Frankl, V. (1946). *Man's search for meaning.* Beacon Press.

Gandhi, M. K. (1999a). *In the collected works of Mahatma Gandhi* (Vol. 25). Publications Division Government of India.

Gandhi, M. K. (1999b). *The collected works of Mahatma Gandhi* (Vol. 68). Publications Division Government of India.

Gandhi, M. K. (1999c). *The collected works of Mahatma Gandhi* (Vol. 60). Publications Division Government of India.

Gandhi, M. K. (1999d). *The collected works of Mahatma Gandhi* (Vol. 23). Publications Division Government of India.

Graham, R. (2021, February 11). Christian prophets are on the rise: What happens when they're wrong? *The New York Times.* https://www.nytimes.com/2021/02/11/us/christian-prophets-predictions.html

Grinberg-Zylberbaum, J. (1994). The Einstein-Podolsky-Rosen paradox in the brain: The transferred potential. *Physics Essays, 7*(4), 25–43.

Iacoboni, M. (2008). *Mirroring people: The new science of how we connect with others.* Farrar, Straus, and Giroux.

Karlis, N. (2021, March 5). *Why some new agers think Trump is a 'lightworker'—In a troubling parallel to mysticism in Nazi Germany.* AlterNet. https://www.alternet.org/2021/03/is-trump-a-lightworker/?utm_source=&utm_medium=email&utm_campaign=6729&recip_id=273702&list_id=2

Kuhn, T. (1962). *The structure of scientific revolutions.* University of Chicago Press.

Lal, V. (2020). *Was Mohandas Gandhi a racist?* https://vinaylal.wordpress.com/2020/06/25/was-mohandas-gandhi-a-racist/

Nagler, M. (2004). Chapter 4: "Work" versus work. In M. Nagler (Ed.), *The search for a nonviolent future: Promise of peace for ourselves, our families, and our world* (pp. 87–130). New World Library.

Nagler, M. (2020). *The third harmony: Nonviolence and the new story of human nature.* Berrett-Koehler Publishers.

Stapp, H. P. (1989). Quantum physics and human values. *Lawrence Berkeley Laboratory Physics Division, 27738,* 1–13.

Stapp, H. P. (n.d.). *On the nature of things: Thoughts, actions, and the fundamentally mental character of nature.*

Tamaret, A. S. (1968). Non-violence and the passover. *Judaism, 17,* 208.

The Wire. (2021, January 29). *Even Gandhi's enemies and critics cannot do without him.*

Tiffany, K. (2020, October 28). This will change your life: Why the grandiose promise of multilevel marketing and QAnon conspiracy theories go hand in hand. *The Atlantic*. https://www.theatlantic.com/technology/archive/2020/10/why-multilevel-marketing-and-qanon-go-hand-hand/616885/

14

From Past to Present: Gandhi's Relevance for Today

David Cortright

Gandhi's model of social resistance has shaped social justice struggles in the United States and throughout the world. He changed the course of history by developing a revolutionary new method of nonviolent action to fight against racial prejudice and oppression. His concept of *satyagraha* ("truth force") combined the quest for moral truth with care and respect for others, through mass disobedience, disciplined self-sacrifice, and a keen sense of political strategy and messaging. I examine these Gandhian principles of strategy, drawing from the work of political analyst Gene Sharp. I also review recent empirical research showing the effectiveness of nonviolent resistance. The methods of Gandhian social action are widely recognized as a "force more powerful," the surest means of achieving justice and peace (Ackerman & Duvall, 2000). They are superior both morally and politically.

D. Cortright (✉)
University of Notre Dame, Notre Dame, IN, USA
e-mail: David.B.Cortright.1@nd.edu

© The Author(s), under exclusive license to Springer Nature Switzerland AG 2022
V. K. Kool and R. Agrawal (eds.), *Gandhi's Wisdom*,
https://doi.org/10.1007/978-3-030-87491-9_14

Gandhi's message and example are more relevant today than ever, as the frequency and scale of nonviolent civil resistance have increased dramatically around the world. In the United States last year, more than 20 million people marched and rallied for Black Lives Matter, the largest wave of mass mobilization in U.S. history. The protests were overwhelmingly peaceful, contrary to government claims of widespread violence and destruction. Scholarly investigation found evidence of more than 7300 protests over a two-month period in 2020. According to the researchers, more than 97% of these actions were nonviolent and did not involve reported harm to persons or property damage (Chenoweth & Pressman, 2020). Rioting broke out in some cities and property damage occurred in a few localities, most notably in Portland, Oregon, but most of the actions were peaceful in nature.

Protesters, today, may not be conscious of Gandhi's influence as they engage in social resistance, but his example and teachings are always with us, offering insights for addressing the most urgent challenges of our time, including climate change, as I note in the final pages. Gandhi's wisdom remains indispensable in guiding us toward a more peaceful, just, and sustainable future.

A Soldier for Peace

My interest in peace and the study of Gandhi came in an unexpected way, when I was drafted into the U.S. Army during the Vietnam War. I grew up in a conservative, Catholic, working-class family of modest means. I had few political interests and as an undergraduate at the University of Notre Dame spent most of my time playing music in the University Band, all the while wrestling with and gradually losing the simplistic religious beliefs that had been drummed into my head in Catholic parochial school. I graduated from Notre Dame in June 1968, which turned out to be an unfortunate time to be an available young man in America. The war in Vietnam was raging and the government needed cannon fodder. Within days of returning home from college I received notice that I was being drafted into the military and within a few weeks was in the Army.

It was a head-spinning experience to go suddenly from a comfortable campus environment to Army training at Ft. Dix, New Jersey. My disorientation deepened when I began talking with other soldiers and returning veterans and learned what was going on in Vietnam. U.S. political leaders said the war was a noble cause to stem communist aggression, but the stories of the veterans and reports from the press told of atrocities and the burning of villages, the bombing of vast stretches of the countryside, and the killing of tens of thousands of innocent civilians. As I began to study the history of Vietnam and the War, my doubts increased. I quickly came to see the war as not only a political miscalculation, but a grave act of profound injustice and cruelty. When I read Noam Chomsky (1970) and other critics I was horrified to learn of the atrocities being committed. The U.S. military—the Army in which I was serving—was responsible for committing war crimes. The war itself was a crime against humanity. For a devastating historic account of the criminal nature of the U.S. war, see Turse (2013).

This was a shattering realization that turned my world upside down. I was part of an Army perpetrating an immoral and criminal policy. I could not continue with business as usual. I could not accept something I knew to be so profoundly wrong. But what could I do? How could I get out of this? I began to have anxiety attacks and feelings of anger and desperation. A colleague told me, years later, I had experienced a crisis of conscience. After much agonizing, I finally decided I had to speak out. I could not remain silent in the face of such atrocities. I became part of the GI peace movement, openly opposing the war while on active duty in the military.

When I arrived at my first duty station at Ft. Hamilton, New York, I found many soldiers who were having similar doubts about the war. From 1968 through 1972 the U.S. military experienced the most extensive period of internal dissent and resistance in its history (Heinl, 1995). Discipline and morale were at rock bottom levels, drug use and racial tensions were pervasive, and many soldiers were resisting military authority and engaging in antiwar dissent. I was one of them and devoted my time to spreading antiwar literature and organizing soldiers to participate in peace rallies and sign petitions against the war. One of the most visible statements of soldier opposition to the war was published in November 1969 as a full-page ad in the *New York Times* signed by 1365 active duty service members.

I was punitively transferred for my antiwar activities and was sent to Ft. Bliss, Texas, where I joined the GIs for Peace group at that base and helped to publish an underground newspaper, *The Gigline,* "printed by and for antiwar GIs," as our masthead proclaimed. Such papers were published at hundreds of military bases and on ships all over the military in those years. I became a full-time antiwar organizer, spending all my time when not on duty (and even some of that time) trying to stop the war. I later wrote about that experience and the broader military antiwar movement in my book, *Soldiers in Revolt: GI Resistance During the Vietnam War* and in the recent volume *Waging Peace in Vietnam: Soldiers and Veterans Who Opposed the War* (Carver et al., 2019; Cortright, 2005).

As my commitment to the antiwar movement deepened, I read more about the causes of the Vietnam War and the larger issues of militarism and peace. When I visited antiwar groups and met movement leaders, I began to notice and feel the presence of Gandhi. His image and influence were everywhere, often in wall posters and in slogans capturing his words. Gandhi's impact was especially strong among the radical pacifist groups that played an important leadership role in the antiwar movement—the War Resisters League, the Fellowship of Reconciliation, and the Quaker-oriented American Friends Service Committee. Always there were frequent references to Gandhian nonviolence and his call for social action to uplift the poor and marginalized. And the knowledge that this frail looking man in loincloth who preached tolerance and love had somehow brought down the mightiest empire on earth without firing a shot. My interest in Gandhi steadily grew, and several years later I began a systematic study of his work. I traveled to India to learn more about the culture and history that shaped Gandhi and to gain a better appreciation of his life and message.

Mentors and Models

I also learned about Gandhi from the peace leaders who mentored and inspired me. One of these was Dave Dellinger, an important leader of the U.S. antiwar movement who is best known today as one of the defendants in the Chicago Seven trial, when antiwar activists were indicted for supposedly inciting a riot at the 1968 Democratic National Convention but were later exonerated. That experience came to life in 2020 through the Aaron Sorkin film, *The Trial of the Chicago Seven*.

Dellinger had a long history of activism for justice and peace, much of it inspired by Gandhi. As a student at Yale University in the 1930s Dellinger read and was impressed by Richard Gregg's 1934 book *The Power of Nonviolence*, which was based on close observation of Gandhi's methods of nonviolent struggle, including seven months in residence at Gandhi's Sabarmati ashram. Gregg was one of the first to provide a systematic analysis of nonviolence, focusing on the psychological dynamics of nonviolent action as a creative and effective means of confronting oppression. Through these and other sources Dellinger came to see Gandhian nonviolence as a new way of resisting injustice and war (Hunt, 2007, p. 28).

Dellinger was imprisoned in 1943 for refusing to register for the military draft. He became a sharp critic of Cold War militarism and racial oppression. He participated in marches for civil rights and throughout his life played a prominent role in mobilizing resistance to war, nuclear weapons, and social injustice.

When I met him in 1971, Dellinger was a co-chair of the People's Coalition for Peace and Justice, PCPJ, one of the largest groups of the antiwar movement. I was invited to be an endorser of PCPJ, which I was happy to do, although my Army duties kept me at Ft. Bliss most of the time. On one of the rare occasions when I was able to travel to Washington, DC for a national meeting I was introduced to Dellinger. He showed genuine interest in me and the efforts of other antiwar GIs and said he admired our courage in speaking out within the military, in the proverbial belly of the beast. That brief encounter had a huge impact on me. I was encouraged and inspired by Dellinger's words of personal support and deeply impressed by the example of his lifetime commitment to justice and peace. His example motivated me to follow a similar path of lifelong commitment to the cause of peace. I also found his ideas valuable in several environmental campaigns in which I participated. Along the journey, I have gained a steadily greater appreciation of the importance of Gandhian nonviolence and the creative ways it can be applied to bring justice and peace.

A Revolution in the Revolution

What impressed me most about Dellinger's philosophy was the combination of radical activism with an insistence on nonviolent methods. He sought to bridge the gap between a commitment to peaceful methods and a belief in the need for revolutionary change. The 1960s were a time of ferment in American society and in many countries—an era of massive growth in the scale of social protest and radical activism, but also a time of deep factionalism within the left. Frustrated by the lack of progress in ending the war and bringing justice to African Americans, some factions began to advocate the use of violent means. Dellinger and others of the older generation agreed with the need for stronger and more effective forms of resistance to militarism and racism, but they remained resolute in emphasizing the commitment to nonviolence. They had studied Gandhi's methods and philosophy and argued that nonviolent means, if applied properly, were more effective than armed struggle and were more likely to bring about a just and democratic society. Dellinger (1970a) synthesized these ideas in an approach he called "revolutionary nonviolence," which was the title of a book of essays he published at the time.

Similar ideas came from Barbara Deming, a writer and critic by profession, who became an activist for racial justice, women's rights, and peace. Like Dellinger and other activists of the time, Deming sympathized with and supported the anticolonial revolutions sweeping Africa, Asia, and Latin America, but she also recognized the profound importance of Gandhian nonviolence. Her eloquent writing on these issues sought to combine the experiences and insights of Gandhi and those of Fidel

Castro. She presented these ideas in her important 1968 essay, "Revolution and Equilibrium." The essay was a response to calls for more militant action from radicals in the United States and in anticolonial struggles abroad (Deming, 1971). She agreed that continued war and exploitation of the poor are unacceptable and that deeply rooted systematic changes are needed in the relations of political power within and among nations. But she insisted that the methods of mass noncooperation and civil resistance pioneered by Gandhi were capable of challenging the most powerful systems of entrenched power and were more effective than armed struggle in bringing about a just and peaceful society.

Deming and Dellinger called for the progressive movement in the United States to go beyond merely symbolic forms of protest to adopt bolder and more creative forms of active resistance. Those who employ nonviolent means have not gone far enough in this direction, Deming argued. Dellinger agreed and called for more effective use of strikes, boycotts, civil disobedience, and mass noncooperation as necessary means of undermining the powers of militarism and social oppression (Dellinger, 1970a, b, p. 249).

More Power Than We Know

I was strongly attracted to these arguments for revolutionary nonviolence. Like many others during those years I felt intense frustration at the continuation of the Vietnam War, despite the massive protests against it. I remember vividly the experience of driving back to New York after the massive November 1969 antiwar rally in Washington, as every car on the highway seemed to be filled with antiwar protesters. My friends and I were elated by the huge turnout and convinced that surely this unprecedented expression of public opposition would impress the Nixon administration and help to end the war. Then came the official White House press announcement on the radio news: the president was said to be watching football games on television and paid no attention to the protesters, and in any case would not be influenced by radicals in the streets. Our elation collapsed.

Later we learned that our actions were indeed having an impact. Despite claims to the contrary, the White House was deeply worried about growing antiwar resistance. Those of us involved didn't know it at the time, but the protests that fall helped to restrain the hand of military escalation and halted plans for a massive bombing attack against North Vietnam. Nixon had campaigned for office on a pledge to end the war, but his supposed peace plan turned out to be a threat of intensified bombing if North Vietnam did not sue for peace on U.S. terms. At the time of the fall protest actions the White House was orchestrating diplomatic and military efforts to threaten the North. Nixon later admitted in his memoirs that antiwar protests undermined his ultimatum to Hanoi: "these highly publicized efforts aimed at forcing me to end the war were seriously undermining my behind-the-scenes attempts to do just that." As Nixon (1978) wrote, "although I continued to ignore the raging antiwar controversy, I had to face the fact that it had probably destroyed the credibility of my ultimatum to Hanoi" (p. 401). This was an admission that antiwar resistance constrained U.S. military options.

One of the critical lessons Gandhi taught is the need for persistence. We should not brood over results or expect that our actions will always succeed, he said. We are committed to the search for truth and justice because it is the right thing to do. It is our moral duty. The struggle continues regardless of whether it is immediately successful or not. Major social change movements may require decades of sustained struggle to achieve their objectives. Gandhi's historic Salt Satyagraha of 1930–1931 mobilized civil disobedience on an unprecedented scale, but in the immediate aftermath the British Raj remained obdurate and unwilling to yield on constitutional issues. Yet the seeds of liberation were being sown in this campaign and others that preceded it, and in 1947 finally bore fruit.

Consider the movement for women's suffrage in the United States, which began in the 1840s but did not realize its objective until 1920. The movement against racial segregation in the United States started long before the Montgomery bus boycott of 1955–1956 and continued for a decade afterward, culminating in the Civil Rights Act of 1964 and sweeping civil rights reforms. The struggle for racial equality continues today in the Black Lives Matter movement and multiple campaigns for economic and social justice.

Social progress may not be evident to those who are in the midst of the struggle. The movement against the Vietnam War continued for nearly ten years and seemed at times to be making no progress. Yet our antiwar efforts, however frustratingly difficult and prolonged, ultimately had a significant impact. As Melvin Small (1988), Tom Wells (1994), Jeffrey Kimball (1998), and other historians have documented, the continuous massive public opposition to the war weighed heavily on decision-makers in the White House. At several critical points during the war, such as the protests of fall 1969, public pressures halted U.S. military escalation. The cumulative effect of social resistance was to force the government to withdraw troops and end the bombing. A few years after the war Dellinger published his important book, *More power Than We Know: The People's Movement Toward Democracy*. Nonviolent mobilization can be effective in constraining injustice and war and is an essential means of achieving social progress (Dellinger, 1975).

Dr. King: The American Gandhi

The most significant influence of Gandhi on the progressive community in the United States came through Dr. Martin Luther King Jr. I never knew Dr. King (although I worked closely with Rev. Jesse Jackson), but his eloquent words and active commitment to justice exerted a profound influence on me and many other Americans. King's deeds and words have been immortalized through the national holiday for his birthday that now exists and the many memorials to him and the civil rights movement in the United States. They are deeply embedded in American culture and social and political life.

Dr. King's thinking was shaped most profoundly by the Christian Gospel. As the son, grandson, and great grandson of Christian ministers, and as an ordained Baptist minister himself, King was immersed in the culture and tradition of Christianity. He absorbed this influence through the particular lens of the African-American experience, which emphasized the Gospel message of caring for "the least of these," of lifting up the downtrodden and feeding the hungry. This was a vision of the Gospel as "preaching good news to the poor," which taught: "Do not be overcome by evil, but overcome evil with good." When King later learned about and absorbed the philosophy of Gandhi he saw significant parallels between those ideas and the teachings of the Gospel. As King wrote, "I came to Gandhi through Jesus" (Garrow, 1988, p. 75).

Gandhi himself was influenced by the Gospel. Christian friends in South Africa introduced him to the teachings of Jesus and tried to convert him, but Gandhi could never accept the religion of those responsible for the colonial oppression of his homeland. He nonetheless appreciated the sublime beauty and power of the Sermon on the Mount and considered Christ a "sower of the seed" of his nonviolent philosophy (Fischer, 1950, pp. 333–334). Gandhi could never confine himself to any one religion. He drew the greatest inspiration from the Jain tradition of his native Hinduism, but he also studied and admired the core messages of justice and love in all the great religions, including Judaism, Christianity, and Islam, believing that the different religions all point toward the same God.

Gandhi's example as a person of color successfully defying the white power system greatly impressed the African-American community. As early as the 1920s the African-American intellectual W.E.B. Du Bois praised Gandhi's method of mass nonviolent civil disobedience as a new form of social struggle that might help to liberate black Americans from the strictures of racial segregation (Kapur, 1993, p. 17). A 1932 editorial by the *Chicago Defender* wrote of the need for an American Gandhi to fight for the cause of the oppressed (Kapur, 1992). Prominent African-American writers and educators traveled to India in the 1930s and 1940s to meet Gandhi and his associates and learn about their methods. Among them were Dr. Benjamin Mays, president of Morehouse College, where King studied as an undergraduate, and Dr. Mordecai Johnson, longtime president of Howard University. It was a lecture by Dr. Johnson that sparked King's interest in Gandhi and set him on a path of studying his methods and ideas. As King later wrote, Johnson's 1950 lecture had a "profound and the electrifying" influence that prompted him to go out and read a "half-dozen" books on Gandhi's life and message (King, 1958, p. 96).

King's study of Gandhi continued for years afterward and included a February 1959 journey to India in which he was fêted by Prime Minister Jawaharlal Nehru and met with members of Gandhi's family and with his former colleagues and disciples. Through his readings, the trip to India, and his discussions with many followers of Gandhi in the United States, King gained an increasingly sophisticated understanding of Gandhi's philosophy and nonviolent action methods. His study of Gandhi ironically deepened his understanding and commitment to the core teachings of Christianity. King realized that Christ's command to love our enemies was not an expression of meekness or submission, but a potent call for the transforming power of love combined with a refusal to accept injustice. He wrote, "Gandhi was probably the first person in history to lift the love ethic of Jesus above mere interaction between individuals to a powerful and effective social force on a large scale" (King, 1958, p. 97). King recognized that the Gandhian method of disciplined nonviolent resistance was a "potent weapon available to oppressed people in the struggle for freedom" (King, 1991, p. 25).

What impressed King and many others about the Gandhian method was not only its proven success in achieving political change, but its ability to win victories without the bitterness and rancor that often accompany revolutionary change. This was crucial to King, who emphasized that racial integration in America could not be achieved without the consent of the majority white population, and that the resort to violence would discredit the freedom movement and harden segregationist resistance. The goal of the movement, he emphasized, was not to defeat the white community, but to seek reconciliation between blacks and whites and gain greater freedom and progress for all. King and his colleagues applied these principles and the specific methods of Gandhian nonviolence in numerous civil rights campaigns in the American South, winning significant political victories that ended the system of legalized segregation. More than any other person, King brought Gandhi's philosophy and method to life in American politics and culture (Ansboro, 1994, p. 6).

The election of Barack Obama as president of the United States both reflected and reinforced the impact of Gandhi and King on the American movement for progress. Obama acknowledged this influence in his historic address before the Indian Parliament in November 2010, "I've always found inspiration in the life of Gandhiji," he said, noting that Gandhi's influence extended to many "champions of equality" in America, "including a young preacher named Martin Luther King." In a dramatic moment of his speech Obama declared, "I am mindful that I might not be standing before you today, as President of the United States, had it not been for Gandhi and the message he shared and inspired with America and the world" (The White House, 2010). The fact that Obama's policies as president often fell short of Gandhian ideals does not negate the importance of Gandhi's influence on his life, nor on the lives of many Americans who have continued to struggle for peace, environmentalism, social justice, and racial equality.

How the Gandhian Method Works

Gandhi was a prolific writer whose collected works total more than 100 volumes, but he never attempted to produce a catalogue of the strategic principles underlying his unique method of nonviolent social action. He was more a doer than a theoretician. He wrote extensively on the philosophy of nonviolence and other subjects, but he did not produce an action guide for others to follow. That task fell to others, most notably the American scholar Gene Sharp, who wrote the three-volume *Politics of Nonviolent Action* in 1973 and over the subsequent decades produced dozens of books and pamphlets on the strategy and tactics of social resistance (Sharp, 1973, 2005). Sharp's work has contributed greatly to my own understanding of the Gandhian method and has been indispensable in spreading knowledge about nonviolent action techniques in the United States and beyond. His publications have been translated into dozens of languages and have become an essential reference and guide to action for nonviolent revolutionaries all over the world.

Sharp was a conscientious objector during the Korean War who spent several years in Norway and England studying the practices of Gandhi and systematically analyzing the principles that made his method successful. He later returned to the United States, taught for a time at Harvard University, and established the Albert Einstein Institution as a center for conducting additional research and disseminating knowledge about Gandhian strategic principles. The central theme of Sharp's work is simple but indispensable: strategy matters. It is not enough to believe in nonviolence and protest against injustice. Real political change depends upon a carefully developed and executed plan of action that seeks to erode the power of oppressors while building social and political support for challengers. It requires understanding and confronting the structures of power.

Sharp identified the core principles of strategy that apply to nonviolent action. He emphasized the importance of clearly defined and achievable objectives, the development of organizational capacity and effective leadership, the cultivation of external support, the application of a diverse array of tactics, and the disciplined adherence to a coherent plan of action. I did not study Sharp's work until after my experiences in the Vietnam antiwar movement and the environmental and nuclear disarmament campaigns of the 1980s. When I examined these strategic principles I found them enormously revealing in helping to explain the successes and failures of the campaigns in which I had been involved. They gave me a more systematic understanding of effective nonviolent action that I could share with students and apply in ongoing campaigns for justice.

Sharp's strategic analysis uncovers the underlying political dynamics that account for the success of the Gandhian method. Nonviolent action movements do not depend upon persuading oppressors changing their minds. They win by challenging the power of oppressive systems. They apply pressure through mass noncooperation. They win the sympathy and support of third parties through a willingness to suffer repression without retaliation. They induce loyalty shifts among those who support or acquiesce to unjust policies. They undermine the legitimacy of power and force decision-makers to accommodate new political realities. On some occasions, when the extent of public noncooperation is sufficiently massive, nonviolent movements can lead to the collapse of authoritarian regimes and pave the way for more democratic rule. This was most dramatically illustrated with the fall of communism in Eastern Europe known as the Velvet Revolution.

Sharp directed our attention to the Gandhian theory of political power. The authority of governments is not a static phenomenon that can be measured solely through coercive power and the size of military and police forces. Power is ultimately about the relationship between the ruler and the ruled. It depends upon the willingness of the governed to follow orders. Even in the most extreme settings of authoritarianism, people have the capability to say no. When large numbers of people stop cooperating, the power and legitimacy of political authority begin to erode. The collective withdrawal of consent is the key to challenging repressive power.

This essential Gandhian insight into the nature of power is appealing and recognizable to me because it reflects what I experienced during the Vietnam War. Large numbers of soldiers and veterans began to resist military authority—sometimes through overt protest, occasionally in direct defiance and refusal of orders, more often through quiet obstruction or intentional incompetence and inefficiency. The U.S. Army ceased to function as an effective fighting force and had to be withdrawn from Vietnam. This was a particularly dramatic example of the nonviolent erosion of power, but there have been many others in military history. Examples include the unwillingness of East German troops to use force against candlelight protesters in Leipzig in the fall of 1989, and the refusal of Soviet troops to follow the orders of their mutinous generals in Moscow in August 1991. Similar dynamics were at work in the overthrow of Slobodan Milosevic in Serbia in 2000. In these and other examples, military and police forces stood on the sidelines and refused to come to the aid of beleaguered regimes attempting to cling to power by stealing elections. Without the backing of their security forces, the regimes were swept aside. The power of armies and the regimes they support can melt away when soldiers refuse to follow unjust orders.

Empirical Confirmation

The effectiveness of nonviolent action as a means of achieving political change has been verified in recent decades by the groundbreaking empirical research of Erica Chenoweth and Maria J. Stephan. They were the first to utilize large-N quantitative social science methods to compare the impacts of violent and nonviolent methods in bringing about social change (Chenoweth & Stephan, 2011). They examined 323 historical examples of civil resistance campaigns that occurred over a span of more than one hundred years. Each case involved an intensive conflict, sometimes lasting several years, in which sociopolitical movements struggled to change regimes or gain major concessions from government adversaries. Comparing the results of violent and nonviolent methods, Chenoweth and Stephan found that nonviolent methods are more effective than armed struggle. In the cases examined, nonviolent campaigns were successful 53% of the time, compared to a 26% success rate when violence was employed. The analysis also showed that the success rate of nonviolent action is not dependent on regime type. Nonviolent methods were equally successful in democratic regimes and in repressive dictatorships. They were also more likely to produce a more democratic society with higher levels of political freedom. The latter finding is presented in Karatnycky and Ackerman (2005). These results are confirmed in Chenoweth and Stephan (2011, pp. 201–219).

In 2016, Chenoweth and Stephan published an update of their research showing that the effectiveness advantage of nonviolence has continued even as the overall number of civil resistance campaigns has increased globally. Success rates for both violent and nonviolent struggles declined over the previous decade but the superiority of nonviolent campaigns in achieving policy objectives increased (Chenoweth & Stephan, 2016).

The work of Chenoweth and Stephan and other empirical scholars revolutionizes the study of nonviolent political change. Previous arguments in favor of nonviolence, as articulated by Gandhi, King, and others, were based on moral reasoning. Many noted, of course, that nonviolent means were proving to be successful in important cases, but no systematic empirical data was available to allow for a definitive judgment on the comparative advantages of nonviolence over violence. That analysis is now available and confirms the core message that Gandhi and King constantly emphasized: nonviolent action is not only the right thing to do, it is also the most effective way of achieving change.

Chenoweth and Stephan (2011) identify the core factors that account for the effectiveness of nonviolent action. The first and most important is what they call the "participation advantage," the ability of nonviolent methods to mobilize massive numbers of people to participate in political struggle. "Large campaigns are much more likely to succeed than small campaigns," they argue. As membership increases, so does the probability of success. Mass participation by diverse sectors of society can erode a regime's legitimacy and main sources of power. Chenoweth has recently identified what she calls the "3.5 percent rule," finding that major civil resistance campaigns typically succeed when they reach that level of social participation (Chenoweth, 2013; Chenoweth & Belgioioso, 2019).

In an armed struggle, by contrast, the resistance is carried out by a smaller, specialized cadre of fighters. An armed insurgency must operate according to military discipline, and its success may depend on the isolation and impregnability of its command structure. In the heat of battle there is no room for debate or dissent. Armed movements are less able to accommodate factions and may turn on themselves in violent purges. Most of the armed revolutions of the twentieth century produced repressive and dictatorial regimes. Those who win by the gun tend to rule by the gun.

Nonviolent movements are also more likely to induce loyalty shifts and defections among government officials and within the security forces (Chenoweth & Stephan, 2011, p. 58). As Gandhi taught, authority systems depend upon the obedience of followers. When that loyalty falters, the oppressive power of the system diminishes. Movements that maintain nonviolence discipline in the face of repression are better able to trigger that effect. By contrast, when resistance campaigns utilize armed struggle they reduce their prospects for success and make it easier for the government to use force against them. When soldiers, civil servants, and third parties are attacked violently they tend to close ranks behind the regime and are less likely to shift their loyalties to the other side. Fear and anger within the population may prompt calls for retaliation and generate increased support for government repression. Officials who are under military attack tend to be less likely to negotiate and make political concessions.

The revelations that come from these empirical studies validate and give greater meaning to the study of nonviolent action. They confirm many of the insights Gandhi and King offered and vindicate the commitment that so many of us have made to the practice of nonviolence. Gandhi always said that nonviolent action is the surest means of achieving justice and upholding truth. He described nonviolence as the most powerful weapon for overcoming oppression. Mightier than the atomic bomb he said in his last years, far more effective than armed violence in enhancing human dignity and political freedom. Gandhi made these claims based on his own experiences in India and South Africa, but he was also asserting a faith in the prospects for future progress. Now we have evidence to confirm that faith and have greater assurance that nonviolent civil resistance is indeed the best means of achieving political change.

Climate Action, Gandhian Ways

Gandhi's wisdom has enormous importance for addressing the urgent challenges of today, especially the human assault on the environment that is causing global climate change. I had the opportunity to discuss these issues in October 2019 when I was invited by the Indian Mission to the United Nations in New York to address an event at UN headquarters commemorating Gandhi's 150th birthday. In my remarks I focused on three dimensions of his message: simple living, social equality, and nonviolence.

Long before the rise of environmentalism and the back-to-the-land movements of the 1960s, Gandhi saw the need to care for the environment and preserve natural systems. He sought to have a light footprint upon the earth. He wrote scathingly in his 1910 book *Hind Swaraj* ("Indian Home Rule") of the excesses of Western civilization and modern technology and warned of the dangers of materialism and greed. If India were to follow the industrialism and economic imperialism of the West, he later warned, it would "strip the world bare like locusts" (Guha, 2019). In the communal ashrams and farming communities he founded, all members were expected to perform manual labor and grow their own food. Gandhi was a strict vegetarian guided by an ethic of avoiding harm not only to humans but all living beings. He emphasized the importance of restraining economic wants and living with less.

In his personal life, Gandhi practiced what he preached. He unburdened himself of possessions and even most of his clothes. At the time of his death all that he owned could fit in a shoebox. In South Africa he moved from the large home where he lived with his family as a successful attorney to the Phoenix farm near Durban where he lived collectively with others and shared in household duties. He shed his three-piece suit to become a man in loincloth, wearing a simple dhoti and shawl of homespun cloth.

In his emphasis on non-possession and living simply, Gandhi was revealing an essential truth about the wasteful forms of economic growth that are at the heart of today's environmental crisis. The overconsumption that has pumped ever-growing volumes of pollution and carbon into the biosphere risks irreparably damaging the planet. Efforts to stem emissions through more efficient production methods are important, but it is also necessary to address the demand side of the equation and explore ways to consume less. The multiplication of wants and pursuit of endless growth are ecologically unsustainable over the long term.

Gandhi's critique of excessive materialism calls us to question our personal choices. Are we consuming too much? Have our wants outstripped our needs? We do not have to follow Gandhi and live in an ashram, but we can commit ourselves to living more simply and modestly. Those of us who enjoy middle-class comfort can afford to demand less for ourselves and share more with others, especially with the poor and marginalized.

Seeking to consume and produce less does not mean abandoning the global struggle against poverty. On the contrary, we must continue and accelerate the work of fulfilling the UN Sustainable Development Goals, which aim for the radical reduction of extreme poverty by the end of this decade. Surely we can find ways to continue lifting people out of poverty without further ruining the environment or undermining the viability of the earth's life support systems.

Gandhi devoted himself to serving the poor. In his famous Talisman for judging what is right or wrong, he asked us to consider how our actions affect the poorest and the weakest. We should act in ways that avoid harm to others, especially the most vulnerable, and seek to help the oppressed. We know that the poor and powerless suffer most from the harmful effects of pollution and environmental degradation. As the climate warms, the rich and well-connected can move to higher ground or cooler climes, but the impoverished do not have that option.

Pope Francis links environmental sustainability to ending poverty and reducing social inequality. He writes in his groundbreaking encyclical *Laudato Si*, "we have to realize that a true ecological approach always becomes a social approach; it must integrate questions of justice in debates on the environment, so as to hear *both the cry of the earth and the cry of the poor*." He calls us to be in solidarity with the *miserando*, the lowly who are "mired in desperate and degrading poverty, with no way out, while others … [are] vainly showing off their supposed superiority and leaving behind so much waste that, if it were the case everywhere, would destroy the planet" (Pope Francis, 2015, pp. 62–63).

Gandhi would have agreed with those sentiments. He thought of excess consumption as thievery. If we appropriate more than is necessary for own needs, he believed, we take it from others. All people deserve an equal opportunity to enjoy the fruits of the earth, Gandhi said. This does not mean that all have the same amount, only that everybody has enough for his or her essential needs.

Gandhi's most important contribution to ecological thinking, I believe, is his philosophy and method of nonviolence. The violence of war inevitably lays waste to the land. U.S. aggression in Vietnam included massive campaigns of chemical spraying and bombing to destroy livelihoods and habitats. As we strive to live peacefully with our fellow human beings, we must also be at peace with the earth and all living beings.

We are inescapably bound together in a web of mutuality through our common humanity and the interdependence of the natural order. To end injustice and the oppression of the poor, we must also help to prevent the exploitation and desecration of the earth. Gandhian methods of nonviolent resistance are necessary for overcoming social injustice, and they are the means by which we can halt environmental ruin and save the planet.

References

Ackerman, P., & Duvall J. (2000). *A force more powerful: A century of nonviolent conflict*. Palgrave.

Ansboro, J. (1994). *Martin Luther King, Jr.: The making of a mind*. Orbis Books.

Carver, R. C., Cortright, D., & Doherty, B. (2019). *Waging peace in Vietnam: U.S. soldiers and veterans who opposed the war*. New Village Press.

Chenoweth, E. (2013, September 21). *TED talk* [Video File]. https://rationalinsurgent.com/2013/11/04/my-talk-at-tedxboulder-civil-resistance-and-the-3-5-rule/#_edn5

Chenoweth, E., & Belgioioso, M. (2019). The physics of dissent and the effects of movement momentum. *Nature Human Behavior, 3*, 1088–1095. https://www.nature.com/articles/s41562-019-0665-8

Chenoweth, E., & Pressman, J. (2020, October 16). The summer's Black Lives Matter protesters were overwhelmingly peaceful, our research shows. *The Washington Post*. https://www.washingtonpost.com/politics/2020/10/16/this-summers-black-lives-matter-protesters-were-overwhelming-peaceful-our-research-finds/

Chenoweth, E., & Stephan, M. J. (2011). *Why civil resistance works: The strategic logic of nonviolent conflict*. Columbia University Press.

Chenoweth, E., & Stephan, M. J. (2016, January 18). How the world is proving Martin Luther King Jr. right about nonviolence. *Washington Post: Monkey Cage*. https://www.washingtonpost.com/news/monkey-cage/wp/2016/01/18/how-the-world-is-proving-mlk-right-about-nonviolence/?utm_term=.f7a9f7b3f811

Chomsky, N. (1970). After Pinkville. *The New York Review of Books*. https://www.nybooks.com/articles/1970/01/01/after-pinkville/

Cortright, D. (2005). *Solders in revolt: GI Resistance during the Vietnam war*. Haymarket Books.

Dellinger, D. T. (1970a). *Revolutionary nonviolence: Essays by Dave Dellinger*. Bobbs-Merrill.

Dellinger, D. T. (1970b). Gandhi's Heirs. In D. T. Dellinger, *Revolutionary nonviolence: Essays by Dave Dellinger*. Bobbs-Merrill.

Dellinger, D. T. (1975). *More power than we know: The people's movement toward democracy*. Anchor Books.

Deming, B. (1971). Revolution and equilibrium. In B. Deming, *Revolution and equilibrium*. Grossman.

Fischer, L. (1950). *The life of Mahatma Gandhi.* Harper & Row.

Francis, P. (2015). *Laudato Si: On care for our common home.* Our Sunday Visitor Publishing Division.

Garrow, D. J. (1988). *Bearing the cross: Martin Luther King, Jr. and the southern Christian leadership conference.* Vintage Books.

Guha, R. (2019, August 14). *India was a miracle democracy: But it's time to downgrade its credentials* [Blog post]. https://www.washingtonpost.com/opinions/2019/08/14/india-was-miracle-democracy-its-time-downgrade-its-credentials/

Heinl, R. (1995). The collapse of the armed forces. In M. E. Gettleman (Ed.), *Vietnam and America: A documentary history* (pp. 323–331). Grove Atlantic.

Hunt, A. E. (2007). *David Dellinger: The life and times of a nonviolent revolutionary.* New York University Press.

Kapur, S. (1992). Prelude to Martin Luther King, Jr.: The images of Gandhi and the Indian independence movement, 1921–1934. *Gandhi Marg, 14*(3), 429–430.

Kapur, S. (1993). *Raising up a prophet: The African-American encounter with Gandhi.* Oxford University Press.

Karatnycky, A., & Ackerman, P. (2005). How freedom is won: From civil resistance to durable democracy. *International Journal of Not-for-Profit Law, 7*(3).

Kimball, J. (1998). *Nixon's Vietnam war.* University of KansasPress.

King, M. L. (1958). *Stride toward freedom: The Montgomery story.* Harper & Row.

King, M. L. (1991). My trip to the land of Gandhi. In J. M. Washington (Ed.), *A testament of hope: The essential writings and speeches of Martin Luther King, Jr.* Harper.

Nixon, R. (1978). *The memoirs of Richard Nixon.* Grosset & Dunlap.

Sharp, G. (1973). *The politics of nonviolent action.* Porter Sargent.

Sharp, G. (2005). *Waging nonviolent struggle: 20th century practice and 21st century potential.* Porter Sargent.

Small, M. (1988). *Johnson, Nixon, and the doves.* Rutgers University Press.

Turse, N. (2013). *Kill anything that moves: The real American war in Vietnam.* Metropolitan Books, Henry Holt and Company.

Wells, T. (1994). *The war within: America's battle over Vietnam.* University of California Press.

The White House. (2010, November 8). *Remarks by the President to the Joint Session of the Indian Parliament in New Delhi, India.* http://www.whitehouse.gov/the-press-office/2010/11/08/remarks-president-joint-session-indian-parliament-new-delhi-india

15

Gandhi's Contribution to a War Free World: My Inspiration

George Paxton

Although in some ways Gandhi was an improbable figure on the world stage—in his mature years, an ascetic, deeply religious Indian of eccentric dress and some decidedly odd ideas and practice—nevertheless, he offered other ideas of potentially universal application which would if adopted transform our world society for the better. And, perhaps most impressively he lived out his principles better than most of us. But he was also liable to a change of mind on issues that confronted him; this is true of his understanding of religion, race, caste, politics, economics, and conflict. Truth was his most fundamental principle but his understanding of particular truths changed over his lifetime.

G. Paxton (✉)
The Gandhi Foundation, Barrington Drive, Glasgow, UK
e-mail: gpaxton@phonecoop.coop

© The Author(s), under exclusive license to Springer Nature
Switzerland AG 2022
V. K. Kool and R. Agrawal (eds.), *Gandhi's Wisdom*,
https://doi.org/10.1007/978-3-030-87491-9_15

My Route to Gandhi

My personal road to Gandhi is a straightforward one. Brought up in the Church of Scotland in the days when most people in Britain had church affiliations, the focus was on the Bible as the 'word of God' and the figure of Jesus who to the minister and most members was the 'son of God'. While admiring the simple sincere life of the minister, I was never convinced of the theology that was taught there, although I retained my admiration for the life and the ethical teaching of Jesus. The teachings attributed to Jesus in the New Testament, especially in the 'Sermon on the Mount' seemed, at once, revolutionary and yet very convincing.

In my later teenage years I sought another religious tradition that was freer in thought and discovered the Quakers who impressed me for their non-dogmatic approach but also because they put a strong emphasis on social issues, especially peace. About the age of 19, I read Louis Fischer's *The Life of Mahatma Gandhi* and was amazed to find that a man who seemed to me as admirable as Jesus in his life and teaching actually died less than 20 years previously.

I was still at university when the British Government abolished conscription so I never had the opportunity to refuse to serve in the armed forces but I have never wavered in my belief that war is one of the worst of human creations. Gandhi's position, I later discovered, was more complex. On finishing university, I obtained a job in medical physics, working in hospitals in the city and around the same time my wife introduced me to the Unitarians, whose openness to ideas suited us. Their pluralistic approach to religion fitted Gandhian philosophy, too. We, also, became vegetarian.

The Cold War dominated international politics around 1960 with the two superpowers facing up to each other, armed with sufficient nuclear weapons to destroy human civilization. In Britain the Campaign for Nuclear Disarmament (CND) was formed in 1958 and it developed into a mass movement for a few years. I joined the local group which attracted, among others, pacifists who had been active in the Peace Pledge Union, trade unionists, Labour Party members, and church members of various denominations. CND's aim was to achieve unilateral nuclear disarmament for Britain which it was hoped would start similar moves in other nuclear-armed states. The most likely route was through the Labour Party taking up these policies and then winning a general election. Some of the nuclear disarmers felt that civil disobedience would be a dramatic way to draw attention to the urgency of the issue and the Committee of 100 was born. Its focus was large-scale civil disobedience such as sit-downs of thousands of people in city centres, particularly in London, or at nuclear bases. The year 1961 saw several sit-down demonstrations in which 100s were arrested on each occasion. However, the hope of attracting an increasing number of participants failed to materialize, neither direct action nor the parliamentary route succeeded.

As the peace movement's activities declined in the later 1960s, I became involved in a group of Amnesty International, and later on, promotion of Fair Trade, among other causes. One might call this Constructive Action, something that Gandhi undertook between satyagraha campaigns.

Around 1985, I discovered that a Gandhi society had been established in Britain following the great interest in Gandhi generated by Richard Attenborough's 1982 film. I joined and have been involved in the Gandhi Foundation since then. The wide scope of Gandhi's concerns and hence of the Gandhi Foundation's was appealing to me. I took on the editing of its quarterly newsletter, suggested a change of name to *The Gandhi Way*, and played my part in spreading knowledge of who is, in my judgment, the greatest human being of modern times.

Gandhi's Adoption of Nonviolence

Gandhi's upbringing and childhood environment predisposed him towards tolerance and nonviolence. Not only was his Hindu vaishnavite family vegetarian but Jains were relatively strong in Gujarat and *ahimsa* (non-harming) was one of their most prominent principles. Moreover, his mother Putlibai was a member of the Pranami sect, which combined elements of Islam and Hinduism and young Mohan was taken to both the Vaishnava temple and the Pranami. Muslims and Jains were also frequent visitors to their home. So appreciation of other religious traditions, although not uncritically, was natural to Gandhi.

Jains believe there is a reservoir of energy which is increased through right action leading to spiritual perfection for the individual. Practice of *ahimsa* is the most important key to this. But a difficulty is that it is impossible to be perfectly nonviolent to all creatures, especially in farming. Gandhi took a less extreme position on *ahimsa*, even abandoning his vegan diet when he, in middle age, became seriously ill. He, also, euthanized a calf who was suffering severely. His ethic was one of the compassions rather than personal perfection—it was directed outwardly to the world rather than remaining inward (Chatterjee, 1983, p. 33). Gandhi's ascetic lifestyle was derived probably even more from the fact that most Indians were extremely poor so using more of the earth's resources than one really needs amounts to theft, thus he advocated *astea* (non-stealing). A simpler lifestyle is, of course, highly relevant to our present predicament of severely damaging the earth's eco-system through what used to be a Western lifestyle now spreading world-wide.

Gandhi's philosophy was also shaped by his contact with Western culture. His first personal contact with Christians was in London when a student of law. It was mostly Protestant Nonconformists whom he met, both in London and later in South Africa. The desire of most of these Christians was to see him convert to what they believed was the one true religion, something which he never accepted. Nevertheless, it was their introducing him to the New Testament that had a profound effect on his spiritual development which reinforced ideas which he had already met in Indian culture. These, he found, were expressed especially in the Sermon on the Mount which includes the passage: 'You have learned what they were told. "Love your neighbour, hate your enemy". But what I tell you is this: Love your enemies and pray for your persecutors …' (Matthew 5:13).

A Church of England clergyman who settled in India and who became Gandhi's closest Christian friend was Charles Freer Andrews (CFA, 'Charlie' to Gandhi, who was 'Mohan' to CFA). Gandhi first met him at the beginning of 1914 when Andrews came from India to South Africa to help with the civil rights campaigns. Andrews was noted for his campaigning against the indentured labour system in British colonies. He had intellectual doubts about some of the core beliefs of the Church and at one time considered leaving the priesthood. Yet to many he was a most Christ-like human being (Chaturvedi & Sykes, 1949). How deeply Gandhi's reading of the New Testament had penetrated can be seen in these words appearing in *Harijan* in 1933: 'Satyagraha is gentle, it never wounds. It must not be the result of anger or malice. It is never fussy, never impatient, never vociferous. It is the direct opposite of compulsion'. It is obviously derived from his reading of I Corinthians 13 (Chatterjee, 1983, p. 91).

Another great Christian, although very different in personality from Andrews and very heterodox in belief, who had a major influence on Gandhi was Leo Tolstoy. The influence in this case came through his writings. In his first year in South Africa, 1894, he began to read various writings of Tolstoy and was most impressed by *The Kingdom of God is Within You*. This book had a descriptive subtitle—*Christianity not as a Mystical Teaching but as a New Concept of Life*. Gandhi said he had been won over to nonviolence by reading Tolstoy (Green, 1998).

In his middle years, Tolstoy became very dissatisfied with his life and turned to a deep study of eastern religions as well as Christianity. He was, already, extremely critical of the institutions of the Russian state and of the Orthodox Church. He concluded that almost no one followed the teaching of Jesus, the teaching of love for others which he interpreted to include non-resistance to evil. And this must apply, he believed, to institutions as well as inter-personal relations. He became what one might call a Christian anarchist who denounced all the institutions of the state— tsar, aristocracy, armed forces, police, courts, and economic structure. He did not stop at denouncing the evil he observed but set about changing his own life: freeing his own serfs, providing schooling on his estate, becoming vegetarian, giving away his wealth. Gandhi's understanding of *ahimsa* broadened to include the concept of love or compassion and is very similar to Albert Schweitzer's expression 'Reverence for Life'.

Towards the end of Tolstoy's life, Gandhi and he had a short exchange of letters. When Tolstoy turned 80 in 1908, being the best known Russian in the world, he received many letters of congratulation including one from Gandhi and another from Taraknath Das, an Indian revolutionary living in USA. Das asked him for an article for Das's magazine and Tolstoy accepted the invitation and eventually sent a letter to Das. Gandhi, somehow, saw a copy of this letter which criticized the Indians for tolerating British occupation. Tolstoy considered that resisting violently would be an adoption of the occupiers' ideology and he appealed to the Indians to adopt non-resistance instead. A key idea was that a country of 200 million could not be ruled by 30,000 unless the population allowed it. In 1909, Gandhi wrote to Tolstoy asking if he could publish the *Letter* (Das did not publish it) and also asked Tolstoy if he in turn could give publicity to the nonviolent resistance of the Indian community in South Africa (Bartolf, 1997, p. 54). Tolstoy replied immediately, in the positive, and a few weeks later Gandhi sent him a copy of Rev Joseph Doke's biography of Gandhi. In April 1910, Gandhi sent Tolstoy a copy of his *Hind Swaraj* (Indian Home Rule), written as a dialogue between an advocate of violent liberation and an advocate of nonviolence, as well as being a sweeping criticism of modern civilization (Bartolf, 1997, p. 58). Great as was the influence of Tolstoy on Gandhi there were differences. Gandhi was never as extreme an anarchist as the Russian, and *satyagraha* was a nonviolent form of resistance rather than non-resistance. Nevertheless, Tolstoy reacted very positively to reading about Gandhi's work in South Africa: '… your work in Transvaal … is yet the most fundamental and the most important to us supplying the most weighty practical proof in which the world can now share' (Bartolf, 1997, p. 64).

Gandhi's first involvement in social/political issues had begun in South Africa when he came face-to-face with racial discrimination. The journey from Durban to Pretoria shortly after he arrived in South Africa was a life-changing one. Firstly, he was ejected from the train at Pietermaritzburg as he, an Indian, was travelling with a first-class ticket. Secondly, on the second lap of the journey which he had to travel by coach he was abused by the driver and later was refused entry to a hotel. These personal insults led him to write to the railway executives to protest at his treatment. His action was in itself unusual as most people of dark skin accepted, albeit reluctantly, that that was the way things were and they had no means to change it.

Gandhi soon developed a characteristic response to personal insults and assaults—he refused to take legal action against the individuals concerned even when urged to do so. This was his reaction when he was pushed off the pavement outside President Kruger's house, or attacked by a mob in Durban on his return from India in 1897, or when some Pathans assaulted him because they thought he had betrayed the Indian community when he reached a compromise in negotiations with General Smuts in 1908.

After a year's work in South Africa and thinking of returning to his family in India, his attention was drawn to a newspaper report of proposed legislation limiting further some civil liberties of the Indian community. This had to be resisted, he felt, and he now set about appealing to members of the government and writing letters to the press. This was the beginning of years of campaigning on behalf of his Indian colleagues using normal channels. For a number of years, he used campaigning methods which kept within the law—letters to public officials and government ministers within South Africa and in Britain, forming bodies representing the Indian community, public meetings, establishing newspapers to educate politically the Indians. However, this proved to be inadequate and more powerful methods needed to be tried.

It was not until a large meeting in the Empire Theatre, Johannesburg, on 11 September 1906 that the Indian community took up civil disobedience. The usual expression for such action was 'passive resistance' but Gandhi felt that a more active word was needed and settled on *satyagraha* or 'holding firmly to the truth'. This was a principled form of nonviolent direct action that aimed at winning the opponent over to one's position or reaching a mutual agreement amicably.

Gandhi, *Ahimsa* and War

Gandhi reached, at least, a rudimentary belief in *ahimsa* while a student in London. His promise to his mother to abstain from meat before leaving India was transformed into a firm ethical belief on reading vegetarian literature. Jesus and Tolstoy broadened the concept. Gandhi embraced nonviolence as a general guide to life and this meant to him a rejection of violence in all its aspects—violence in speech, in thought, as well as physical violence.

There was however a complication. Perhaps he imbibed the concept of multifaceted truth (*anekantevada*) from his Jain environment. Gandhi's most fundamental concept was *satya* or truth, that's what he sought. But it was clear to him that human beings by their limited nature cannot know absolute Truth but rather only the truths that are understood by different women and men at particular times. From this one can see the necessity of tolerance since no one person possesses the whole truth of anything (Chatterjee, 1983, pp. 32–33). One has to respect another person's position and hence nonviolence is demanded. However, most people believe that it is acceptable to defend oneself against attackers, physically if need be, and that can, sometimes, mean war. Gandhi, in time, developed a nonviolent method of defense, satyagraha, but that developed gradually.

Gandhi was first faced with a war situation in 1899 when the English-speaking South Africans clashed with the Afrikaans speakers or Boers. Although he did not believe in violence himself he, nevertheless, accepted that most people are not pacifists and have the right to use violence in a just cause. Gandhi also believed, at this time, that the British Empire was, essentially, a good institution and where it had defects it could be reformed. In addition, he saw an opportunity for the Indian community to improve their position by supporting the Government and, hopefully, win the respect of the Europeans and after the war would be offered better conditions.

He, thus, offered to raise an Ambulance Corps to serve on the British side. The British army commanders were initially not interested but as the war was not going well they eventually accepted the offer and about 1100 Indian men volunteered and were given elementary training. They were led by Gandhi and performed their duties well, mainly carrying the wounded soldiers to the medical stations. Although the Indians were recognized for their service by the army command, the Government showed no signs of improving the Indians' legal, social, or political position.

Four years after the end of the Anglo-Boer War, a smaller conflict arose in Natal. Some Zulus protesting against taxation killed two policemen and this started the 'Bambatha Rebellion'. The Government launched a punitive expedition and Gandhi again offered to raise an ambulance corps. This was a small unit of only 20 with Gandhi as sergeant-major. They discovered that many of the Zulus were being flogged and their wounds were untreated. The Indians were willing to treat them and that became their main task for which the Zulus expressed their gratitude by their gestures. This war, although only brief, disturbed Gandhi much more than his first experience of war—'The Boer War had not brought home to me the horrors of war with anything like the vividness that the rebellion did' (Gandhi, 1940, p. 233).

During the following eight years, Gandhi developed satyagraha as a means of combating the attempts of the South African Government to restrict Indian civil liberties and this met with some success. Considering his task at last done, he and his wife Kasturba with colleague Hermann Kallenbach left South Africa for Britain intending, after a short stay there, to sail for India. Just before they arrived, Britain declared war on Germany. Once more Gandhi felt drawn to do what he could in support of Britain and again he thought of an Ambulance Corps. He got the support of the Government and put out an appeal for volunteers which attracted sufficient Indians, mainly students studying in Britain. A first group of 30 of the Corps was sent to a hospital near Southampton, its task being to treat Indian troops who had been wounded in France.

Gandhi's reasons for this action were very similar to the two earlier occasions. On this occasion he added that the navy was used to protect supplies of food and other essentials, therefore, he was implicated in the war by living in Britain. But, one could point out that while he wished to give support to Britain even in its wars he was at least providing medical aid on all three occasions, saving life rather than destroying it. He did not, however, make this distinction. Some of his colleagues did not like his association with the military, such as Henry Polak who cabled from South Africa, and Pragji Desai, a leading satyagrahi, took a similar position (Brock, 1983, p. 70).

He and Kasturba sailed, finally, for India arriving there at the very start of 1915. During the remainder of the European war Gandhi was reacquainting himself with his country and people and before long he involved himself in social disputes which he contributed to solving. But, in the last year of the First World War he once more allowed himself to be drawn into a war situation.

Crisis

Early in 1918 the European war was not going well for Britain. Even more Indian troops would be useful and so the Viceroy Lord Chelmsford called a War Conference at Delhi for 28 April and tried to persuade Gandhi to attend. Chelmsford used an argument that was difficult to resist: '… would you not admit that it is the duty of every Indian citizen to help the Empire in the hour of its need'. But this time the men were to fight and kill. Gandhi thought that serving in the armed forces would encourage bravery, a virtue that he greatly admired. He agreed to recruit Indians for the British Army. Not surprisingly, there were protests again from colleagues including Esther Faering, a Danish woman missionary who joined Gandhi's ashram, and Charlie Andrews who was not convinced that learning to kill was a good way to develop the courage needed for a *satyagrahi* (Brock, 1983, p. 61).

Gandhi's thinking at this time was remote from that of Tolstoy and Jesus. He seemed to have believed that the Indian people were timid and passive and that they would never achieve independence without a change of character. Perhaps his own timid character when young had something to do with his elevating the virtue of courage. But he went further, even telling Andrews: 'You cannot teach ahimsa to a man who cannot kill' (Brock, 1983, p. 62).

Gandhi proceeded to recruit choosing the district of Kheda in Gujarat where there had been a recent satyagraha campaign and so he expected a positive response. He travelled village to village in the district but was usually met with a lack of enthusiasm and surprise that this man who so praised the virtues of nonviolence was recruiting for the British Army. Few volunteered. In mid-August Gandhi's health broke down, something that he attributed to carelessness in his diet, but also implied that mental conflict was a contributing factor. His illness gave him time for reflection and he began to emerge from a period of mental turbulence. He wrote in September:

One need not assume that heroism is to be acquired only by fighting in a war. One can do so even while keeping out of it. War is one powerful means [for this] among many others. But if it is a powerful means, it is also an evil one. (Brock, 1983, p. 66)

On the ending of the War in November Gandhi was greatly relieved and turned his mind to other matters. But in 1928, Bart de Ligt, the leading Dutch anti-militarist and anarchist, wrote to Gandhi about his earlier attitude to war. Although greatly admiring Gandhi he was disappointed that he had, in effect, supported war on four occasions. This developed into a dialogue in the pages of *Young India*. De Ligt gave a convincing answer to Gandhi:

... the present governments from time to time, maybe even as a rule, do good more or less. But that can never be for us a sufficient motive for collaborating unreservedly with them in all their enterprises. I am supposing for instance, that someone—or some government—does me a great service. Am I then obliged, from the moral point of view, to come to his assistance even when he acts badly, offends and kills, and forms schemes which are in flagrant opposition to any religious or humanitarian conceptions? No, quite the contrary. The more grateful I feel towards him, the less can I collaborate with him in evil work. (Bartolf, 2000, p. 44)

Vladimir Chertkov, Tolstoy's former secretary, wrote in the same year to Gandhi expressing similar views (Bartolf, 2000, p. 35).

In a letter of November 1928 to De Ligt, Gandhi, after repeating his reasons for supporting governments on four occasions, finished with:

But the light within me is steady and clear. There is no escape for any of us save through truth and nonviolence. I know that war is wrong, is an unmitigated evil. I know too that it has got to go. I firmly believe that freedom won through bloodshed or fraud is no freedom. (Bartolf, 2000, p. 33)

In 1931, at the Second Round Table Conference held in London to consider the future governance of India, Gandhi declared ' ... I am here very respectfully to claim, on behalf of the Congress, complete control over the army, over the defence forces and over external affairs'. But on his way home he passed through France, Switzerland, and Italy and in Lausanne he met De Ligt who asked him:

> 'What would you do if an eventually free India were to enter into a war?' Gandhi replied that he was convinced that, if India freed itself by nonviolent means, she would never more go to war. If however, contrary to all his dreams, an eventually free India should go to war, he hoped—with divine assistance—to have the strength to rise up against his government and to stand in the way of violent resistance. (Bartolf, 2000, p. 71)

A Greater Challenge

In late 1935 Italy, with Mussolini as head of the Fascist Government, invaded Abyssinia. Villages were bombed including with poison gas. Gandhi reflected on the invasion in *Harijan* in 1938:

> ... if the Abyssinians had adopted the attitude of non-violence of the strong ... Mussolini would have had no interest in Abyssinia. Thus if they had simply said: 'You are welcome to reduce us to dust and ashes, but you will not find one Abyssinian ready to co-operate with you', what would Mussolini have done? He did not want a desert. (Gandhi, 1994, CWMG Vol. 67, p. 76)

The Czech crisis of 1938 brought a similar response from Gandhi—to resist the Nazis nonviolently.

The plight of the German Jews also prompted Gandhi to give similar advice in 1938, which, in general, was not welcomed by the world Jewish community who considered him naive:

> But the German persecution of the Jews seems to have no parallel in history. The tyrants of old never went so mad as Hitler seems to have gone. ... If ever there could be a justifiable war in the name of and for humanity, a war against Germany, to prevent the wanton persecution of

a whole race, would be completely justified. But I do not believe in any war. (Gandhi, 1942, NVPW Vol. 1, p. 171)

In early July 1940, when the Battle of Britain between the German and British air forces was about to begin, Gandhi published a message 'To Every Britton':

> I appeal for cessation of hostilities, not because you are too exhausted to fight, but because war is bad in essence. You want to kill Nazism. You will never kill it by its indifferent adoption. Your soldiers are doing the same work of destruction as the Germans. The only difference in that perhaps yours are not as thorough as the Germans. If that be so, yours will soon acquire the same thoroughness as theirs, if not much greater. On no other condition can you win the war. In other words, you will have to be more ruthless than the Nazis. (Gandhi, 1942, NVPW Vol. 1, p. 297)

It is clear from the advice to the Czechs, to the Poles also and to the British that Gandhi's belief in the power of nonviolence had solidified. Although none of the governments that soon were invaded by the German forces considered nonviolent methods of resistance nevertheless certain sections of the occupied populations took up nonviolent resistance as pragmatic responses to occupation.

On 3 September 1939 the Viceroy Lord Linlithgow announced that India was at war with Germany. At the Congress Working Committee (CWC) Gandhi advocated unconditional nonviolent support for Britain but most of the CWC members did not hold to nonviolence as a fundamental belief but only an expedience (Abdul Ghaffar Khan did support Gandhi) and thus were prepared to offer military support in return for concessions.

As the threat to India from the Japanese advance grew Gandhi wrote in April 1942:

> … non-violent resistance could commence the moment they effected a landing. Thus nonviolent resisters would refuse them any help, even water. For it is no part of their duty to help anyone to steal their country. But if a Japanese had missed his way and was dying of thirst and sought

help as a human being, a non-violent resister, who may not regard anyone as his enemy, would give water to the thirsty one. (Gandhi, NVPW Vol. 1, p. 417)

Gandhi's close colleague, Mirabehn, had at this time been asked by Gandhi to go to Orissa to prepare the population for nonviolent resistance in the event of Japanese troops landing on the east coast. But realizing how unprepared the Indian population was for nonviolent defense he conceded to Congress.

The Modus Operandi of Satyagraha

Gandhi's satyagraha is an ideal form of nonviolent action. It seeks to use highly ethical means to win over the opposition with a dialectical approach. The aim is to reach an outcome to the conflict which is satisfactory to both sides. Contact between the sides is necessary for this to happen as well as open minds. On the other hand, there are certain positions which are not to be compromised. Gandhi believed that satyagrahis should be prepared to die resisting and this would be likely to bring desirable change in the aggressor—a conversion. The suffering endured, he believed, would melt the heart of the aggressor. But is this realistic in most cases? Is there not another way in which nonviolent resistance works? Thomas Weber examined one of Gandhi's best known campaigns—the Salt Satyagraha of 1930 and in particular the attempt to take over the Dharasana Salt Works. He deduced that the effectiveness of the action came primarily from the publicity it generated world-wide and not the suffering endured by the satyagrahis converting the police who were defending the Salt Works (Weber, 1993).

It is likely that there are many routes that bring about change depending on the particular case. Gene Sharp, who has made the most extensive study of nonviolent action in its many forms, sees the operation of power as the most significant factor. A most important part of this is that a degree of consent by the populace is necessary for control by the elite to be effective. But the withdrawal of consent is always possible. Sharp lists the many forms of nonviolent action that can be used to weaken control and identified 198. Sharp believed that his pragmatic approach to nonviolent action would be more readily adopted around the world if it was detached from the cultural and ethical beliefs of Gandhi (Sharp, 2005). Someone who disagreed with Sharp was the philosopher Howard Horsburgh. Horsburgh thinks Sharp's avoidance of discussion of ethical qualities in the resisters—such qualities as 'truthfulness, good-will, courage, self-reliance, patience, readiness, concern for justice' and his concentration on technique is a weakness (Horsburgh, 1975). However, there is much common ground between both of them in addition to avoidance of violence—they agree that sabotage should not be used, and nor should secrecy.

I believe that Gandhi sometimes underestimated the effectiveness of pragmatic nonviolent resistance by focussing particularly on suffering and conversion as the means. Norman Finkelstein points out that Gandhi's own campaigns often displayed elements of coercion (Finkelstein, 2012). We now know of many examples of pragmatic direct action not using violence in many parts of the world, a significant proportion of which were successful. My own interest in resistance in Nazi Germany and occupied Europe has revealed cases of resistance in this very repressive situation (Paxton, 2016). Although not sufficient to defeat the oppressor, the potential to do so is demonstrated, especially as Nazi Germany was overstretched economically and administratively and was heavily dependent on collaboration by the occupied population—which was not guaranteed in the long run. That Germany's defeat by the Allied forces cost a huge number of lives running to the tens of millions and vast material destruction in addition should also be given consideration in any comparison of violent and nonviolent means of liberation.

We now know, thanks to the research of Erica Chenoweth and Maria J. Stephan, who examined more than 300 large cases of violent and nonviolent change in the twentieth century that nonviolent campaigns are statistically about twice as successful as violent ones (Chenoweth & Stephan, 2013).

A War-Free World

To most people the absence of war seems pure fantasy. Yet, so many activities that were normal and apparently permanent have disappeared from human society, or almost so. I am thinking of such practices as human sacrifice, slavery, rule by inheritance, judicial torture, the inferiority of women, the superiority of the white race, and many more. War is another that needs to be consigned to history.

Admittedly, there is no single solution for abolishing war—many factors need to be combined. Here are some: the reduction and eventual abolition of the arms trade which is kept at such a high level because of the profits to be made by arms manufacturing corporations; general disarmament starting with nuclear disarmament as the most dangerous weapons; the further development of international law and strengthening of the International Court of Justice; and a reformed United Nations. Klaus Schlichtmann has pointed out that Gandhi was not averse to a United Nations as an aid to world peace and he quotes several speeches/interviews made during the Second World War. In a speech to the All India Congress Committee in Bombay on 7 August 1942 Gandhi said: 'We are aiming at a world federation in which India would be a leading unit. It can come only through non-violence' (CWMG, p. 381; Gandhi, 1994). A reduction in armaments could release large sums for positive uses such as health and education especially for less developed countries.

The adoption of some of Gandhi's other principles could encourage a more just and peaceful world such as *sarvodaya* (the welfare of all); *satya*—the search for truth leading to tolerant and pluralistic societies; *aparigraha* (non-possessiveness) to counter the desire for more and more goods that underlies current economics; and employee ownership (trusteeship) in place of individual ownership of businesses thus giving more freedom (*swaraj*) to more people and encouraging equality. These would lead to a genuine security rather than the false and dangerous 'security' of the armed state. This approach would also fit into a simpler lifestyle than most people in the developed countries 'enjoy' at present, an absolute necessity for our planet's health and survival of the living beings on its surface.

Gandhi's most original contribution to creation of a war-free world is satyagraha, a moral equivalent of war (Horsburgh, 1968). This is always available for use by those who wish to live in a non-repressive society and have the determination and courage to use it. However, it may be that something short of the high standards set by Gandhian satyagraha, that is, a more pragmatic nonviolent resistance, can often be effective too.

References

Bartolf, C. (Ed.). (1997). *Letter to a Hindu, Taraknath Das, Leo Tolstoy and Mahatma Gandhi.* Gandhi-Informations-Zentrum.

Bartolf, C. (Ed.). (2000). *The breath of my life, The correspondence of Mahatma Gandhi and Bart de Ligt.* Gandhi-Informations-Zentrum.

Brock, P. (1983). *Gandhi's non-violence and his war service.* Navajivan Publishing House.

Chatterjee, M. (1983). *Gandhi's religious thought.* MacMillan Press.

Chaturvedi, B., & Sykes, M. (1949). *Charles Freer Andrews.* George Allen & Unwin.

Chenoweth, E., & Stephan, M. J. (2013). *Why civil resistance works: The strategic logic of nonviolent conflict.* Columbia University Press.

Finkelstein, N. G. (2012). *What Gandhi says about nonviolence, resistance and courage.* OR Books.

Gandhi, M. K. (1940). *The story of my experiments with truth.* Navajivan Publishing House.

Gandhi, M. K. (1942). *Nonviolence in peace and war* (NVPW) (Vol. 1). Navajivan Publishing House.

Gandhi, M. K. (1994). *Collected works (CWMG).* www.gandhiheritageportal.org. Accessed 21 Dec 2020.

Green, M. (1998). *Tolstoy and Gandhi: Men of peace.* Harper Collins India.

Horsburgh, H. J. N. (1968). *Non-violence and aggression: A study of Gandhi's moral equivalent of war.* Oxford University Press.

Horsburgh, H. J. N. (1975). Politics of non-violent action. *Inquiry, 18,* 103–112.

Paxton, G, (2016). *Nonviolent resistance to the Nazis.* YouCaxton Publications.

Schlichtmann, K. *Gandhi and world peace: A federation of the world.* Found on www.academia.ed. Accessed 21 Dec 2020.

Sharp, G. (2005). *Waging nonviolent struggle: 10th century practice and 21st century potential*. Extending Horizon Books.

Weber, T. (1993). "The marchers simply walked forward until struck down"—Nonviolent suffering and conversion. *Peace & Change, 18*(3).

Part IV
The Interminable Wisdom of Gandhi

16

Gandhi's Wisdom in the Twenty-First Century and Beyond

V. K. Kool and Rita Agrawal

One of the editors of this book, Kool, was addressing a small group of wealthy people who were interested in helping needy children. When he asked each one of them to take an initiative and invite a young child and keep him/her for a day at their affluent homes, very few showed spontaneous and instant readiness. While they had genuinely meant to help the needy, their own comfort and identity in interacting with a poor child for the entire day at their homes became the issue. One member was concerned about her image in society, another with hygiene, and more.

At this point, we are reminded of what Gandhi had said: "recall the face of the poorest and the weakest man who you may have seen, and ask yourself, if the step you contemplate is going to be of any use to him"

V. K. Kool (✉)
SUNY Polytechnic Institute, Utica, NY, USA

R. Agrawal
Harish Chandra Post Graduate College, Varanasi, Uttar Pradesh, India

© The Author(s), under exclusive license to Springer Nature
Switzerland AG 2022
V. K. Kool and R. Agrawal (eds.), *Gandhi's Wisdom*,
https://doi.org/10.1007/978-3-030-87491-9_16

(Gandhi, August 1947, p. 125). Psychologists such as Skinner had used this quote of Gandhi to support the theory of reinforcement, but in the absence of any development of identity with the person, the authenticity of wisdom fails to bring the desired results. No wonder, as stated earlier, Skinner was not successful in sustaining his community as compared to what Gandhi did at the Tolstoy Farm in South Africa or at Wardha ashram in India.

Any understanding of the need for wisdom hinges, basically, on our survival and adaptation to an ever changing physical and social environment, which, in turn, helps to forge our personal identity. Further, personal identity has important links to two domains: first, the core of communal culture and, second, its representation in human cognition. Together, they form, guide, and monitor our experiences, helping us to build a super identity that provides the abstraction of who we are and who we want to be, maybe God-like, a Rocky, an Avatar, or Gandhi.

Even those living beings that are placed lower down in the phylogenetic scale and are unable to use language are gifted with several forms of behavior leading to their survival. Scholars in the field of comparative biology and related disciplines have been, constantly, extrapolating information about them, and with recent advancements, there is considerable that can be learnt from their ways of adaptation and survival, making us wiser in the process (for more details, see Kool & Agrawal, 2010, 2011). Therefore, it is important to begin with asking a question: what happens when we think that we are wise even though we may not be so?

Why Do We Need Gandhi More Than Ever Before in Our Search for Wisdom?

The trajectory for the study of wisdom has been overshadowed by issues from its very inception. Firstly, human beings engage in discrimination by considering themselves wiser than other living beings. This tendency escalates, further, to the intra-human level leading to feelings such as White versus Black, mature versus immature, or, young versus old, leading to the switching off of the default mode of our wisdom and, believing falsely, that our lives are more significant than that of others.

Often, we kill other living beings without any remorse. Make a visit to a slaughter house to know the value of life and what do you find? Should we call ourselves wise consenting to what is happening around? Sure, we may say, we or they are wise but helpless. Is there wisdom in inaction? At the same time, putting wisdom into action has its own problems (Boulware, 2019). But, according to Gandhi, wisdom is no wisdom if it does not seep into action. "Walk the talk" is the motto of wisdom.

Secondly, whether there is consensus regarding a common definition and measurement of wisdom or not, Hume's contention, that, while values are represented in the state of mind, it is the affective responses which determine the perceived value of properties around us, has to be agreed upon. In this respect too, the core issue for understanding wisdom requires inputs ranging from those of lower levels of organisms to that of the godfathers of humanity. One such example of how organisms lower down in phylogeny struggle to survive and create desirabilities for augmenting and demonstrating their wisdom is provided by a 60 minutes-CBS program journalist who visited an island, unsullied by human presence, and was amazed to be shown a bird who had created a huge six feet tall nest and danced, incessantly, to lure a mate to its own Taj Mahal (for details see Kool & Agrawal, *Psychology of Technology*, 2016).

Such creatures in nature lack human intelligence and are unable to construct mansions but offer useful information for the study of wisdom. Thus, phylogenetically and incrementally, conceptualizing or measuring wisdom involves a trajectory, different from the traditional approach, for exploring the affective and emotional nature of wisdom manifested in self sacrifice, altruism, and more. It is precisely for this reason, that Gandhi remarked in an interview with Benjamin May on December 31, 1936 at Wardha, India and reported in his book, *Born to Rebel: An Autobiography*:

Nonviolence is not passive resistance but rather an active force. It is three fourths invisible, one quarter visible. Likewise its results are likely to be invisible and not capable of measurement........ when one retreats in nonviolent effort, he must never retreat out of fear, nor because he believes the nonviolent technique will never win. His faith must teach him that nonviolence can never lose because three fourths of it is invisible and cannot be measured. So it can never be said that the method is impractical, or that it has failed, if a campaign is called off. (May, 2002/1936).

The above position of Gandhi might appear troubling to those who specialize in wisdom and its measurement. More recently, sensing the need for focusing on the affective aspect in wisdom studies, Grossman (2017) has proposed the concept of emodiversity (reported in Chapter 1 of this book), illustrating how the experiencing of diverse emotions becomes an integral part of wisdom. Both cognitively and emotionally, wisdom is a behavioral feature that defines our potential for existence and often expands our cognition, on one hand, and relieves us from the burden of those limitations that had, hitherto, appeared irreversible, on the other. Therefore, the range of study of wisdom is complex and it is not surprising that Gandhi had expressed his reservations on having some set exactitude and parameters of wisdom. In fact, even today, its quantification eludes scientists.

Thirdly, the history of psychology is replete with the overemphasis on various forms of pathological behaviors and the identification of organic disorders that are associated with such behaviors. It is difficult to believe, but true, that as late as until the end of the previous century, psychologists were preoccupied with the study of self control in the context of the breakdown of normative behaviors, leading to criminality and other forms of deviancy (for example, work by leading scholars such as Roy Baumeister, 1999). On the other hand, a cursory glance at the role of self control in situations beyond our normal repertoire of behavior, for example, in yoga, mindfulness, silence, fasting, and other myriad forms of behavior that communities around the world, and, religions in particular, have offered to us through the ages reveals the positive nature of self control. In several chapters of this book, readers will find examples of how Gandhi demonstrated his wisdom through such nuanced forms of behavior.

More specifically, Gandhi's wisdom is rooted in one's ability to manage, monitor and test self control in the most arduous conditions, imaginable. With temptations constantly surrounding us, the chances of the depletion of self control, as reported in numerous modern psychological researches (also reported in other chapters of this book) are high, but to manifest self control in the face of adversity is challenging for not only expanding cognition (for example, how to continually use fair means to achieve our goal), but also for managing the ambivalent emotions (for example, controlling our anger and disgust and loving the perpetrators of violence, at the same time).

On examining the event of the historically famous Dandi March organized by Gandhi for the making of salt and defying British law, it is clear that the abundant exuberance of self control, as manifested by the scores of nonviolent marching protesters who succumbed to the brutality of British led police, became the cardinal expression of the identity of millions who found their communal identity merging with their personal identity of freedom (Kool & Agrawal, 2018). The journalists witnessing the event got so emotional that they declared, instantly, that the West had lost its moral superiority and that India had become a free country, there and then, using the moral weapon of nonviolence. Self control helps to create affordances that demonstrate the wisdom of nonviolence and expands human cognition in the face of emotions that continue to flood us.

A close examination of the life and work of Gandhi illustrates that he not only focused on the carving of human cognition in relation to a variety of emotions, or as modern psychologists present them in the context of emodiversity, as mentioned in Chapter 1, but he also realized that the driver of nonviolence must have enough intrinsic motivation, in the form of will power, to steer the movement in the right direction (Kool, 1993, 2008; Kool & Agrawal, 2013). For this purpose, his experiments with truth provide strength to his followers to test themselves in several domains but especially, in remaining nonviolent even in the face of being annihilated (Kool, 2013). Thus, by focusing on self control as a cardinal form of behavior, Gandhi engaged and enmeshed the subtle threads of human cognition, emotion, and motivation for engineering and demonstrating human wisdom.

On Moving Away from the Study of Negative Forms of Behavior: The Context of Gandhi's Wisdom

Since its inception, the science of psychology has been simultaneously preoccupied with the study of pathological behavior on one side and that of the intellectual and creative aspects of the human mind, on the other. In its applied form, the practitioners of psychology have advocated, directly or indirectly, that the elimination of unwanted behavior and the availability of creative intellectuals, scientists, professionals, and community leaders in key positions would help in solving problems at all levels, both individual and social (Kool & Agrawal, 2006). However, it was not until the beginning of the current century that the flagship journal of the American Psychological Association, the *American Psychologist*, published its first complete issue on positive psychology with topics such as happiness, resiliency, and more. Even at this stage of the growth of psychology, it is difficult to convince most intellectuals and policy makers that the control of war, violence, hostilities, and other such forms of negative behaviors are no definite or sustained corollaries to well being, peace, and development.

At an interview in the 1980s, when Kool was asked about his specialization, he replied, "human cognition and the psychology of nonviolence". The committee members began questioning his specialization by saying: "oh, we have psychology of industry but not non-industrial psychology"; another said, "we understand psychology of violence, but are you going to set up a course/program on non-cognitive psychology as well", and more. The counter argument that Kool presented was whether non-vegetarians would eat the meat of pets such as dogs and cats? The answer, obviously, was an emphatic "no". In much the same way, Kool told them that the adding of the prefix "non", does not necessarily, make a concept the mirror opposite of another.

From the above and many other illustrations, it is clear that understanding and finding interventions for the enhancement of wisdom is not easy, since comparisons with its flipside, for example, the comparison of "wise" with "unwise" is not only risky but also leads to dubious contentions. In the context of multicultural training programs it would, unquestionably, be a disaster. And yet, in program after program, an integral part of the training is to enhance the thinking in terms of opposites. We were surprised to find that it is difficult to complete a certain executive program of Cornell University without identifying the opposites of the presented concepts/scenarios. Recently, Grossman (2017), a leading scholar on wisdom, has offered inputs for the understanding of the context of wisdom, but it needs greater elaboration and authenticity in view of the above argument.

For Gandhi, wisdom comes not by simply eliminating the negative aspects of life, but by realizing the yin and yang of life, as Barbara Fredrickson (2001) conceptualized in her Broaden and Build theory, highlighting both the upper and lower spirals of well being. In terms of Grossman's description (refer to Chapter 1 and Grossmann et al., 2020) of the components of wisdom in terms of moral grounding, encompassing the pursuit of truth, shared humanity, and common good orientation, the weights assigned to each category by different individuals were found to vary, offering plasticity in the understanding and the seeking of applications of research on wisdom. Such plasticity corroborates the idea that with changing context, culture, or the core of consciousness, wisdom may not remain wisdom.

Gandhi's wisdom, rooted in nonviolence, has a moral grounding but offers little plasticity as we move away from its default mode of nonviolence. For this reason, psychologists such as Kolhberg (1976) placed Gandhi in the highest tier of moral development attained by hardly 5% of people, and, even at that level, the moral development attained by Gandhi would not be easy to measure. It is difficult to categorize people such as Gandhi, wrote Owen Flanagan (1991) in his book, *Varieties of moral personality*, because, though they are viewed to be at the apex of human existence, they do not operate in terms of a single or a predetermined multiple set of moral standards. Nagin Sanghavi, eminent historian and writer on Gandhi had exactly the same belief regarding Gandhi: when interviewed by Rita Agrawal in 2017 (and described in our book, *Gandhi and the Psychology of Nonviolence*, 2020) he contended that mahatmas (great souls), such as Gandhi, are difficult to describe and measure.

Wisdom can be seen emerging in a variety of forms including,

- The clergy way: do as it has been prescribed by the holy books or social order,
- The saint way: apply ethics and find the right thing to do,
- The hermit way: live and be guided by your conscience; becoming a loner but never disavow your responsibility toward the community.

In his search for truth, Gandhi never hesitated to find solace in any of the above stated categories because relativism is the basis of the idea that truth is endless and provides further meaning to our navigation through life. Psychiatrist Jeste, in his description of positive psychiatry and as mentioned in Chapter 1, contends that there is considerable to be learnt from our grandma's wisdom (Jeste & LaFee, 2020). It is also true, that such wisdom is acquired from the combination of any or all the above stated experiences. Unfortunately, Western dictionaries define a hermit in the context of a schizoid personality disorder. Raghavan Iyer (1983) was so correct in his assessment that for Westerners, Gandhi, in the role of a hermit, would be impossible to understand.

The silver lining in the research on wisdom is the category of meta-wisdom according to Baltes and Staudinger (2000) and Gugerelle and Riffert (2012). They have found uncertainty, relative values, and context to be salient features of wisdom. Any conceptualization of human life is impossible in the absence of choices, but hermits, unlike ordinary human beings, become reclusive and discard material life following their own choices in life. Yet, they never step away from the highest grounding of human virtues, tried and tested in the most compelling circumstances of life. Gandhi took a leaf from hermits, laid his hands to the study of various religious books including the Bible and the Gita and interacted with religious leaders in the three continents of the world where he had lived and operated. Gandhi determined that by being in the company of such people around him, he could observe behaviors such as silence, fasting, and vows so as to keep the essence of a hermit in his character. He enjoyed moral engagement with people around him but at the same time displayed features of behavior so typical of a hermit. This is the nature of authentic wisdom of a super human being (Ferrari et al., 2016).

By living like Gandhi, we experience his wisdom, as is amply demonstrated in the chapters presented in the third section of this book: Nagler's interpretation based on the Hindu holy book, the Bhagwada Gita, and his establishing of the Metta Center for Nonviolence (Box 16.1); Cortland as protester; and Paxton on war. In many ways, among those who emulated Gandhi in their life and work, for example, Karve, Bhave, and others, had an opportunity to experience Gandhi directly and found ways to advance his wisdom through doosri azadi (second freedom), that is, freedom from poverty coupled with rural development, literacy, and self governance. Gandhi's wisdom, rooted in the soil of nonviolence, is a human ontogenetic foresight characterized by least uncertainty as long as we do not replant it in the soil of violence.

Box 16.1 Michael Nagler's Metta Center for Nonviolence and the Third Harmony

Michael Nagler, the contributor of a chapter in this book, is the founder of the Metta Center for nonviolence in California and has advocated nonviolence based on Gandhian principles for decades (Nagler, 1990). He has offered a path of nonviolence following a harmonious way of life into the mainstream of our culture:

Harmony 1: with all there is (universe)
Harmony 2: harmony with the earth, and
Harmony 3: focusing inwards

According to him, with the above in harmony, we would contribute to the future of nonviolence, which is being proven by the decades of scientific research on quantum physics and brain science.

Source: Nagler, M. N. (2020), The third harmony: Nonviolence and the new story of human nature. Berrett-Koeler audio; Sandra Bass, Berkeley blog, November 30, 2020.

Nagler's conceptualization of human nature, rooted in the current stream of scientific research and thinking, is an invitation to focus on the relevance of human behavior in dealing with issues concerning harmony at the above three levels and to seek lessons from Gandhi in cultivating our wisdom by unfolding the layers of our coexistence as seen in the moral grounding of Gandhi as a cleric, saint or sage (Box 16.1). Through his experiments with truth, Gandhi offered a trajectory to expand our cognition in seeking such harmony, which, modern scholars of the psychology of wisdom also find handy. For instance, procedural knowledge regarding the planning, understanding, and finding of meaning in life, claim psychologists, are the basic parameters of wisdom, but it, definitely, requires a person to invent and impart these elements of wisdom. Following nonviolence, Gandhi amply demonstrated these attributes of wisdom but where is Gandhi in the psychology of nonviolence? The proof is in the pudding, as Murray et al. (2014) wrote in their chapter, *Toward a psychology of nonviolence*. While summarizing the status of research and publications on the psychology of nonviolence, let alone, specifically, covering the wisdom of Gandhi, they write:

> Although there have been some efforts to develop a psychology of nonviolence (e.g., Kool, 2008), and the APA has had a division of peace psychology since 1988, the potential for contributions of psychology to the study and practice of nonviolence has been largely untapped. The possibilities, however, are exciting. We have only enough space to make a few suggestions. Kool (2008) gives a far more extensive discussion. (p. 179)

Faith, Wisdom, and Gandhi

Let us narrate the story of a 10 year old boy who bought an umbrella when it had not rained for five years and the community members gathered to pray to God to bestow them with plenty of rain for their survival. While the boy covered himself with the umbrella, others looked at his weird behavior because it had not rained for five years. But soon, it started raining. Only faith defines the genuineness of wisdom. We know several family members and health professionals who risked their lives to save patients suffering from the recent COVID pandemic. Similarly, think of Schindler's list and the saving of Jews from Hitler's genocide. It is our faith in the sanctity of life that guides such behavior.

If it is misdirected, it could create rebels, terrorists and other similar agents. Therefore, Gandhi, a rebel himself, taught us to never switch off the default mode of the wisdom of nonviolence in our cognitive system and to keep respecting the sanctity of life at all levels (Vasudhaiva Kutumbakam).

No matter what the form of faith—religious, political, or any other—it is a fact that it eases the cognitive load by acting as a heuristic, and thereby, facilitates the faster processing of information. So, meeting a member of our own church helps in the effortless perception of certain group attributes. Social identity theory, as described elsewhere in this book, provides ample evidence on how unknown individuals form groups even for simple tasks such as counting dots and making other judgments. With sentiments and emotions accompanying a faith, the pace of information processing increases, becoming a precursor for the forging of an identity in the context of violence or nonviolence. Faith in a violent group may make one a terrorist while faith in a nonviolent group makes one a Gandhian nonviolent protester.

Another hallmark of wisdom as exemplified by Gandhi is humility, so often ignored by politicians and leaders the world over. Gandhi has offered us innumerable examples, but we tend to simply ignore them or learn nothing from his life and work (Box 16.2).

Box 16.2 Following Gandhi's Wisdom Has Its Own Rewards

1. While educating inmates of a youth correctional facility in NJ, USA, Mark Edwards (2020), a Princeton University faculty, asked them to think of their prison as Gandhi's Ashram and encouraged them to focus on Gandhi's life and work and be like him during their remaining time in prison. Not surprisingly, Edwards noticed that the mode of their cognitive appraisal of violence reversed and they began to appreciate and value nonviolence. Similar effects were reported by Cervantes (2020, April 20) while teaching degree courses such as *Waging Nonviolence* in a program offered to prisoners in Chicago. Using Kool and Sen's test of nonviolence, scholars at the University

---

of Maryland found that when nonviolence was primed at the cognitive levels of inmates, it helped reduce violence among the inmates of three prisons of Maryland (for details, see Kool & Agrawal, 2020).

2. While stalwarts in business and industry have long believed that Gandhi's views are not practical, contributors in this book such as Graeme Nuttall show how Gandhi's wisdom of aparigraha helps in increasing productivity in UK and Australia; Nachiketa Tripathi demonstrates that the calling orientation contributes to greater morale; Tej Prakash shows its relevance to the International Monetary Fund (IMF). Using Kool and Sen's test of nonviolence and by designing their own tool for relevant measurement in industry, Bhalerao and Kumar (2015) revealed how testing employees in the domain of nonviolence helps to break the cycle of violence.

3. A number of concepts of Gandhian nonviolence, such as tapas and anasakti appear exotic, but several scholars have empirically tested and demonstrated their usefulness(for details, see Kool, 2008; Kool & Agrawal, 2020). Manickam (2014) created a test of Sahay, meaning tolerance, which is relevant for the understanding of Gandhi's wisdom.

4. While it is inspiring to learn from scholars who go beyond words and writings to emulating Gandhi's life and work, and provide opportunities of witnessing the authenticity of his wisdom, there are countless people who could be rated as being less if not at all familiar with Gandhi's life and work. One such example is Lisbeth Ejlertsen (2017), of Denmark, who has written a book on spirituality, recently and has visited India several times. When Kool requested her to relate her thinking with Gandhi, she found wisdom in Gandhi and stated her willingness to communicate about him.

As stated in the opening chapter of this book, while scientist Einstein, President Obama, and prominent intelligence scholar Howard Gardner, intend to seek inspiration from the life and work of Gandhi, placing Gandhi in an island of the moral world of our time that is getting lonelier by the day will be unwise. Further to President Obama's remark in his book (2020), that Gandhi had set the moral tone of the previous century, it is mandatory that we must not only hear the tone but also continually test it through our cognition and behavior in the current millennium.

Faith is a facilitator of cognitive activity. With faith in nonviolence, wisdom widens its scope in relationships with community members. In his balance theory of wisdom (reported in Chapter 1), Sternberg (Sternberg, 1998; Sternberg et al., 2019) refers to this scenario of wisdom as the extra-personal aspect, in addition to the intra-personal and inter-personal (e.g., dyadic relationships) domains. While it is logical to argue that the context and attributes of wisdom vary as we move from intra- to extra-personal levels of wisdom, the question with which wisdom scholars have been grappling is about the identity it generates, particularly in the noosphere, allowing and stamping their existence, and viewing oneself as an individual and in relations with his/her community. Erikson (1969) was very clear on this issue as he pointed out that identity without affiliation has no meaning. He argued further that with affiliation to Gandhi's nonviolence—the cardinal virtue of coexistence, the emerging identity mitigates the boundaries at all levels—intra-, inter, and extra-personal. The individual finds himself or herself in the core of community and vice versa.

Throughout human history, faith has been the mainstay of wisdom, helping people in testing their individual effectiveness and collective survival. Attesting to Gandhi's trajectory of wisdom and in making it appear isomorphic, Raghavan Iyer (1983) wrote:

> Although Gandhi based his faith in the supremacy of the individual on his view of conscience and of the duty that a man owes to himself, his stress on action rather than thought led him to assert that the duty that a man owes himself is also owed by him to his fellow men.... This is, as Adam Smith pointed out, the only looking-glass by which we can, with the eyes of other people, scrutinize the propriety of our own conduct. (pp. 133–134)

Let us examine how the faith of two leading thinkers of the previous century, Marx and Gandhi, differed: while Karl Marx called violence the midwife of human history, Gandhi substituted nonviolence for the same expression. Marx was against any role of religion in human life as he considered it the opium of humankind and clubbed nonviolence with religion. In contrast, while extolling nonviolence, Gandhi viewed violence as regressing to animality and a threat to existence. Was Karl Marx violent at home? Was Hitler, either, violent at home? In analyzing violent behavior of nonviolent individuals vis-a-vis nonviolent behavior of violent individuals, Kool (2008) concluded that there are several gray areas in viewing violent and nonviolent behaviors (see also Chapter 2) and observed that while Hitler was very kind and loving at home, he was brutal at work in contrast to Gandhi who kept nonviolence as his default mode at all levels. Again, a faith is no faith when it is planted differently at different places and times. Not surprisingly, William James, like Gandhi, was also concerned about the dual self of modern human beings.

With Gandhi's nonviolence as the default mode of our cognition, it is not difficult to understand how faith, created in view of one's own conscience and aligned with duty, would be the cardinal test of wisdom. Gandhi, therefore, advised each satyagrahi to search their conscience to determine their faith in truth and nonviolence, before they sign up for their participation in his movement. Did Karl Marx or Hitler impart the same wisdom to their followers? The reader will notice that the default mode of cognition of nonviolence did not shift while shifting from the personal to the social levels, in the case of Gandhi. He was critical of the external inducements offered by the media, politicians, and others holding power in corrupting the innocence of the masses who believed and trusted them.

Like Seligman's authentic happiness, if there is a need to find authentic wisdom, Gandhi certainly heralded it and with no secrets around, made it transparent at all levels—intra-, inter-and extra-personal. This was Gandhi's "un-othering", a topic discussed in another chapter of this book. Gandhi is a perfect example of Kaufman's (2020) transcendental personality.

On the other hand, we invite readers to evaluate Gandhi's well-known example of ordering the killing of a terminally ill calf upon the incessant crying of her mother. He stood against his own faith of nonviolence, culminating in a number of his followers abandoning him. He acted like a hermit who would prefer to remain aloof than to succumb to the desirabilities around him.

Gandhi, as we learn, found wisdom in creating upper spirals of virtues and contended that faith could monitor and guide behavior but the genuineness of love and search for truth must keep updating our wisdom. When faith reaches a cross road, wisdom steers it in the direction of cardinal virtues—albeit, not instantly visible on the navigational system. But the human being must keep moving on and experimenting. There is wisdom in such progression and the killing of the sick calf should not be construed, dogmatically, as regression to animality.

Wisdom Is Psychological and Yet Not so Psychological

Like many other concepts in psychology such as sensation, perception, memory, intelligence, and motivation that usually contribute to the core of an introduction to psychology, concepts such as compassion, forgiveness, empathy, and wisdom, while forming the substance of positive psychology, are equally important and are rooted in our relationships with others. With the wisdom of nonviolence as the default mode of cognition, the study of activities of the newer prefrontal cortex is as relevant as the operation of the subcortical centers in the limbic and hippocampal areas of the brain. Emotions have evolutionary significance as they bond us, positively, negatively, or both, with people and things around us. Wisdom manages the tsunami caused by emotions and with self control intact, resists the evil of violence and guides us toward the appreciation of coexistence. Therefore, while wisdom is psychological, it also calls for inputs from external agents and could remain in moratorium in the absence of feedback from others.

More than our perceptual and intellectual processes, wisdom creates affordances in seeking feedback from others or nature, both in micro and macro forms. In our daily lives, it is wise to follow the norms as we do in following the traffic rules. However, is it wisdom if a surgeon drives over the speed limit while rushing to save the life of an injured patient admitted in a hospital? A surgeon friend of ours has asked us this question numerous times after receiving speeding tickets. However, while he received speeding tickets from only a small number of police personnel, several acquitted him, while a few not only acquitted him but also escorted him to make sure that he reached the hospital at the earliest. Scholars engaged in wisdom research in particular, and moral psychology in general, have sought answers to such moral conflicts for decades but judging wisdom in such scenarios has remained elusive, leaving its interpretation to the eyes of the beholder. Our surgeon friend continues to defy the speed limits, for he finds wisdom in saving a life rather than caring about his driving record, fines, and insurance issues. For Gandhi, virtue and wisdom are interchangeable as long as both tend to address the larger interest of humanity.

Kenneth Boulding, former president of American Association of Advancement of Sciences and known as half Mahatma Gandhi and half Milton Friedman, encouraged psychologists, at a conference in Wisconsin in 1988, to lay greater focus on Gandhian psychology. Along with him, others also felt the need for the establishment of an independent peace psychology division in the American Psychological Association. It was, indeed, a pleasure to all those concerned that this was established soon after. Kool invited him, again, at a conference in 1992 in New York to assure him, in the presence of several distinguished members of this division, that psychologists had, indeed, begun their work in this new sub-field of psychology of nonviolence and peace. In his inaugural speech, Boulding remarked (and, on the same day, also, reiterated his viewpoint while addressing the local Chamber of Commerce) that at least 90–95% of human activity is nonviolent, or call it unviolent, but it was Gandhi who formally laid the foundation of organized nonviolence (Boulding, 1993). Out of the three faces of power, physical/military, economic and integrative (reported in Chapter 1), Boulding (1990) contended that integrative power has strong psychological roots for organized nonviolence. He illustrated how Gandhi won the hearts of the British labor class even after boycotting British textile products which were hurting their livelihood. Did Gandhi not notice the impact of his wisdom of nonviolence and truth as presented in Box 16.3? It was the charisma emanating out of his integrative power based on love for his adversaries, the seeking of truth, and the adherence to nonviolence.

> **Box 16.3 Boulding: An Eyewitness of Gandhi's Influence in UK**
> "I remember Gandhi making his famous visit to Lancashire when I was young. In spite of the fact that his boycott of imported British textiles in India was affecting the Lancashire economy adversely, he made a great impression on the people. I remember a popular song which went something like this: We don't like the black shirts, we don't like the brown shirts, we don't like the white shirts, but here is to Gandhi with no shirt at all" (p. 204).
> Source: Chapter by Boulding, K. E. (1993): Nonviolence in the twenty-first century. In V. K. Kool (Ed.), *Nonviolence: Social and Psychological Issues*. Latham: University Press of America

As stated in Chapter 1 of this book, Gandhi's wisdom of nonviolence is as important for human cognition as homeostasis is to the balancing and functioning of the body. Take away nonviolence and everything becomes chaotic and threatens survival. Nonviolence is akin to the default mode in machine language or homeostasis in physiology: it is the cardinal basis of human existence and leads to authentic wisdom. It is because of this that we regard him as one the wisest of human beings and a father figure, an architect of human psychology in the East, much like we have known William James for decades in the West.

On the Wisdom of Machines

In the above context, Boulding also invited us to examine the cognizance of nonviolence in the twenty-first century through popular songs. As the reader can easily figure out from Box 16.3, Gandhi's wisdom worked like magic and resonated in the songs of the British labor class. In contrast, Boulding noted that the World War II produced hardly any songs while the Gulf War, though raising considerable enthusiasm, did not generate any songs at all. Israel's social scientist, Moerk (2002), noted that folklores, including songs, offer scripts to the cognitive framework of a culture and tend to honor their leaders. Just as national songs arouse nationalism, folklores, and songs with violent leaders, such as Hitler or Stalin, in the driver's seat could cause enormous suffering to humanity.

Further, Moerk contended that such folklores have evolutionary significance for the survival of a community and they are here to stay, even with the arrival of the new millennium. What is significant is that we will soon be in the company of robots and a beginning has been made with the awarding of citizenship by South Arabia to Sophia, a humanoid.

The reality of the presence of such mechanical artifacts has already bombarded us and their presence is being acknowledged by expressions such as, "hi Siri" or "hello Google". Sherry Turkle's view of the emergence of the second self in the context of technology is, definitely, gaining in prominence in our cognition (Turkle, 2011). Our dependence on machines has become so pervasive that we tend to look for our own phone number in our mobile phone, or require a calculator for adding 54 and 21!

Not in the very distant future, we would be in the company of intelligent robots capable of showing and sharing our emotions. Like our pets, they would be like members of our family, but with a difference. They could be more intelligent and sophisticated than us and could control us. In Chapter 10 of this book ("Turing Testing and Gandhi's Wisdom in the era of Cognitive Computing" by V. K. Kool & Rita Agrawal), we have raised the issue of survival in the company of humanoids. Thankfully, we can kill them by deleting the source of their energy. There would be no remorse in such violence nor would Gandhi be unhappy in his grave.

However, arguments such as the above come with a caveat. What if we fall in love with the humanoid Sophia? Unable to differentiate between the living and the lifeless, a baby cries when the mother begins to dust her doll, believing that it is getting hurt. But, even adults, who are able to differentiate between the living and the lifeless, are behaving in similar ways. People in Japan have been offering Buddhist funeral services for robot dogs and a Japanese astronaut bade farewell to a robot companion. In the company of such mechanical devices, we expect new folklores to emerge and become a part of our life and culture. So long as they promote nonviolence and are given positive treatment through funerals, etc., such expressions are manifestations of the core of humanity, namely, compassion. However, in the context of the current culture, they might also appear weird.

The management and control of the artificial intelligence of robots could become problematic as humans lose control over the data mined from their systems (for further details see other chapters in this book). Can machines become spiritual, as discussed by Kurzweil (1999, 2005), and can they be made to follow nonviolence as the default mode? As current experts of technology believe, it is likely that robots could kill us.

At some point in the twenty-first century, Gandhi's spinning wheel could take the shape of a robot for wise interaction and improvement in the quality of life. For Gandhi, the charkha (spinning wheel) is not just a machine, it is a source of livelihood, easy to operate without intimidation and education, a source of appreciating physical work, boosting our self esteem, and a collective endeavor for experiencing humanity. Maybe, such a scenario could be nomenclatured authentic human–machine wisdom, should we be getting ready to address various other forms of wisdom such as collective wisdom, cultural wisdom, religious wisdom, and so on. Following the findings of the National Science Foundation (Rocco & Bainbridge, 2002), it would be difficult to predict our interaction with machines beyond a period of 20 years, but the usefulness of Gandhi's wisdom of nonviolence can certainly be predicted lasting till human life is wiped out from the face of the earth.

Therefore, we invite the readers to use the lens of nonviolence to visualize Gandhi's wisdom.

Wisdom, Nonviolence, and Happiness: Gandhi's Seasons of Life

Walt Whitman, known as the first poet of democracy in the USA, wrote eloquently about the seasons of nature: "many a changeful season to follow, and many a scene in life". Gandhi's truth and nonviolence, too, are bound to show countless seasons as we navigate through life with wisdom as our scull. Unlike intelligence, wisdom has a greater collective orientation and acts much like a brilliant sailor who knows the finer differences between sailing a ship in a calm sea and that during the worst of storms. Wise people may appear enigmatic and mysterious as they sense changes in the season around them. British journalist and educationist Candler (1922) and Gregg, American author of the well-known book, *The Power of Nonviolence* (1958), both of whom had met Gandhi in India, write that though they found him wise, he was also very enigmatic. Candler wrote in the *Atlantic*, in July 1922:

> Probably there is no figure in contemporary history who means so many different things to so many different people. To the incurious Westerner, the name of Gandhi calls up the picture of a saint, or a charlatan, art ascetic, fanatic, or freak. If he reads many newspapers, the Mahatma will appear in turn as patriot, martyr, high-souled idealist, and arch-traitor; evangelist, pacific quietist, and truculent tub-thumper and revolutionist; subverter of empires and founder of creeds, a man of tortuous wiles and stratagems, or, to use his own phrase, 'a single-minded seeker after truth'; generally, in the eyes of the tolerant who are without prejudice, a well-meaning but mis-guided politician. Certainly a complex figure.

Further, Candler wrote very candidly that "I must confess that I never believed in Mr. Gandhi until I met him". .... and added, "Happily or unhappily, the common man in the street does not understand Ahimsa or Satyagraha".

We are not surprised to find that Gandhi's wisdom has often been taking the shape of collective violence in the garb of peaceful protests around the globe (Stengel, 2011; *Time*—"Person of the Year: The protester"). The essence of his message has been lost and it is being used for political, bureaucratic, employment, or other purposes, as opined by Weber (2018) (known as the Australian Gandhi).

Life is about generating happiness. It comes with faith in humanity as in raising a child. It has its own cost and rewards. Gandhi's happiness lay in nonviolence and in finding the means to attain it, without worrying for the goal per se. For him, it is a process, not a state. There is no absolute truth nor is there absolute happiness.

For Gandhi, there can be no compromise as far as seeking and deploying nonviolence as the corner stone of human cognition, replete with the tested and continually refined scripts and schemas of nonviolence and generating individual happiness in tandem with his/her role in the community (one example of how this can be done is by Roy, 2011). This is the essence of Gandhi's psychology, so significant at both theoretical and applied levels: to bring together authenticity of wisdom, happiness, and nonviolence and to keep on experimenting with truth and love as the default mode of cognition.

And then, one may find wisdom in Whitman's "many a scene in life".

Recently, leading scholars on the psychology of wisdom, such as Robert Sternberg, have argued that the issues concerning wisdom remain ill-defined and more so, at the curriculum levels in the schools where formats of testing such as multiple-choice examinations do not afford opportunities to explore and examine real life problems. In his article, "*Where Have All the Flowers of Wisdom Gone*", Robert Sternberg (2019) reported that stories that relate to wisdom in imparting education to children in schools have declined, significantly, over the years. According to Sternberg, such a scenario does not help them to think wisely.

It is our contention that neither have the flowers of wisdom and nor its seeds or the emphasis on "the moral skill" gone, as far as our institutions are concerned. Our contention is further reinforced by that of Schwartz and Sharpe (2019) through their article, *Practical Wisdom: What Aristotle Might Add to Psychology*. The missing link is our focus on nonviolence, placed, as it has been, in the back seat, and, the presence of mighty war weapons, international rivalry, and corrupt politicians and media (Kool & Agrawal, 2020). With such a scenario, accepting nonviolence as the default mode of cognition becomes problematic. Not surprisingly, children are primed to either adhere to violence or find themselves in a state of aphantasia, a state in which they are unable to carve a solution to the problem.

Through his experiments with truth and nonviolence, tested and experienced in three continents of the world, Gandhi demonstrated that the gap between theory and practice could be narrowed through our action evidenced in our conduct, but certainly not by merely holding on to beliefs. How far would our imparting of instructions take us? As illustrated in Box 16.2, when Edwards (2020) asked the prison inmates to think of their prison as Gandhi's ashram and follow Gandhi, the default mode of cognition changed from violence to nonviolence. How was he able to accomplish this? First and foremost, he must have had the approval of the prison authority to test Gandhi as a model in the prison. Mere instructions in the prison would have had a limited effect in the absence of an unaligned social policy, the creation of feasible curriculum instructions, and the motivation of the learner.

On the other hand, before psychology, as a science, offers recipes for wisdom, it needs introspection regarding its own wisdom. Did we learn from Milgram's disobeying participants in his experiments who refused to deliver shocks to the learner in a simple task? Have we highlighted and given preference to nonviolence, as championed by William James, the founding father of modern psychology in the west? Has psychology integrated the views of leading interdisciplinary scholars such as Galtung (1996), Boulding (1993), and more in its growth and as veteran scholar Sharp (1960) contended that Gandhi would be helpful in developing the theory and practice of social sciences, including psychology (Kool & Agrawal, 2020)? Has psychology not ignored Erikson's contention offered more than 50 years ago that Gandhi's work has great insights for the growth and development of modern psychology?

Nonviolence is the precursor of wisdom and while its correlates have been explored in bits and pieces by contemporary psychologists, a comprehensive examination of the psychology of nonviolence does not appear to be in the main menu of psychologists. This is clearly recognized when we scroll down the history and growth of modern psychology and as Murray and coworkers (2014) wrote:

> Although there have been some efforts to develop a psychology of nonviolence (e.g., Kool, 2008), and the APA has had a division of peace psychology since 1988, the potential for contributions of psychology to the study and practice of nonviolence has been largely untapped. The possibilities, however, are exciting. We have only enough space to make a few suggestions. Kool (2008) gives a far more extensive discussion. (p. 179)

The above observation is further reinforced by Arnett (2008) in a paper published in the *American Psychologist* that while the American Psychological Association has been the leading body of psychologists in the globe, it has also been neglecting the remaining 95% of the population of the world. Is there wisdom in neglecting learnings from the rest of the world or in fulfilling its obligation by showing its alignment with the rest of the world by offering mere passing references, as we find in the case of Gandhi and the psychology of nonviolence? While we applaud the American Psychological Association for inviting Martin Luther King to address its convention shortly before his assassination in 1968, works on Gandhi and the psychology of nonviolence need to be enlivened in psychology, in general, and in wisdom research in particular.

Gandhi's wisdom is like a rose bud ready to flower with its petals of compassion, love, forgiveness, and the humanness within us. To find it you do not have to separate it from the thorns around it. For Gandhi, wisdom is about understanding the lack of understanding. Wisdom needs to be preserved but also expanded over time, much like the rose, whose fragrance is expanded through the experiences of holding it in our hand fingers despite the bleeding caused by its thorns. It may be visible to others or not, but phenomenologically, it is about knowing what we know about the lack of understanding. This is not only the root of human cognition but is, in essence, wisdom emanating from the life and works of Gandhi in whom Western Psychology might find the iterant, incomer but convincingly, the founding father of modern psychology in the East with a genuine calling. As Obama had stated, ever so succinctly, "Gandhi had set the moral tone of the previous century".

References

Arnett, J. J. (2008). The neglected 95%: Why American psychology needs to be less American. *American Psychologist, 67*, 602–614.

Baltes, P. B., & Staudinger, U. M. (2000). Wisdom: A metaheuristic (pragmatic) to orchestrate mind and virtue toward excellence. *American Psychologist, 55*, 122–136.

Baumeister, R. F. (1999). *Evil: Inside human violence and cruelty*. Freeman.

Bhalerao, H., & Kumar, S. (2015). Nonviolence at workplace—Scale development and validation. *Business Perspectives and Research, 3*(1), 36–51.

Boulding, K. (1990). *Three faces of power*. Sage.

Boulding, K. (1993). Nonviolence in the 21st century. In V. K. Kool (Ed.), *Nonviolence: Social and psychological issues*. The University Press of America.

Boulware, J. M. (2019, December 6). *Solving the problems of the world through wisdom*. Centerfor Practical Wisdom, The University of Chicago.

Candler, E. (1922). Mahatma Gandhi. *The Atlantic*. theatlantic.com.

Cervantes, H. (2020, April 20). I teach nonviolence in the prisons hit hardest by COVID-19. Here's why we must decarcerate now. *Waging Nonviolence*. wagingnonviolence.org.

Edwards, M. (2020, January 29). *Reading Gandhi: Creating an 'ashram' in a youth correctional facility*. princeton.edu/news.

Ejlertsen, L. (2017). *The spiritual wisdom of India, Volume 1: About my search for happiness and truth in life with Indian gurus and palm leaf astrologers*. Author House.

Erikson, E. (1969). *Gandhi's truth*. Norton.

Ferrari, M., Abdelaal, Y., Lakhani, S., Sachdeva, S., Tasmim, S., & Sharma, D. (2016). Why is Gandhi wise? A cross-cultural comparison of Gandhi as an exemplar of wisdom. *Journal of Adult Development, 23*(4), 204–213.

Flanagan, O. (1991). *Varieties of moral personality*. Harvard University Press.

Fredrickson, B. (2001). The role of positive emotion in positive psychology: The broad and built theory of positive emotions. *American Psychologist, 56*, 218–226.

Gandhi, M. K. (1947). *The collected works of Mahatma Gandhi, 89*. https://www.gandhiashramsewagram.org.

Galtung, J. (1996). *Peace by peaceful means: Peace and conflict, development and civilization*. Sage.

Gregg, R. (1958). *The power of nonviolence*. Navajivan Publishing House.

Grossman, I. (2017). Wisdom in context. *Perspectives on Psychological Science*. https://doi.org/10.1177/1745691616672066

Grossmann, I., Weststrate, N. M., Ardelt, M., et al. (2020). Wisdom science in a polarized world: Knowns and unknowns. *Psychological Inquiry, 31*(2), 103–133. https://doi.org/10.1080/1047840X.2020.1750917

Gugerell, S. H., & Riffert, F. (2012). On defining wisdom: Baltes, Ardelt, Ryan and Whitehead. *Interchange: A Quarterly Journal of Education, 42*(3), 225–259. https://doi.org/10.1007/s10780-012-9158-7

Iyer, R. (1983). *Moral and political thought of Mahatma Gandhi*. Concord Grove Press.

Jeste, D. V., & LaFee, S. (2020). *Wiser: The scientific roots of wisdom*. Sounds True.

Kaufman, S. B. (2020). *Transcend: The new science of self actualization*. Penguin Random House.

Kohlberg, L. (1976). Moral stages and moralization: The cognitive-development approach. In T. Lockina (Ed.), *Moral development and behavior*. Holt, Rinehart, and Winston.

Kool, V. K. (Ed.). (1993). *Nonviolence: Social and psychological issues*. University Press of America.

Kool, V. K. (2008). *The psychology of nonviolence and aggression*. Palgrave Macmillan.

Kool, V. K. (2013). Applications of Gandhian concepts in psychology and allied disciplines. *Indian Journal of Psychiatry, 55*, 235–238.

Kool, V. K., & Agrawal, R. (2006). *Applied social psychology: A global perspective*. Atlantic.

Kool, V. K., & Agrawal, R. (2010). The psychology of nonkilling. In J. E. Pim (Ed.), *Toward a nonkilling paradigm* (pp. 349–367). Center for Global Nonkilling.

Kool, V. K., & Agrawal, R. (2011). From empathy to altruism: Is there an evolutionary basis for nonkilling. In D. J. Christie & J. E. Pim (Eds.), *Nonkilling psychology* (pp. 65–93). Center for Global Nonkilling.

Kool, V. K., & Agrawal, R. (2013). Whither Skinner's science of behavior, his assessment of Gandhi, and its aftermath? *Gandhi Marg, 35*, 487–518.

Kool, V. K., & Agrawal, R. (2016). *Psychology of technology*. Springer.

Kool, V. K., & Agrawal, R. (2018). Gandhian philosophy for living in the modern world: Lessons from Satyagraha. In S. Fernando & R. Moodley (Eds.), *Global psychologies: Mental health and the global South*. Palgrave Macmillan.

Kool, V. K., & Agrawal, R. (2020). *Gandhi and the psychology of nonviolence, Volume 1 and 2*. Palgrave Macmillan.

Kurzweil, R. (1999). *The age of spiritual machines*. Viking Books.

Kurzweil, R. (2005). *The singularity is near*. Viking Books.

Manickam, S. (2014). The development and validation of the questionnaire measure of Sahay/tolerance. *Journal of Psychological Researches, 58*(2), 75–83.

May, B. (2002/1936). *Born to rebel: An autobiography*. University of Georgia Press.

Moerk, E. I. (2002). Scripting war entry appearing it unavoidable. *Peace and Conflict: Journal of Peace Psychology, 8*(3), 229–248.

Murray, H., Lyubansky, M., Miller, K., & Ortega, L., et al. (2014). Toward a psychology of nonviolence. In E. Mustakova-Possardt & M. Lyubanski

(Eds.), *Toward socially responsible psychology for a global era* (pp. 151–182). Springer.

Nagler, M. N. (1990). Nonviolence as new science. In V. K. Kool (Ed.), *Perspectives on nonviolence* (pp. 131–139). Springer.

Obama, B. (2020). *A promised land*. Crown.

Rocco, M. C., & Bainbridge, W. S. (Eds.). (2002). Converging technologies for improving human performance: Nanotechnology, biotechnology, information technology and cognitive science. *NSF/DOC-sponsored report*. National Science Foundation.

Roy, S. (2011, October 21). Learning from a barefoot movement. TED talk. Retrieved from www.ted.com.

Schwartz, B., & Sharpe, K. E. (2019). Practical wisdom: What Aristotle might add to psychology. In R. J. Sternberg & J. Gluck (Eds.), *Cambridge handbook of wisdom*. Wiley.

Sharp, G. (1960). *Gandhi wields the weapon of moral power*. Navajivan Publishers.

Stengel, R. (2011, December 14, Wednesday). Introduction: Person of the Year. *Time*.

Sternberg, R. J. (1998). A balance theory of wisdom. *Review of General Psychology, 2*, 347–365.

Sternberg, R. J., Nusbaum, H. C., & Gluck, J. (2019). *Applying wisdom to contemporary problems*. Palgrave Macmillan.

Turkle, S. (2011). *Alone together: Why we expect more from technology and less from each other*. Basic Books.

Weber, T. (2018). *The Mahatma, his philosophy and his legacy*. Orient Blackswan.

Author Index

Freeden, M. 243
Freter, F. 116

G
Gaertner, S.L. 116
Galtung, J. 19, 20, 30, 115, 230, 234, 235, 332
Gardner, H.E. 4, 12, 203, 208, 224, 322
Garfinkel, H. 210–212, 224
Garrow, D.J. 278
Garza, A. 229
Gearhart, S. 110
Gelderloos, P. 229
Ghosh, B.N. 176, 178
Ghosh, E.S. 113, 116
Gibson, S. 208
Gilbert, S.J. 222
Ginsberg, B. 229
Glassman, M. 200
Goffman, E. 210
Goodwin, M.H. 214
Gould, S.J. 188, 189
Goyder, G. 128–130
Graham, R. 251
Green, M. 295
Gregg, R. 273, 330
Gregoire, C. 61
Grinberg-Zylberbaum, J. 264
Grossmann, I. 18
Gugerelle, S. 318
Guha, R. 285
Guru, G. 111, 114

H
Haksar, N. 100
Hall, G.S. 11

Harvey, K. 99, 100
Heidegger 186
Heinl, R. 271
Heritage, J. 209, 214, 216
Hirschi, A. 152
Hofstede, G. 154
Hollander, M.M. 208
Hook, S. 187
Horsburgh, H.J.N. 305, 307
Huang, M. 196, 197, 202
Hunt, A.E. 273
Huxley, A. 10, 85

I
Iacoboni, M. 264
Illes, K. 155, 159
Ingrams, A. 158
Ishii, K. 177
Iyer, R. 34, 40, 41, 63, 64, 197, 318, 323

J
James, W. 9, 15, 30–33, 194, 324, 327, 332
Jeste, D.V. 14, 15, 318
Joel, B. 160
Jones, G. 130
Jordens, J.T.F. 95, 96
Joseph, S.K. 128, 129

K
Kadambi, R. 57
Kahneman, D. 31, 35, 36, 38, 39
Kakar, S. 119
Kapur, S. 114, 278
Karatnycky, A. 283

Subject Index

9 783030 874933